THE CASE FOR THE FACE

1684513

Scientists Examine the Evidence for Alien Artifacts on Mars

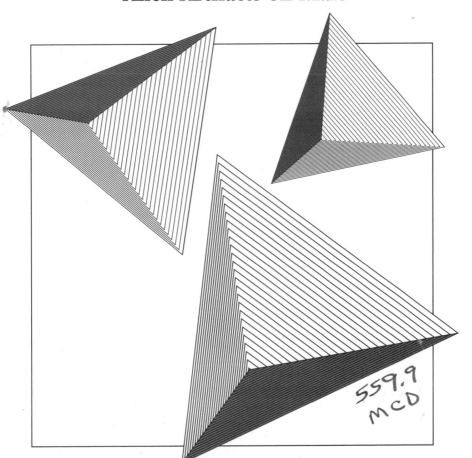

The Case for the Face:
Scientists Examine the Evidence for Alien Artifacts on Mars

Printed in the United States of America.

Published by
    Adventures Unlimited Press
    One Adventure Place
    Kempton, IL 60946 USA

Book development by Mind Into Matter, Chicago, IL

Cover and interior design by Monica Rix Paxson

The Case for the Face logo design is trademarked.

Photo and Image Credits: Front cover face images and interior
images © Dr. Mark Carlotto; back cover illustration of ancient
Mars © Grace DiPietro; and images used throughout courtesy of
the numerous contributors and courtesy of NASA/JPL/Cali-
fornia Institute of Technology. Also, please note individual credits
assigned to specific images and illustrations throughout the text.

Library of Congress Catalog Number: 98-84516

ISBN 0-932813-59-3

First Edition: March 1998

To Dr. Bartholomew Nagy

——quite possibly the first person to discover signs of past life on Mars.

In in his book, *Carbonaceous Meteorites,* Dr. Nagy claimed that research he began in 1966 showed that fossils found in carbonaceous chondrite meteorites were remains of extraterrestrial organisms. It is now believed by a number of authors in this book and others, that these meteorites may have originated on Mars.

Regretfully, Dr. Nagy passed away several months before the August, 1996 announcement by NASA scientists of a similar discovery in the ALH84001 meteorite, also thought to have originated on Mars.

Contents

A Picture's Worth...

Evidence of Alien Artifacts?

OLD MARS: ALIVE AND GREEN?

Rhapsodies on Mars

Coming to a Planet Near You...

Cydonia, Viking, Pathfinder Geology

Statistical Evidence

APPENDICES & REFERENCES

Introducing
Planetary
SETI

C an we find a net to capture the meaning
of a glowing star? What bridge spans the vast
space we must cross to reach understanding?
How small are we who attempt the journey!
And yet somehow we learn to find our glory
in a brave and endless struggle to comprehend
eternal mysteries. We are voyagers in an
infinite sea, our destination always beyond
the horizon. But we are voyagers.

—Gates of Prayer

An Introduction

David C. Webb, Ph.D.
Member, National Commission on Space
appointed by President Ronald Reagan

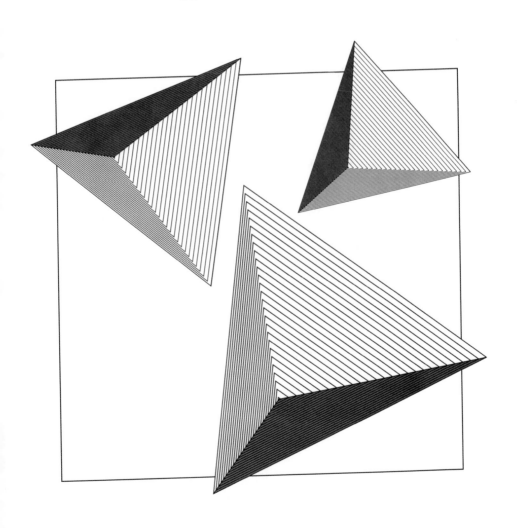

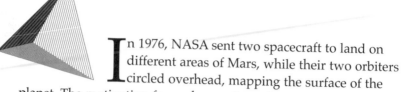

In 1976, NASA sent two spacecraft to land on different areas of Mars, while their two orbiters circled overhead, mapping the surface of the planet. The motivation for such a costly and complex mission (with a price tag of over 2 billion dollars) was to learn more about this most Earthlike of the other planets in the solar system, and to determine whether there was now, or ever had been, any life on Mars. Each of the two landers was equipped with a sampling arm to scrape the surface and a miniature biological testing chamber.

No definitive signs of life were found by the two landers, although controversy still exists about the results that were achieved. A number of researchers believe that if there had been chemical assaying equipment on board, the results would have been conclusively positive.

The real success of the Viking missions lay in the images of the surface of Mars that were received on Earth, revolutionizing our knowledge of the planet's topography and geology. Over a period of approximately four years, the two orbiting spacecraft transmitted a total of 51,539 images. These were to be scientifically evaluated for content. Unfortunately, only some 25% of this evaluation had taken place when the program's operating funds ran out. The remaining images were placed in storage. There they remain to this day, waiting for an examination that most likely will never take place.

A number of the more interesting images that were found were published by NASA in one form or another in the following years. One of the early images to be released showed an area of the planet's Cydonia region covered by an unusual number of large mesas or "knobs," one of which had the appearance of a giant sculptured face staring upward. This picture was picked up by the media and was widely distributed, generating considerable public interest: Was it really an artifact of an intelligent society, or a natural landform that looked like a face? If it was an artifact, what sort of civilization constructed it and when? These and similar questions quickly started to emerge in public discourse, but were equally quickly cut off when NASA announced that they had found a second image of the area taken from a different sun angle, which plainly showed the object to be an ordinary hill. Apparently it was only the interplay of light and shadow on the first picture that gave the illusory impression of a face.

This is the original image of "The Face" first shown to the media and the public. It is peppered with transmission errors and a regular grid of dots.

Most people were satisfied with this explanation and thought little more about it. A year or two later, however, two aerospace researchers, Vincent DiPietro and Gregory Molenaar, applied their newly-developed image enhancement software to the face-like feature. The Starburst Pixel Interleaving Technique (SPIT for short) produced a stunning result: far too many details were displayed by the new process to so casually dismiss the object as a hill. They requested that NASA supply them with the raw data of the second image. To their chagrin and dismay, they were told that the image had been misfiled and could not be found. Not content with that answer, DiPietro kept searching the files, eventually coming up with a total of ten images, of which eight confirmed the existence of the Face. (The remaining two images were obscured by clouds). Although most of the eight images were taken at a resolution too low to be conclusive, one of them (VIKING frame 70A13) was at approximately the same resolution as the earlier image. The presence of a second eye socket and various other elements of symmetry were confirmed. Clearly the likeness to a face was no trick of light and shadow.

DiPietro and Molenaar wrote up their research and presented it in a paper at the 156th Meeting of the American Astronomical Society. Instead of eliciting some interest within the planetary science community, they were subjected to a barrage of personal and subjective criticism regarding both their capabilities and the reasons they had carried out this work. So vicious and continuous were these attacks, that their health, their family relations, and their subsequent careers were greatly affected.

What, one might ask, would cause such a virulent reaction from supposedly rational scientists? The most likely answer is what can best be termed as the "Percival Lowell syndrome." Lowell was a famous astronomer who established the Lowell observatory at Flagstaff, Arizona. In the early years of this century Lowell observed what appeared to be numerous criss-crossing lines on the Martian surface. Because these seemed extensive and orderly, he concluded they were really canals dug by an intelligent species to convey water from the Martian poles to the remainder of the planet. As he was an eminent scientist, many people—including some other eminent scientists of the day—accepted his theory. Lowell's views remained controversial until the Mariner missions to Mars in the 1960's, when it was found that the "canals" Lowell insisted he had seen in his telescope were evidently an illusion. The only thing resembling canals on Mars were the signs of some former natural watercourses, none of which have the regular and orderly appearance of artificial canals. Contrary to the Lowell scenario, Mars appeared to have been a lifeless world from the beginning, peppered with craters, resembling Earth's equally lifeless Moon.

The resulting shock to the general public, and most particularly the planetary science community, was so great that for the remainder of the twentieth century, the possibility of life on Mars has been considered a taboo subject in scientific circles. So firmly entrenched has this reaction become that NASA itself was later to feel its impact, when in 1996, a team of NASA scientists proposed that a meteorite presumed to have come from Mars contained fossilized microorganisms, proving that life must have once existed on that planet. A controversy erupted that is ongoing.

It is then no surprise that for twenty years, most members of the planetary science community have refused to admit the possibility that any of the images of Mars show anomalous objects worthy of additional research or scrutiny. The present book, however, the product of four years of activity by a multidisciplinary scientific research team, Society for Planetary SETI Research (SPSR), plainly demonstrates the fallacy of this position. The team's research shows not just one (the so-called "Face"), but a number of objects, both in Cydonia and other regions of Mars, that deserve to be labeled anomalous and worthy of serious scientific attention.

This important work comes at a critical time in our ongoing attempt to learn more about Mars. We have already seen the success of the Pathfinder mission, the "little spacecraft that could"-and did. Now, a second spacecraft, the Mars Global Surveyor (MGS), is in orbit around the planet. As its name implies, the mission of MGS is to survey and map the entire Martian surface, an essential first step for the coming decade that will see a concerted international effort to not only map, but to also land roving craft similar to Pathfinder, and to obtain and return to Earth samples of Martian soil. All these efforts will be precursors to a possible manned landing on the planet in the second decade of the next century.

The mapping and imaging of the Martian surface to be carried out by the Mars Global Surveyor is similar to that of the Mars Observer spacecraft which was inexplicably lost, presumably to an explosion, just prior to its arrival at the planet in August, 1993. The Observer had a complete suite of surveying and imaging equipment, so its loss was a major blow to the entire Mars exploration effort. In an attempt to make up in part for this loss, NASA developed MGS on a fast-track, with exactly the same two imaging capabilities as Mars Observer: one, a wide-angle, relatively low resolution system, which will produce images with decidedly less image resolution than the Viking system; the other, a high resolution system which will provide approximately fourteen times Viking's resolution, but with a significantly narrower field of view. Due to this reduced coverage, the high-resolution system is to be used only on priority targets, which will have to be selected and their coordinates downloaded to the spacecraft via radio broadcasts from Earth. Therefore, to image Cydonia or any other area of Mars at high resolution, there must be a specific set of instructions sent to the Surveyor from Earth. Due to the distances involved and other parameters, this is not a simple issue.

It is important that the Cydonia region be imaged at high resolution in order to finally put an end to the ongoing disagreement
between those (the majority of planetary scientists) who believe that
there is no evidence of artificiality in the area, and those who believe
that there are several anomalous features there and elsewhere on the
planet that deserve proper scientific evaluation. Even Carl Sagan,
one of the leaders of the former group, after ten years of actively
opposing the possibility, agreed. In 1995, shortly before his untimely
death, he wrote in a new book, *The Demon-Haunted World,*

> "Even if these claims are extremely improbable —as I
> think they are—they are worth examining....I therefore
> hope that forthcoming American and Russian missions
> to Mars, especially orbiters with high-resolution televi-
> sion cameras, will make a special effort—among hun-
> dreds of other scientific questions—to look much more
> closely at the pyramids and what some people call the
> face and the city..."

That is why, when MGS was launched in 1996, members of
the SPSR research team attempted to ascertain whether the
Cydonia region was included in the targets slated for high-
resolution imaging. Mixed responses were received from NASA,
with the administrator saying yes, Cydonia was on the list; only to
be corrected by his chief scientist who gave the vague response
that "it may not be so." Meanwhile, the principal investigator of
the imaging team, Michael Malin, (whose company provided the
camera system), used his web site to further confuse the situation,
by writing that, as the people of America apparently wanted this
data, it would be provided; but avoiding the critical issue of priorities. Instead he gave a rambling (and apparently inaccurate)
account of how, as the cameras were affixed to the spacecraft, it
was not possible to guarantee any specific object at high resolution, because the spacecraft would have to fly directly over it and
with the uncertainties of orbital drift and other characteristics, this
could not be guaranteed. We later discovered that the spacecraft
can be swung in orbit, to approximately 14 degrees on either side
of its track, by means of on-board momentum wheels put there for
just such a purpose. Even without using this capability, however,
the high-resolution camera is able to take a series of image "strips"

which could effectively blanket the area in question and provide a rich new store of data for Mars anomaly research.

The SPSR team, greatly disturbed by the various confusing and inconclusive positions taken in various NASA statements, decided to contact NASA at the highest levels to try and lay this matter to rest. After several fruitless attempts, Dr. Carl Pilcher, acting Director of Solar System Exploration, invited a delegation to come to his office and make a presentation. Six SPSR members, including myself, Professor Stanley V. McDaniel, Mr. Vincent DiPietro, Dr. John E. Brandenburg, Dr. Mark J. Carlotto and Dr. Horace W. Crater, all gave short summaries of their findings. Afterward, Dr. Pilcher informed them that Cydonia was to be placed on the list for high-resolution imaging each time the spacecraft passes over the area. He also stated that Dr. Malin had signed on to the new policy.

This book is going to print before any of the findings are in, and so the question of whether there are, or whether there are not, anomalous objects on Mars, is still open. The members of SPSR are content, however, that the hypothesis is being fairly tested and that the twenty-year old battle will shortly come to an end—one way or another.

Preface:
Meeting With NASA

Professor Stanley V. McDaniel

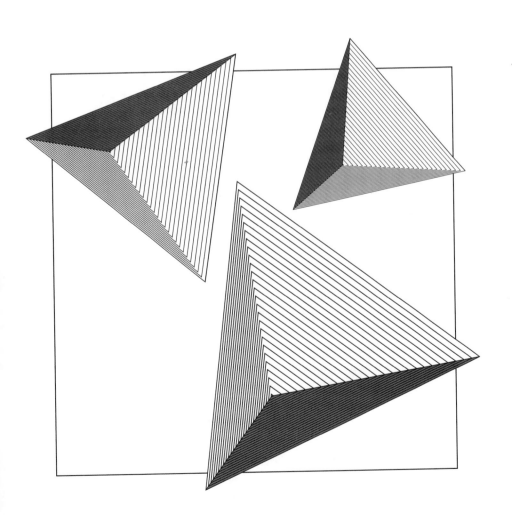

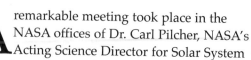

A remarkable meeting took place in the NASA offices of Dr. Carl Pilcher, NASA's Acting Science Director for Solar System Exploration, on November 24, 1997. The meeting's purpose—to discuss research showing the probability of artificial structures on Mars and to discuss how this research might impact NASA's targeting plans for its Mars Global Surveyor spacecraft, which arrived to map the Red Planet in September, 1997. Attending the meeting with Pilcher and Dr. Joseph Boyce, a program scientist with NASA, were six members of the Society for Planetary SETI Research (SPSR), whose members had fought to legitimize research on this highly charged subject for the past twenty years.

Whatever the outcome of the current wave of Mars exploration—a ten-year program begun with NASA's Mars Pathfinder robotic mission in 1997—this meeting was already of historical importance. It marked the first time since the Viking Mars missions in 1976 that NASA had shown a willingness to take seriously studies of the unusual surface features in the Cydonia region of Mars. The meeting signified a new attitude of openness and inquiry on NASA's part, sparked by the pioneering policies of NASA Administrator Daniel Goldin.

Prior to this meeting, the official NASA position toward the anomalous features on Mars had been one of ridicule, governed by the bias that Mars was always the same apparently lifeless orb we see today. The only other explanation, then, for artificial structures on Mars, was that visitors from interstellar space had established a colony or base on Mars in ancient times, and here NASA's official view was that there could be no propulsion systems adequate to make interstellar travel possible. The argument seemed to be: "There could have been neither visitors to Mars nor native Martians. Therefore there could be no ruins of ancient structures on Mars."

All this has now changed. On January 8, 1998, Administrator Goldin said in a speech to assembled astronomers at the annual meeting of the American Astronomical Society that NASA itself is now interested in the development of propulsion systems to carry spacecraft to the planets of nearby stars. He also stated that NASA's data policy will no longer allow private contractors to sequester spacecraft data. In the past, NASA's contracts with private contractors had allowed contractors to sequester data for as long as two years.

Mark Carlotto's awesome rendering of the Cydonia Plain shows much of the anthropomorphic imagery that the SPSR's team was able to interest NASA in, seemingly for the first time, in their Nov., 1997, meeting. It is viewed as if you were flying toward it from the South at a lower elevation than the angle of the original NASA photos. In this view, the "Face" is in the upper right corner, the "D & M Pyramid" is in the lower right corner and the area referred to as "The City" is in the lower left. North is toward the top of the photo.

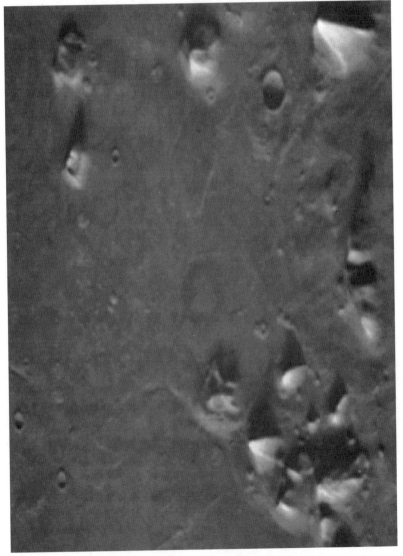

In previous statements as early as October of 1996, Administrator Goldin had indicated that the Mars Global Surveyor spacecraft would assuredly attempt to take new photos of the mysterious object that has been called "The Face on Mars." However, a number of questions remained unanswered. It was unclear from Goldin's statements as to whether the promised photos would be taken by Surveyor's high resolution camera or simply the much lower resolution mapping cameras. There was also a question as to both coverage and priorities: Would the attempt be made to image only the one object (the Face) or would the entire area, containing multiple objects of interest, be covered? Also in question were what priorities would be assigned to these objects by the MGS camera operator, a private contractor with NASA.

These questions were of considerable importance. If the attempt were made with the low resolution cameras only, the returned data would be no advance on currently existing images. If the attempt were confined to the Face alone, there would be a high chance of not capturing an image of the Face with the high resolution camera. Again, if insufficient priority were assigned to the anomalies, other targeting priorities might override them and no images of Cydonia might be taken at all.

The answers to these questions were hard to come by. Numerous letters written to NASA by SPSR failed to get a definitive answer. It was then that SPSR president Horace W. Crater began an effort to bring SPSR scientists to NASA for a meeting to discuss the research and the questions. Dr. Crater's requests for a meeting were rejected on four occasions by Wesley Huntress, NASA Assistant Administrator. Just as SPSR was about to give up, Dr. John E. Brandenburg, a plasma physicist and member of SPSR, succeeded in securing the Nov. 24, 1997 meeting with Drs. Pilcher and Boyce.

Representing SPSR at the meeting were members Vincent DiPietro, Dr. Brandenburg, SPSR President Dr. Horace W. Crater, Dr. Mark J. Carlotto, Dr. David Webb, and myself. We were greeted with considerable cordiality. Presentations of statistical studies by Drs. Carlotto and Crater were met with apparently intense interest. At the close of the meeting, Dr. Pilcher answered the important questions mentioned above. He assured us that image strips would be taken on every occasion that the Global Surveyor crossed over the region of interest, using the high resolution camera. In a follow-up telephone conversation between Dr. David Webb and Dr. Pilcher, Dr. Pilcher stated that this was "official NASA policy" and that the camera contractor had "accepted" that policy. We were given the OK to make that statement publicly.

It seemed to the SPSR members at the meeting that scientists at the NASA administrative levels had not previously been aware of the extensive research carried on over the past years by scientists such as Dr. Mark Carlotto and Mr. Vincent DiPietro. In addition to the statistical results indicating a reasonable probability that some of the Martian objects may be artificial, Mr. DiPietro pointed to the elements of coherent detail in the Face that are extremely difficult to account for by appealing to simple erosion. The reader will find accounts of both statistical and image enhancement studies in this present volume.

All of the image enhancements and charts presented to the NASA officials were viewed with clear indications of serious interest. We were later given to understand that although many within NASA still view the issues with great skepticism, there are also others who find the evidence intriguing. Both groups have good reasons for wanting new high resolution images: the former in order to prove the hypothesis of artificiality wrong; the latter in order to find out the truth, however it may fall.

At the present writing, there remains a knotty issue having to do with the relation between the Camera operator, a private contractor, and NASA. Although Dr. Pilcher has assured us that Dr. Michael Malin of Malin Space Science Systems, who has charge of the Camera on board the Global Surveyor, has agreed to the policy, Dr. Malin's own public statements as seen on his World Wide Web pages indicate an extremely negative approach to the topic. Dr. Malin has also stated that he has a high degree of autonomy in the choice of targets and the prioritizing of targets. Some uncertainty still exists regarding the ultimate control of image data acquisition and retention: Does the data "belong" to NASA and through NASA to the public, or is it in some sense restricted by the conditions of a private contract between the Jet Propulsion Laboratory and Malin Space Science Systems?

As this book goes to press, these unanswered questions still shadow our expectations regarding the ultimate success of the Global Surveyor mission in providing new data on the mysteries at Cydonia. It is our fervent hope that the interest shown by NASA in those anomalies will prevail. We also hope that Dr. Malin, being apprised of the legitimate research material conveyed to NASA by SPSR scientists, will take on a more accommodating attitude of scientific curiosity in the matter of the Cydonia objects—it will, after all, be to Dr. Malin's credit as well if the high resolution images confirm Cydonian anomalies as artificial.

The answers await us in the near future. They may change our essential understanding forever. Come join this great adventure with us as we await a possible answer from NASA to space science's greatest mystery.

The Society for Planetary SETI Research

> It is not at all true that the scientist goes after truth. It goes after him.
>
> —Kierkegaard

In light of the statement above, this book introduces you to the research work of the Society for Planetary SETI Research (SPSR). SPSR is an organization composed of PhDs, scientists, academics and professionals devoted to analyzing possible evidence of past or present extraterrestrial activity on planets of the solar system. Planetary SETI (Search for Extraterrestrial Intelligence) differs from Radio SETI, which searches for radio messages broadcast by intelligent beings from beyond our solar system.

SPSR's multidisciplinary research has focused on unusual features discovered in photographs taken by the NASA Viking Mars Mission in 1976. This intensive work has resulted in four separate and distinctly different statistical analyses which show high probabilities that several objects in the Cydonia region of the Martian northern plains are either non-random (not in accordance with chance expectation) or artificial. As such, it is possible to hypothesize that they could be the ancient ruins of intelligently designed structures. If confirmed by current or future NASA missions, such a discovery will have far-reaching implications for humanity's perception of its place in the universe, as well as for the future of space exploration.

SPSR includes experts from such diverse disciplines as physics, space science, astronomy, computer imaging and photographic analysis, geology, engineering, archaeology, philosophy, and anthropology. Organized in 1993 by Professor Stanley V. McDaniel of Sonoma State University, its distinguished membership includes a member of the National Commission on Space, a quantum physicist at a leading university Space Science program, a Fellow of the Royal Astronomical Society, a leading rocket scientist and meteorite researcher, a former member of NASA's astronaut corps, and a number of space industry employees among many others. It also includes the authors of virtually every peer-reviewed paper ever published about the anomalies, the world's two leading image analysts of the Martian photos, the authors of six separate books on the Martian anomalies and the NASA engineer who first brought the Cydonia anomalies to public awareness.

Planetary SETI:
An Adventure
In Science

Professor Stanley V. McDaniel
& Dr. Mark J. Calotto

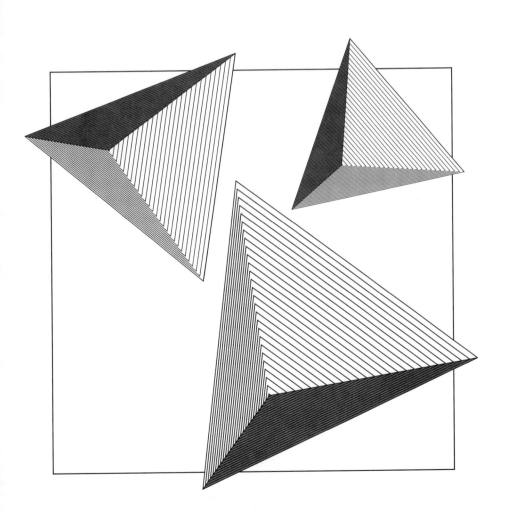

Professor Stanley V. McDaniel

For most of us, when we see the acronym SETI, we think immediately of giant radiotelescopes searching the skies for those elusive signals that might introduce us to intelligent life "out there." SETI, the Search for Extraterrestrial Intelligence, has been confined exclusively to groping among the distant stars.

Yet reputable scientists, including those who wrote the prestigious Brookings Institution report on space policy for NASA in 1960, have felt that artifacts of extraterrestrial origin may be found in our own solar neighborhood. Despite that report, NASA has paid little or no attention to this possibility.

When, in 1976, Viking Orbiter A returned controversial images of the Cydonia region of Mars, it remained for independent researchers outside NASA to respond. Because one of the formations had the unmistakable look of a sculptured humanoid face, and NASA scientists believed such a thing cannot exist, the official position was that the image was an accident of lighting that would "disappear" in different images. They even began to tell the public that there were images in which the object disappears, even though no such images exist.

But it was not an accident of lighting. Independent researchers began taking a closer look. At that moment these courageous scientists had the daring to defy the official position, the real study of Planetary SETI began. They began painstakingly working out techniques to extract as much information as possible from the images. They were embarking on an unparalleled scientific adventure.

Meanwhile NASA scientists acted as though their work simply does not exist. A virtual censorship had been imposed on papers dealing with the subject, and officials had repeatedly attempted to create the impression that only "believers" and charlatans take the images seriously.

Here we endeavor to correct that impression with an historical collection of articles by members of the Society for Planetary SETI research (SPSR), whose roster includes only academically or professionally qualified scientists. Recently Dr. Carl Sagan, in his last book, conceded that the Face and other Cydonian features were a proper subject for scientific study. In these pages you will find the work of the scientists who knew that from the beginning.

Dr. Mark J. Carlotto

Speculation about extraterrestrial life goes back to ancient times. Greek philosophers thought the sun and the moon were inhabited by spirits and demons. Belief in a "plurality of worlds," other worlds like our own, began to take root around the time of the Renaissance.

The nineteenth century saw new speculation fueled by advances in science, especially the telescope. An astronomer by the name of Franz von Paula Gruithuisen claimed that he had found a walled city on the moon. Scientists like Gauss and Littrow thought about ways of communicating with the inhabitants of other worlds using mathematics. Toward the end of the nineteenth century a series of developments lead to the first demonstration of radio waves by Heinrich Hertz. Shortly thereafter, Nikola Tesla, who had been conducting experiments with high voltage alternating currents, predicted that messages could be sent great distances, even to Mars.

Around the time of the great Martian canal controversy at the beginning of this century, scientists began to realize that the other planets in our solar system could not support life—at least not life as we knew it. Attention was beginning to turn toward the stars. Starting in the 1960s, the modern-day search for extraterrestrial intelligence (SETI) began. And interestingly enough, it was based on the same general idea proposed by Tesla half a century earlier.

When SETI got underway, many scientists thought the same extraterrestrials that they were trying to contact might have visited our solar system and left behind artifacts. In fact thirty-five years ago, in a speech to the American Rocket Society, Carl Sagan stated, "It is not out of the question that artifacts of these visits still exist or even that some kind of base is maintained, possibly automatically, within the solar system, to provide continuity for successive expeditions."

Back in the early days of SETI we didn't have the spacecraft and imaging technology to look for these artifacts. But today we do, which leads to this perplexity—if planetary SETI was thought to be a legitimate scientific topic then, why isn't it today?

Perhaps Mars Global Surveyor may change all of this. In the meantime, please join us in this inquiry to learn what we have already found on Mars and what could be awaiting us when we return.

In Pursuit
of the
Mystery

‸

As a famous nuclear physicist once put it, science is often the pursuit of the elusive obvious. In the stories that follow, you will hear how the siren song of Cydonia has compelled so many good scientists to pursue its elusive allure, often in spite of threats to jobs, professional standing and relationships. For twenty years, the quixotic photos have pointed again and again, without respite, to evidence of long dead builders on a planet now frozen and almost airless, (and, ominously, our nearest neighbor). For these brave people, the mystery is just too big not to pursue.

As with any ongoing scientific pursuit, no absolute final answers can yet be drawn. However, the data is marshaled, and studies point strongly to nonrandom features on Mars. Either someone or something once built on the surface of Mars, or Mars holds evidence for a regular geological process on a scale never before encountered. Either conclusion will be remarkable and open new doors of understanding about the wild and ever-changing solar system of humanity's nascence. The still shrouded conclusion to this search awaits the release of the higher resolution pictures from NASA's Mars Global Surveyor. However, what is best told now is why the marvels of Cydonia led so many scientists to doggedly risk threats to careers, relationships and professional respect to find its answers, and why there's a mystery out there that won't go away until final, irrefutable data is received.

Mars:
The Planet
of Mysteries

Vince DiPietro

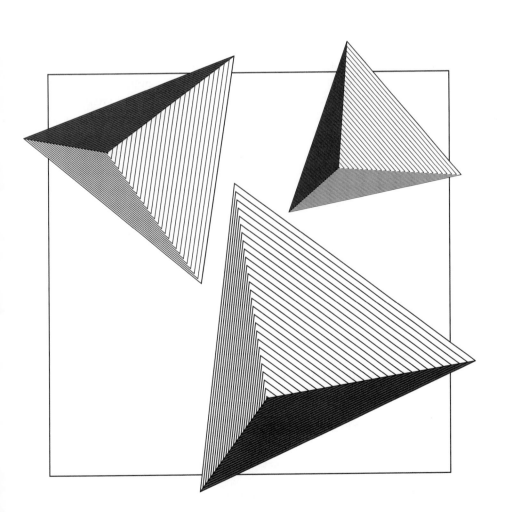

The Original Mars
Anomaly Investigation

For many years now I have been involved in a project which is frowned upon by some scientists and admired by others. I believe that there may have been an ancient civilization on Mars about one billion or more years ago. The circumstantial evidence is growing almost daily. First, conditions favorable for life existed there in the distant past. Data from Mars shows the presence of water, oxygen in the atmosphere, and now organic carbon—a billion years old—found in meteorites that came from Mars and landed on the Earth in Antarctica.

Second, unusual features, appearing to have been the work of intelligent design, have been identified on the Cydonia plain of Mars. I and my colleague Gregory Molenaar did the first serious study of the "Face on Mars" in 1979–1980. We obtained digital tapes of Viking data, then converted the data to computer images—long before home computer equipment was so easily attainable. We borrowed and rented computer time to generate the images, developed the Starburst Pixel Interleaving Technique (SPIT) for image clarification, and made our own photo prints of the data we processed. Several years later the raw data was re-examined by many other scientists and engineers, confirming our original work.

The SPIT process improves the quality of digital images and reveals additional detail. SPIT has been used on satellite images of the Earth's surface as well as satellite data from Mars. The book Unusual Mars Surface Features describes the process and provides examples that demonstrate the accuracy of its results. *(See "Image Enhancement: What It Is and How It Works" on page 47.)*

The best speculation about any of the objects, such as the Cydonia Face, is that they were intentionally carved. Many NASA scientists consider the Face "a trick of lighting." NASA Headquarters recently released a complete list of images made over the Cydonia region by the Viking spacecraft in 1976. In addition to the six images we located originally, these included four new images, making the total of ten images over the region of the Face. These ten images are taken at varying camera angles, altitudes, and lighting conditions. All but two (where clouds obscure the image) confirm the existence of an object that looks like a "Face." The facial appearance is definitely not a "trick of lighting."

Sometimes the Face has been compared with New Hampshire's "old man in the mountain," a rock formation that looks like a face in profile when viewed from a particular angle. This is a faulty comparison, since the Face in Cydonia is a full frontal view. Its three-dimensional shape has, furthermore, been corroborated by several independent tests.

In addition, significant items of detail have been found on the Face, which are highly unlikely for an accidental freak of wind erosion. Among these details are the teeth-like structures in the mouth area (found by Dr. Mark J. Carlotto) and the "eyeball" feature that I discovered.

The Cydonian Hypothesis

Gregory Molenaar and I were joined later by Dr. John E. Brandenburg, a plasma physicist. Together we framed "The Cydonian Hypothesis" which we published in the peer-reviewed Journal of Scientific Exploration in 1990. On the basis of our evidence, we proposed that the Face on Mars and other Martian formations may have been created by native Martians who had a neolithic-level culture during an extended period of warm climate. We further proposed that these inhabitants were human-like, based on what is called the "principle of mediocrity"

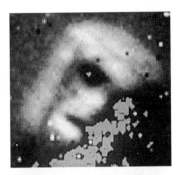

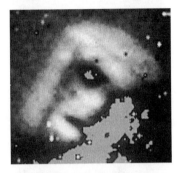

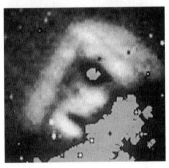

The Face on Mars is shown using a new software technique called "bit-slicing" which was applied to the eye area. By applying false blue color (shown here as light grey) to discrete levels of grey not ordinarily visible to the eye, a rounded structure resembling a pupil was found to exist within the eye socket. The three images reveal successive "layers" or contours of the object, indicating a rounded, dome-like shape. Bit-slice processing by Vincent DiPietro (copyright 1997).

or the principle that life throughout the universe will tend to develop along similar lines to that found on the Earth.

There have been several scientists during the last century who have examined meteorites that were found to contain organic carbon and fossils from places other than the Earth. Well before the Mars meteorite announcement by NASA scientists on August 7, 1996, there was the work of Dr. Ian Wright of the Open University, England, who published his research in the journal Science in 1989. Dr. Wright examined a younger class of Martian Meteorite (160 million years old). Dr. Wright's analysis of the trapped gases within the meteorite officially designated EETA79001 are an exact match to the gases in the Martian atmosphere as the latter was analyzed by the Viking spacecraft. Dr. Wright also found traces of organic carbon.

Prior to Dr. Wright, in 1975 another scientist, Dr. Bartholomew Nagy of the University of Arizona, published the book, *Carbonaceous Meteorites*. The research he reported there was the culmination of work dating as far back as 1966. The book describes his findings for 4-billion-year-old Martian meteorites discovered in Orgueil, France; Ivuna, Africa; and Revelstoke, Canada. What appear to be fossil remains of creatures, including cellular structure, are pictured in the book.

Further evidence indicated the DNA found in the meteorites is "right-handed" (referring to the twist in the spiral chain of DNA molecules). Earth's biological organisms exhibit "left-handed" DNA. Dr. Nagy believed that the meteorites had to be of extraterrestrial origin. It was not until recently that these same meteorites were identified as having their origin on Mars.

Unfortunately for science, the meteorite from Orgueil sat around in a museum for many years and had been handled by a great number of people. It was eventually found to be contaminated with earth organisms, and thus Dr. Nagy's entire report was discredited. Dr. Nagy passed away in 1995 and is not able to defend his pioneering effort. Prior to Nagy's death, Dr. John Brandenburg had several conversations with him. Dr. Nagy insisted that he had indeed shown that the fossils were not from this Earth. In his book he states "Perhaps it is well not to draw conclusions, but it appears most likely that the carbonaceous compounds and small carbonaceous objects found in these meteorites would be confidently assumed to be of biological origin if found on earth."

But Dr. Nagy was not the first to investigate meteorites bearing signs of organic material. Another scientist found fossils that were not from this Earth 116 years ago. Dr. Hahn, a German geologist, discovered a series of organics—sponges, corals, and crinoids—in meteorites from the great meteoric fall of June 9, 1866 at Knyahinya, Hungary, near Nagybereszna, Ungvar, Ukraine, USSR. Hahn believed that the the fossils were "the remains of other celestial bodies—probably those of a destroyed planet." His article appeared in Popular Science for Nov., 1881. Dr. Hahn was ridiculed for his ideas and findings. Possibly Dr. Nagy followed up on Dr. Hahn's work; both individuals were originally from the same geographical area near Nagybereszna in the USSR.

When Was Mars Inhabited?

The age of the Cydonia site, according to what is known as the "Hartmann Model," is about 600 million years. (*See timescale chart on pages 28–29.*) This refers to the time after which geological activity in the area came to an end. The meteor that caused the crater Lyot (pronounced LEO) may have been responsible for damage to the planet, loss of atmosphere, and the eventual extinction of life there. Crater Lyot dates at 300 million to 900 million years old. If Lyot was the reason Mars lost its biosphere, habitation of Cydonia would likely have been prior to this time period.

Yet it is possible that some type of living organism still exists on Mars. In 1980 Dr. Leonard Martin of the Lowell Observatory in Flagstaff, Arizona discovered what may have been large water spout erupting in two Viking images. His work was published in the NASA Activities, Dec. 1980, vol.11, no.12. The images, from Viking frames 775A10 and 775A11, were two overlapping photos taken 4.5 seconds apart which clearly show what appears to be a column of steam from a geyser.

If NASA is truly serious about retrieving possible living specimens from Mars, the location of these water spouts is the place to go. But, like the work of Dr. Nagy, Dr. Martin's work also dropped out of sight and has been ignored. When I visited the Lowell Observatory a few years ago, the attendants at the visitor's center disclosed that Dr. Martin was still resident there, but none of them had ever heard of the water spout and the pictures were not on display.

Meteorite Evidence for Life/Extinction: Mars/Earth

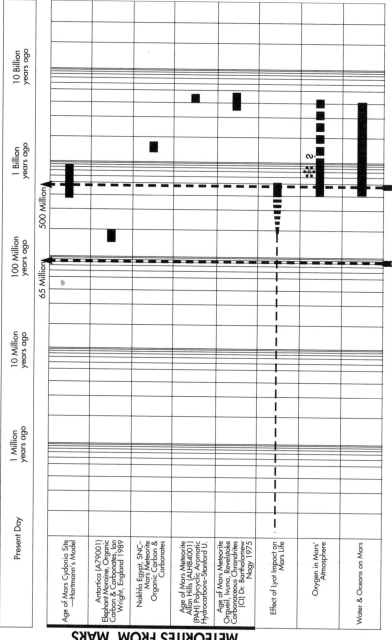

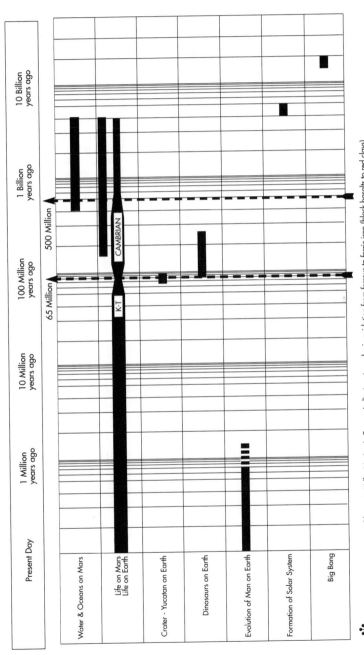

✳ Layers of ferric iron in exposed layers in Valles Marineris Canyon indicates atmospheric oxidation from ferrous to ferric iron (black basalts to red clays).

Each major vertical division on this logarithmic scale starts with time today and progresses to past increments of 1 million, 10 million, 100 million, 1 billion, 10 billion years ago. The other two dotted vertical lines at 65 million and 500 million represent catastrophic events for the two planets: the extinction of the dinosaurs on Earth and the probable extinction of life on Mars by the meteor that made Lyot crater.

Two successive Viking images from frames 775A10 and 775A11 suggest an explosive water spout or steam vent (just above and to the left of the large crater). Taken 4.5 seconds apart, a marked difference is seen in the shadow of the object. The shadow is initially smaller and pointed (left image). Less than five seconds later the shadow broadens and the object's diameter increases (right image). Estimates based on the size difference indicate the cloud is rising at a velocity of over 200 feet/second.

A Nuclear Blast on Mars?

Another more serious finding was first brought to our attention by Dr. John Brandenburg. The element Xenon 129, the second generation of a radioactive component produced when nuclear fission occurs, is found in abundance in the Martian atmosphere. Nuclear fission, such as that from a reactor or bomb, produces Iodine 129 with a half life of 17 million years, releasing beta particles and Xenon 129. The latter element is stable and lasts forever. Has nuclear fission taken place on Mars?

There is an accepted scientific explanation for the presence of Xenon 129 on Mars. But it is only a theory. Billions of years ago while the sun and solar system formed, there may have been a supernova which produced Iodine 129, later transformed into Xenon 129. Supporting this view is the fact that remnants of Xenon 129 are found all over the solar system, But the theory does not account for the fact that there is 3 times more Xenon 129 on Mars than on Earth. Where did all of the extra Xenon 129 come from, and why on Mars?

The Russian Mars96 probe, which failed to leave Earth orbit and plunged into the ocean, may have been looking for Xenon 129 on Mars, either in the atmosphere or on the surface. The probe carried a sophisticated instrument package including instruments capable of detecting Xenon. This very capable Russian spacecraft was outfitted with many more instruments than NASA's current Mars Global Surveyor. The high resolution cameras on board the

Russian craft, unlike those on the Global Surveyor, had pointing capability and more scan lines (5184 pixels per scan line) for greater resolution of the imagery. The American spacecraft has only 2096 pixels per scan line.

The failure of this spacecraft is still unexplained. According to one of the Russian scientists involved with the project, as reported at the George Washington University in late 1996, all went well with the launch. At the final stage of rocket propulsion, the payload separated from the rocket motor, and then the rocket motor fired. But these events occurred in the wrong order; the result of an out-of-sequence software program. The instructions being reversed, the rocket sped off to Mars, while the payload fell back to Earth. Was this simply a lack of quality control, or was there a more sinister reason (perhaps sabotage?) for the software problem? We can only hope that the Russians will find out what happened and why.

Loss of the Russian Mars 96 Probe

Nuclear fission, such as that from a reactor or bomb, produces Iodine 129 with a half life of 17 million years, releasing beta particles and Xenon 129. The latter element is stable and lasts forever. Billions of years ago while the sun and solar system formed, there may have been a supernova which produced Iodine 129, later transformed into Xenon 129. Remnants of Xenon 129 are found all over the solar system. But the supernova theory does not account for the fact that there is 3 times more Xenon 129 on Mars than on Earth. Was there a nuclear explosion on Mars in the distant past?

The failed Russian Mars 96 probe carried a number of instruments capable of detecting radioactive Iodine 129, the precursor to Xenon 129. Below is a list of the instruments that would have gone to Mars if the Russian probe had not failed. Those that might have detected radioactive Iodine 129 are starred. The loss of the Mars 96 probe is all the more unfortunate because the current NASA spacecraft, the Mars Global Surveyor, does not carry such instrumentation.

PFS - planetary IR Fourier spectrometer
TERMOSCAN - mapping radiometer
SVET - mapping high-resolution spectrophotometer
SPICAM - multichannel optical spectrometer
UVS-M - ultraviolet spectrophotometer
PHOTON - gamma-spectrometer*
NEUTRON-S neutron spectrometer*
MAK - quadrupole mass-spectrometer*
ASPERA-C - energy-mass ion spectrograph and neutral-particle imager
FONEMA - fast omnidirectional non-scanning energy-mass ion analyzer*
DYMIO - omnidirectional ionospheric energy-mass-spectrometer
MARIPROB - ionospheric plasma spectrometers
MAREMF - electron analyzer and magnetometer
SLED-2 - low-energy charged particle spectrometer*

What Happened
to the Mars Observer?

Another Martian mystery occurred on August 21, 1993, when NASA's Mars Observer spacecraft, after a successful journey to Mars, lost all radio contact with Earth. The Mars Observer Spacecraft was traveling in a solar elliptical orbit, designed to intercept the orbit of Mars. A planned thrust from the on-board rockets would slow down the spacecraft when it approached the point of insertion into an elliptical orbit around Mars. Further rocket firings at later times would finally adjust the orbit of the spacecraft to a more circular path. The plan was to accomplish this orbital insertion about a month before the spacecraft would go into solar conjunction (when Mars would be behind the Sun with respect to Earth). After the spacecraft emerged from behind the Sun, an uninterrupted two years of scientific experiments would commence. This was to include imaging with the on-board cameras.

Loss of contact occurred just after the command sequence was given to pressurize the fuel chamber. Prior to the pressurization of this fuel chamber, after the commands were given to the on-board computer, and by the direction of the manufacturer (Martin Marietta), the radio transmitter on board the Mars Observer was turned off. The spacecraft was never heard from again.

The probable cause of the failure may have been the leakage of fuel from holes which might have developed in the fuel chamber as a result of micro-meteorite impacts. The fuel, squirting out these holes, would impart a slight circular thrust to the spacecraft, sending it and the transmitting antenna in a spinning motion, causing loss of communications. The actual reason for failure may never be known.

How Mars Observer
Might Have Been Saved

The real story behind "What happened to Mars Observer" was the unwillingness of NASA's Jet Propulsion Lab (JPL) to ask the Russians to turn on their "black box" radio transmitter, riding piggyback on board the Mars Observer, before the spacecraft's trajectory took it behind the Sun. One of the instruments on board was a Russian "Black Box" containing its own power supply and an omni-directional low power transmitter and receiver. This was to be used in conjunction with the French Balloon Experiment. It was intended to be activated in 1995 when a Russian probe, a different spacecraft carrying the French Balloon Experiment, would rendevous with Mars. The high gain directional beam radio antenna on board the Mars Observer and the Russian Black Box would relay the Russian data back to Earth.

The urgent need to utilize this device as a beacon was apparent from the moment the spacecraft failed. The Black Box contained all of the necessary elements—power supply, radio receiver, radio transmitter. It seemed logical that this device could be turned on and arrangements for detection could be made using a very large array antenna on the Earth. This might have determined the whereabouts of the Mars Observer, in the same fashion as a survivor at sea in the dark of night might be found if the survivor turned on a light beacon.

Since Mars was rapidly approaching solar conjunction, a limited time was available to turn on the Black Box. By doing so the spacecraft's position and orbit could possibly have been determined. Then by manipulating certain positioning elements (gyros or thrusters) the spacecraft might have been returned to Earth orbit, where it could have been retrieved and repaired.

Although I voiced my opinion to several sources capable of initiating a rescue by turning on the Black Box, action was delayed by what appears to be a political decision as to whether to ask the Russians for help or feign ignorance. I called the Russian Embassy, some of its scientists, Goddard scientists involved with the Mars Observer, and Martin Marietta engineers in New Jersey. None of these persons responded to my request to turn on the Black Box.

The Mars Observer failed on August 21. It was not until 2:20 p.m. PDT on Tuesday, September 21, 1993 that an attempt was made at to turn on the Black Box. By that date Mars and everything in its vicinity was at or near solar conjunction, creating a very high degree of undesirable signal-to-noise ratio. Had this experiment been initiated in August when the accident occurred, the chances would have been much more favorable for contact and response.

Additionally the battery power supply for the Black Box had a finite life span. If by some chance, the transmitter had managed to be turned on, the transmission signal may have been lost in the transit behind the Sun for the months that followed. When Mars finally cleared the interference of the Sun, early the following year, the battery on the Russian Black Box may have expired. From this perspective it was very possibly the tardy decision of JPL, a contractor to NASA, that lost the one opportunity we may have had to discover the fate of the spacecraft.

What Will We Learn from the Global Surveyor?

On Sept. 5, 1996, Dr. John Brandenburg and I went to NASA headquarters. in Washington, D.C., and spoke with Dr. Jergen Rahe. We laid out all of the photo enhancements and I made a prediction: "If the camera on the Global Surveyor does indeed image the Face in Cydonia, you will find the eyeball and the teeth." Let us hope that this prediction will be fulfilled.

BIOGRAPHICAL NOTE

Vincent DiPietro is an engineer who designed, built, tested, and ran the digital image recorders for the Landsat and Nimbus programs for the NASA Goddard Spaceflight Center.

How I
Came To Cydonia

Dr. David Webb

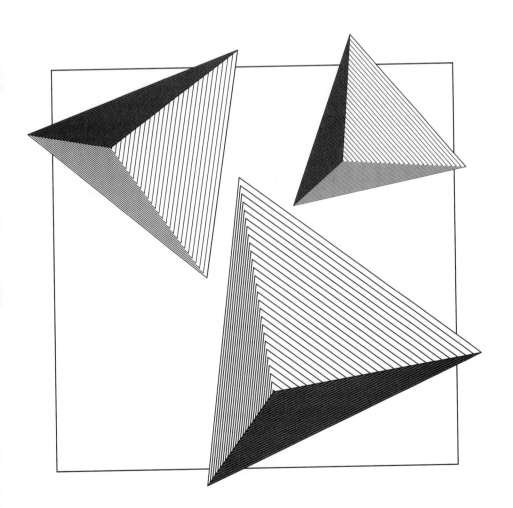

I am an aerospace and technology development consultant living in Daytona Beach, Florida. My major efforts over the past 25 years have been directed toward furthering humankind's efforts in space. In 1984 I became interested and involved in the controversy surrounding the Cydonia region, not only because of its impact on future exploration efforts to the Red Planet, but also because of a long-time interest in the manner in which new discoveries are or are not assimilated into a society. This was the major emphasis of my college and university studies: most particularly, the manner in which science and technology can be used to further (or hamper) national and international development activities.

This subject matter crosses so many disciplinary boundaries that in the sixties (and even today) there were no academic programs encompassing such concepts. This resulted in a constant struggle throughout college and university to have existing disciplines open up to these new ideas and incorporate them into their thinking and programs. In the process I learned much about how difficult it is to persuade those trained in an existing academic discipline to lift up their eyes and view horizons outside of their own narrow background.

In 1985, I was appointed by President Reagan as one of 15 members of the National Commission on Space established by the Congress to develop a 50-year agenda for the U.S. in space. This provided an opportunity for me to show some of Dr. Mark Carlotto's exceptional computer-enhanced images of the Cydonia region to Carl Sagan, with the hope that he would acknowledge the need for the planetary science community to undertake a rigorous analysis of the apparent anomalies on Mars.

Unfortunately, although finding the images "exceedingly interesting," Dr. Sagan decided for whatever reason not to press for such an examination. In fact, shortly thereafter he wrote an article for *Parade Magazine,* in which he derided the efforts of those who held the belief that these might be of artificial origin, as nothing more than wishful thinking. It was to be nearly ten years before he reversed this position (in 1995) and stated that, although he personally did not believe the anomalies were artificial, they were of legitimate scientific interest. We had the imaging capabilities to prove this issue one way or another, so it should be done at the earliest opportunity.

In 1993, after Professor Stanley V. McDaniel issued his rigorous examination of the unfortunate and unscientific manner in which this issue has been treated by NASA and the planetary science community generally, I joined a number of scientists who had communicated to Professor McDaniel their interest in rigorously evaluating the data from Cydonia. In this way SPSR was born. I am honored to be a part of this effort and am hopeful that as a result of the ongoing work of the group that at long last the Cydonia anomalies may receive the attention they deserve from the larger science community.

BIOGRAPHICAL NOTE

Dr. David Webb is an internationally known figure in the field of space policy, development and education. He was Chairman of the United Nation's Conference on the Peaceful Uses of Space and is a member of the National Commission on Space which was appointed by President Ronald Reagan under Congressional mandate to prepare a 50-year agenda for the US in space. He also has been tremendously influential in US space education having now helped start up three collegiate-level space studies programs.

Carl Sagan & I:
On Opposite
Sides of Mars

Dr. Brian O'Leary

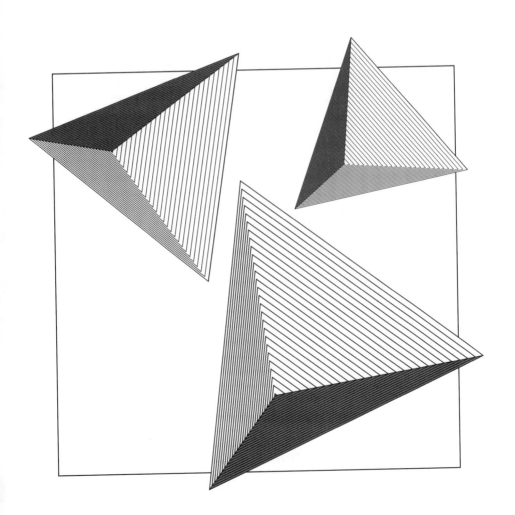

Dear Carl,

Wherever you now are, I wish you well and I am sorry we didn't have a chance to connect in person before you passed on. Both of us have had a long-standing connection through our interest in Mars. It sometimes amazes me how many times our paths have crossed through the decades while we were researching and teaching about the mystery of the next world beyond ours from the Sun. During that one generation, knowledge about Mars has exploded from almost nothing to a stunning array of facts leading directly to the likelihood that life was present there at least once.

As individuals, our fascination with Mars goes back even further, approaching a half century. My own interest began as an eight-year-old boy at an open house at Harvard College Observatory in 1948. It was the night Harry Truman upset Thomas Dewey in the American presidential race. I recall gazing through the telescope that night at the shimmering red disk with a polar cap, and I wanted to go there. Or, if I couldn't, I at least felt moved to find out what the place was all about, whether this world was Earthlike or could harbor some kind of life.

You were later to become an Assistant Professor of Astronomy yourself at Harvard, and that is where we first met in person as colleagues. I walked into your office one day in 1965, when I was working on a Ph.D. thesis at the University of California at Berkeley. The dissertation concerned what we could infer about the composition of the Martian surface and atmosphere from its optical properties.

I remember that great big globe of Mars you had in your office with its vague features deduced from centuries of painstaking visual and photographic observations through telescopes. This was on the eve of opening our eyes to orders of magnitude more surface detail soon to be revealed by spacecraft cameras. I also noticed a tension between us, perhaps a Harvard-Berkeley rivalry in ideas. Beginning in those times and for years to come, your name and mine were probably on more published papers about Mars than any other two individuals.

Just as I was completing my Ph.D. work in 1967 I landed what seemed to be the ultimate job: I was appointed as the first (and, in retrospect thirty years later, only) astronaut appointed by NASA specifically to go to Mars. But within a few months, the manned Mars program was canceled and I resigned. I am grateful that you seized on the opportunity and were the first to call me to invite me to join the faculty of Cornell University's astronomy faculty, which you had just joined yourself. I accepted your offer and so began our three exciting and productive years as close colleagues in the rapidly expanding new field of planetary science. Remember how we worked together with NASA, bringing in lucrative grants as team members on a number of historic planetary missions, publishing dozens of papers, many of them collaborative? Those certainly were the halcyon days for all of us in this field.

In 1976 you were a Viking scientist close to those who first analyzed the photographs that came in from the orbiter. You joined in the chorus that the picture of the infamous Cydonia "face" released to the public was a "trick of light and shadow." Being a professional practicing planetary scientist myself, I presumed your assessments were correct and that, indeed, under further scrutiny, the face would "disappear."

It wasn't until 1984 when Richard C. Hoagland, Vincent DiPietro and others pointed out to me a much different story: that the suggestive features of the face did not disappear on a second image taken under different illumination. They convinced me that these images were worth researching further, and so a number of us began what has been an effort spanning over a decade of scientific investigation. We had access to the data tapes and state-of-the-art image processing techniques which culminated in the rich tapestry of results presented in the present publication.

I certainly agree with you that many speculations that have arisen about the "face" and nearby features are weak, at best. But through the years several of us have also concluded a number of substantial studies, many of which have appeared in the peer-reviewed literature. For example, DiPietro, his colleague Gregory Molenaar, Dr. Mark J. Carlotto, and Ananda Sirisena (in England) have given a very careful look at the shape of the face itself. Carlotto and I published suggestive evidence for a face-like three-dimensional structure by comparing images under two different illuminations. Carlotto's fractal analysis, a quantitative test for possible artificial origin, is also very significant work. The statistical study of mound geometry performed by Dr. Horace Crater and Professor Stanley V. McDaniel strongly indicates nonrandom distribution of features. These and many other approaches described herein give an impressive, albeit not airtight, case that some of these objects may be artificial..

W hy is it, then, in 1985 you ridiculed and misrepresented this evidence in your popular article "The Man in the Moon" in *Parade Magazine*? Why do mainstream planetary scientists not enter into serious research on this subject? Why do your colleagues continue to present shallow arguments against our work, pointing out such trivia as the "happy smiling face" and "Kermit the Frog" as equally plausible artificial structures on Mars?

Before leaving us, you may have seen Dr. Louis Friedman of the Planetary Society in a recent televised debate, suggesting one possible reason for such ridicule. He said that inquiry into these matters might threaten the careers of the scientists involved. I can vouch for that from personal experience, because entering into this research did in fact distance me ever further from you and your colleagues.

A deeper problem becomes revealed: does NASA have an alternative agenda we don't know about? Have they tightened the reins on the scientists they fund, preventing them from looking at these questions? With all their resources at their fingertips, why have they not pursued and published their own research? Why have they debunked responsible outside inquiry into the matter, as documented in *The McDaniel Report*? Is there something they (or you) don't want the public to know? Or is it just a basic conservative scientific bias in which, as Friedman said, "we need to look first for more ordinary explanations, and in this case it seems clear we're dealing with a random pile of rocks that happen to look like a face."

This bias is consistent with your oft-quoted statement "Extraordinary claims require extraordinary evidence" (really a non-scientific double standard). But the Cydonia situation appears to be even more extreme, because you and your colleagues have gone so far as to deny any existing evidence, and have come to a negative conclusion without proper analysis.

Carl, I apologize for expressing anger in the past toward you on this and other scientific questions. For the moment, I would like to grant the assumption that we are in a clean debate among colleagues, and as Lou Friedman suggested, it is not easy for a

mainstream planetary scientist on the NASA payroll to venture
into such controversial topics when there are plenty of other
worthwhile issues to address. I can certainly understand the conservative bias of scientists when first confronting an anomaly.
After all, Galileo's colleagues refused to look through his telescope. We all make mistakes.

Regarding questions such as these, it is easy for a scientist to
formulate a premature negative position from which it may be difficult to retreat for political reasons. You may be familiar with
Thomas Kuhn's classic text, *The Structure of Scientific Revolutions*,
which states that leading scientists during any time of great
change may become among the last to embrace a new paradigm or
world view, because many of their own hypotheses and theories
may be threatened.

But what question can be more intriguing than the possibility
of intelligent life having occupied Mars, even though in
your mind that possibility is a long-shot? The members of
the Society for Planetary SETI Research are here to say that it isn't
such an extreme possibility; that in fact the evidence is sufficient to
warrant an aggressive look at Cydonia in general and the "Face"
in particular. Now that we have cooperation from NASA after
twenty-one years of ambiguity, we at last have the opportunity to
obtain very high resolution photographs via the Mars Global
Surveyor if the mission is successful.

In our free society, the American people deserve to know the
truth. We both can acknowledge that NASA is a civilian agency
supported by taxpayers, but I'm afraid that, in the past, vested
interests entered into the process, and NASA seemed to have lost
their vision. I noticed some of the beginnings of empire-building
and planetary politics during the booming years around 1970,
which seemed to have created an unwitting alliance between special interests and scientific conservatism.

I appeal, then, to your curiosity and ethical sense. We have a
spacecraft going to Mars that can probably resolve the Cydonia
issue, and we now have quite reliable guarantees that NASA will
give highest priority to targeting the face, and that the pictures
will be released to the public (acknowledging engineering constraints, of course). This letter is an appeal to your spirit, and to

those colleagues you have left behind, to help ensure that the truth in this matter be revealed.

I am grateful for the many collaborations we had and the opportunities you gave me to participate in pioneering planetary exploration. You were one of the great educators of the cosmos in our time. You had the courage to take some unpopular positions on many issues, including that of the "Face on Mars." Having taken such positions, you leave us with the possibility of further dialogue, from which an enlightened consensus may come.

Perhaps it was to stimulate that dialogue that in your last book *The Demon-Haunted World* you came forward to offer belated (if guarded) praise to the independent researchers who have studied the Cydonia objects for so many years. In that book you also admitted for the first time that NASA was mistaken when it judged the facial appearance to be a "trick of light and shadow." Your last word on the subject was that it is one that qualifies as a scientific study. You called for a closer look at Cydonia. I and my colleagues, who have worked so long and hard on this topic, thank you deeply for that final turn of phrase.

May our paths once again cross in a magnificent universe illuminated with truth.

BIOGRAPHICAL NOTE

Dr. Brian O'Leary is the author of several books on space exploration and New Science. He received his Ph.D. in astronomy from the University of California at Berkeley in 1967, and has since published over 100 peer-reviewed articles in planetary science and astronautics. He was a member of NASA scientist-astronaut corps during the Apollo program and was deputy team leader of the Mariner 10 Venus-Mercury television science team.

A Picture's
Worth...

A thousand weeks—plus. For that long (more than twenty years) the arguments have raged. First they were about the validity of two images showing what seems to be a monolithic face created by some long-dead builders. Later that argument expanded to include the many remarkable anomalies in the Cydonia area-features which were given suggestive names like the D & M Pyramid, The City, The Fort. On one extreme were establishment scientists who insisted the images simply couldn't be of artificial objects, no matter how provocative: On the other extreme, many non-scientists offering outlandish speculations. In the middle ground, the voices of many serious scientists, willing to look objectively at the evidence, were drowned in the cacophony of claims and counterclaims.

But still, after twenty years, it comes down to the images. Either the Viking images accurately reflect evidence of alien intelligence or they don't. Ultimately there is only a debate because these remarkable images exist. Until men and women walk the surface of Mars at Cydonia, or new data from the Mars Global Surveyor is successfully returned to Earth, the processing and analysis of the existing images remains paramount. The articles here let you know how the clarity of images is enhanced without distorting the integrity of the original data. Other articles show you how the experts are able to derive such powerful images from such distant data, and how to then view it in simulated 3-D.

A final article tells of the young science students at a secondary (High) school in Scotland who were able to render very recognizable images of the Face and several of the other Cydonian images; showing that while the images are a result of rocket science, it doesn't take a rocket scientist to figure out that the images look tantalizingly like artificial features.

Image Enhancement:
What It Is
& How It Works

Stanley V. McDaniel

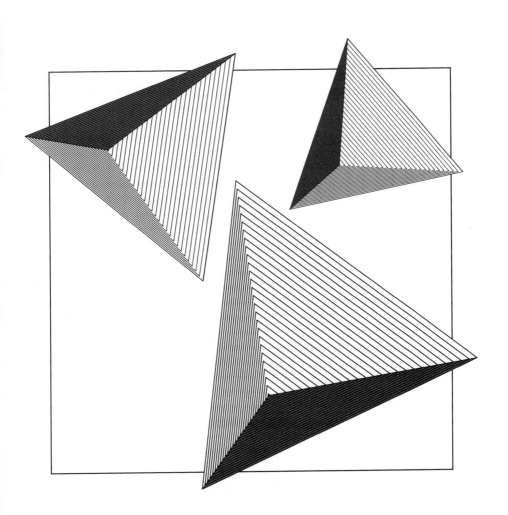

"Raw Data" vs. Enhancement

Recently, while delivering a lecture on the Mars anomalies to an audience at Imperial College in London, I was taken aback at the end of the lecture. A member of the audience asked me if the slide images I had been showing were enhanced. When I answered "yes," the questioner said "Well, you can do anything with enhancement." The implication, of course, was that the researchers who had produced the images had deliberately faked them.

No doubt the person who asked this question did not intend to insult the researchers. He may have been influenced by skeptics who have taken advantage of the ambiguous term "enhancement" to criticize the Mars anomaly investigation. The word "enhancement" can mean many things, including the addition of ornament. But in the world of digital data processing, the term means something very specific—the use of various techniques to clarify and bring out detail not easily seen in the raw data. The question is: Which is more informative, the raw data, or the enhanced image?

What is "Raw Data?"

Images from the Viking spacecraft were returned to Earth in the form of eight-digit binary numbers representing shades of gray from total black to total white in 256 gradations (extrapolated from an original 128 grey levels recorded by the camera.) These binary numbers are the actual "raw data." To turn these numbers into visible images, their values are converted into "pixels." Each pixel is a square area containing a single grey-scale value derived from a binary number. The shade of the pixel represents the integrated average shade, or "value," of all the details in the area it covers. The final image is built up out of such pixels.

The human eye can detect only about 32 different levels of grey, so digital imaging and subsequent processing constitutes at least a fourfold improvement over visual seeing, especially when enhancement techniques are applied in the computer. These pixelated images may be improved for viewing by increasing its contrast (the raw Viking image has very low contrast and its contents are hard to discern otherwise). Additionally, "pixel replication" may be employed to enlarge the image. In pixel replication, each pixel is simply enlarged. This form of enlargement has no effect on the resolution of the image. It merely makes it larger.

Although technically not quite correct, it is reasonable to refer to the image after pixel replication as "raw data." Little is changed in the image other than to convert the binary numbers to pixels, enlarge the pixels and apply appropriate contrast control. Hereafter when I refer to "raw data" (in quotes) I will mean the image after pixel replication and contrast control. The image prior to these modifications will be referred to as raw data (without quotes).

What Does Pixel Interpolation Do?

What is most commonly called digital image enhancement is a process known as pixel interpolation. This is a step beyond pixel replication, and it is here that critics of "enhancement" would like to believe that distortion occurs. They imagine that "raw data" contains the total amount of information that can be derived from the original binary coding. If this were true, it would follow that any fiddling around with the image past mere pixel replication is somehow not legitimate.

But then the widespread use of pixel interpolation throughout government and industry would be hard to explain. To understand how pixel interpolation works to clarify an image and make detail visible that cannot be made out in the "raw data," it is important to get an idea of how the spacecraft camera converts its view of the terrain beneath it into units having particular shades of grey (represented, we recall, by binary numbers).

In the case of the key images taken by the Viking spacecraft over the controversial Cydonia region of Mars, the camera resolution was about 47 meters or approximately 150 feet. This means that as the camera "looked" at the area below it, it had to choose a grey scale value for each 150-foot square unit. In the figure on the following page we see the "camera track" for an individual line of pixels recorded as the camera passes over the physical land form, represented by the irregular gray area. The "recorded data" shows the values that the camera records for each pixel as it passes over the object. As the diagram shows, an integration of values occurs where the edges of the darker object fall within the area of

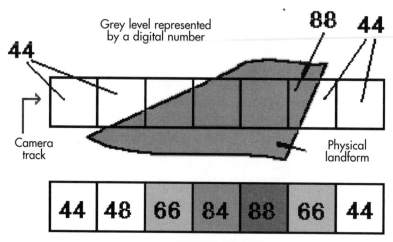

44

88   44

Grey level represented
by a digital number

Camera
track

Physical
landform

44	48	66	84	88	66	44

RECORDED DATA
Pixel values returned after averaging for
the scanned area.

Averaging or integration of values for each pixel occurs as the camera passes over irregular terrain. To some extent the original contour can be recovered by applying an appropriate interpolation algorithm.

the camera's pixel definition. In the figure, the camera records a value of 66 instead of either 88 or 44. In the recorded ("raw") data the sharp edges of the object are therefore "lost" and the object may be unrecognizable. The complex set of pixel shades shown represents such an averaging, or integration, of values as the camera responds to variations in the actual contour and shadows of the terrain.

More than Meets the Eye

The relations of values between the pixels contain more information about the original shape of the object than is visible to the eye. Because the specific variations of pixel values were originally derived from an averaging of the values in the actual scene, an appropriate interpolation algorithm often can recover the original shape of the object with reasonable accuracy. According to imaging experts Vincent DiPietro and Gregory Molenaar, interpolation actually amounts to a statistical analysis of the data provided by the pixel relationships.

Such a procedure involves the original pixel and the values of immediately surrounding pixels. The original pixel is divided into smaller pixels, whose new values are derived (interpolated) from the partially-shared values of the adjacent original pixels.

There are several types of pixel interpolation, some more sophisticated than others. Bilinear interpolation utilizes just the four pixels bordering directly on the one to be interpolated, while more sophisticated algorithms may reference more. Cubic Spline interpolation, the one used by Dr. Mark J. Carlotto in his definitive enhancements of the Martian anomalies, utilizes weighted values from twelve surrounding pixels.

When Vincent DiPietro and Gregory Molenaar turned their attention to the Viking images in 1979, the algorithms available to them were insufficient. They developed a new algorithm which they titled the "The Starburst Pixel Interleave Technique (SPIT)." This method uses data from eight surrounding pixels. The interpolation algorithm examines each pixel of the raw data one by one and queries the chosen surrounding pixels, which cast their weighted votes to produce values for new pixels to interpolate into the area originally represented by the one raw data pixel. The process then moves on to the next raw data pixel, queries the adjacent pixels around it to redefine new values for this raw pixel, and so on.

If the interpolation algorithm employed is one that has been tested for accuracy against actual features, and it is used with appropriate care, the result is to yield information inherent in the relationships between the various pixels, which is ultimately a function of the way the camera data is gathered in the first place.

By using such an algorithm, for example, the genuine circularity of a crater rim can be recovered, even though in the "raw data" the shape is visually unclear. Very little can be determined from the pixel pattern in A, which is taken from a very low-resolution Viking image, frame 561A25. The resolution in this image is about 535 feet, 3.5 times lower than the primary reference frames for the Cydonian anomalies on Mars. Nevertheless, application of the SPIT algorithm brings out the basic contours of a crater located in this position B. For confirmation, the same crater as resolved in higher-resolution Frame 70A13 is shown in C. This illustrates the efficacy of tested methods of enhancement for bringing out detail even in very low resolution images.

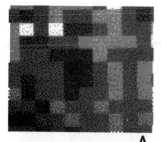

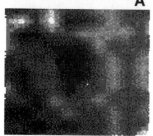

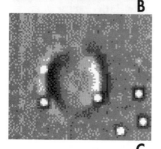

Testing interpolation for accuracy. Image (A) is a portion of very low resolution Viking frame 561A25. After applying the SPIT algorithm, the basic shape of a crater can be seen (B). Confirmation of this result is provided by a much higher resolution image (C) from Viking frame 70A13. Some details clearly visible in (C) can also be seen in (B).

Production of artifacts (false data) as a result of enhancement is always possible, but this does not mean that enhancement by interpolation is a useless procedure or that under controlled circumstances it cannot bring out the contours of real features that are not clearly visible in the "raw data." The Mars anomaly investigators Dr. Mark J. Carlotto, Vincent DiPietro, Gregory Molenaar, and Ananda Sirisena in England are all highly experienced professionals who have worked with state-of-the-art interpolation algorithms to bring us the best possible and most reliable images of the mysterious objects on the Martian Cydonia plain.

BIOGRAPHICAL NOTE

Professor Stanley V. McDaniel is the author of *The McDaniel Report* and is the former chairman of the Department of Philosophy at Sonoma State University in northern California.

Enhancing
the Subtle
Details in the Face

Mark J. Carlotto

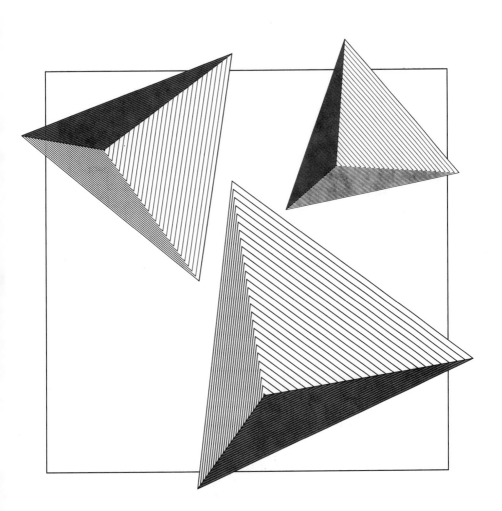

The Presence of Subtle Details
Adds to the Mystery

I magery released by NASA of the Face on Mars shows us little more than a gross representation of a humanoid head. But close up, the Face possesses subtle details that are not obvious in NASA photographs—details that one does not expect to find in a geological formation: a dark cavity within the eye socket that looks like an eyeball, broad stripes across the face reminiscent of Pharaonic death masks, thin lines that intersect above the eyes in the style of a ceremonial headpiece or crown, and fine structure in the mouth that look like teeth. This article describes how the imagery of the Face has been processed and argues that these facial details are probably real surface features at or slightly below the resolution of the Viking Orbiter's camera.

Image Enhancement
of the Face

E arly investigators found the Face to be an extremely sophisticated object in terms of its architectural symmetry, facial proportions, and artistic impression (Pozos 1987). When I began examining the Viking Orbiter imagery in 1985 my initial goal was simply to produce the best quality enhancements of the Face using the two available images, 35A72 and 70A13.

Both images were corrupted by random "salt-and-pepper" noise caused by data transmission errors. An image restoration algorithm was developed to clean up the imagery by detecting noise pixels and filling them in with values computed from the surrounding pixels. The processing involved:

1) Running a 3×3 averaging operator to the original Viking image;

2) Computing the absolute value of the difference between the image produced in 1) and the original Viking image;

3) Thresholding the above difference image to separate "signal" and "noise" pixels ("signal" pixels are by definition below the threshold and "noise" pixels are above);

4) Computing the local median of the original Viking image in a 3 × 3 pixel window;

5) Using the threshold image produced in 3) to combine the original Viking image and the median filtered Viking image computed in 4).

The last step keeps signal pixels in the original Viking image and fills in noise pixels with the median value of the surrounding 3 × 3 block of pixels. Although special-purpose computer hardware and software were required at the time, today the above processing can be easily performed using most commercial image processing packages.

Because of the limited dynamic range of the sensor and the large field of view (about 50 × 50 kilometers), image contrast is not optimal in all parts of a Viking image. After cleaning up the imagery, a local contrast stretch operation was applied to adaptively adjust the contrast within a window about the size of the features of interest (65 × 65 pixels). The processing involved:

1) Computing the local average of the restored image using a 65 × 65 pixel window;

2) Subtracting the image computed in 1) from the restored image;

3) Scaling the range of pixel values in the above image to occupy the full range of the display.

Figure 1 shows the two images of the Face extracted from frames 35A72 and 70A13 after image restoration and a local contrast stretch (Carlotto 1988). The images have been registered to each other and magnified 4× to facilitate subsequent

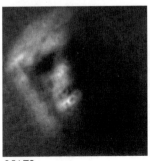 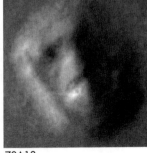

Figure 1

Restored and enhanced images of the Face.

35A72   70A13

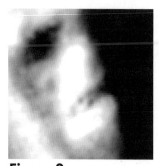

Figure 2

Enhancement of "iris" detail within left eye cavity.

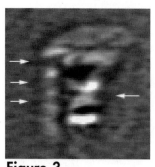

Figure 3

Enhancement of lateral stripes in 35A72.

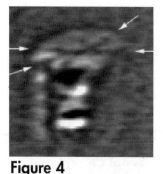

Figure 4

Enhancement of crossed lines above the eyes in 35A72.

processing and analysis. Registration was performed by selecting common points between the two images, and warping one image to match the other using a first order polynomial transformation. Output pixel values were computed using bicubic spline interpolation.

Independent Verification of "Eyeball"

I was intrigued by certain details in the restored and enhanced images—details that should not be there. But I was not the first to notice them.

DiPietro and Molenaar first detected a dark cavity in the eye socket on the left sunlit side of the Face which they called the "eyeball" (DiPietro and Molenaar 1982). Using a technique known as false-color enhancement, they found evidence of this feature in both 35A72 and 70A13.

False-coloring assigns color to gray tones so that subtle differences in gray tone can be better discriminated. But finding evidence of a feature in two images of the same object suggested another enhancement strategy. Figure 2 shows the result of averaging together the two registered views of the Face from 35A72 and 70A13 shown in Figure 1. Averaging increases the signal to noise ratio, emphasizing features that are common in the two images (the "signal") while de-emphasizing features that are different

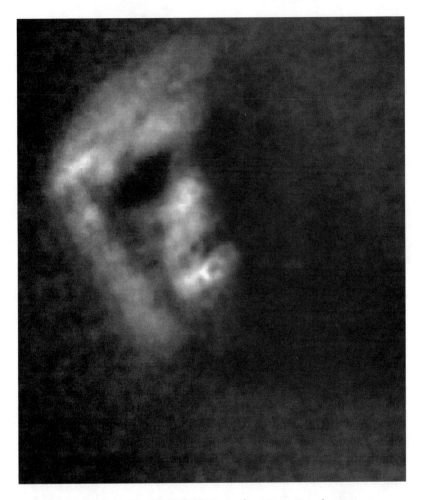

A bove is an enlargement of the left side image from Figure 1 on the previous page (Viking image 35A72) which allows a greater examination of the details mentioned in Mark Carlotto's article—the crossed lines above the eyes, the clearly defined left eye socket, and the tooth-like features of the mouth.

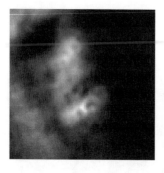 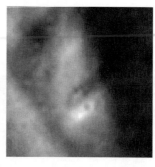

Figure 5

Features in mouth
in 35A72 (left)
and 70A13
(right).

(the "noise"). The result shows what appears to be a "iris" within
the left "eyeball" of the Face.

Linear Features

RichardHoagland first identified several broad stripes across
the Face that suggested to him a style found in the
Pharaonic art of Egypt. To better see these stripes, the
35A72 image of the Face is rotated so that they are aligned in the
horizontal direction. Horizontal averaging is performed to
enhance linear features in that direction (Figure 3). It is important
to note that the stripes are not aligned in the same direction as the
Viking camera's scan lines and so cannot be camera artifacts.
Interestingly, these features are not particularly clear in 70A13
which was taken at a higher sun angle. This suggests that they
might be caused by slight depressions in the surface rather than by
different surface materials having different reflectivities because
the former would be less evident at higher sun angles.

Several thin lines which cross over the forehead area were
also detected early in the investigation (Pozos 1987). These features which can be seen in both 35A72 and 70A13 are suggestive
of a ceremonial headpiece or diadem (Figure 4). The lines in 35A72
(the horizontal line in particular) were enhanced by horizontal
averaging as above. None of these lines are aligned in the same
direction as the scan lines in either 35A72 or 70A13 and so cannot
be sensor-related. Since they can be seen in both images of the
Face they must be real surface features.

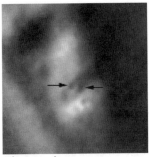

Features in the side left side of the mouth are present in both images of the Face.

Malin's "teeth" are on the right side of the Face and are present in only 70A13.

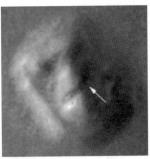

Figure 6

Figure 7

Controversy Over the "Teeth"

O f all the details, the most controversial are the "teeth" which can also be seen in both images of the Face (Figure 5). That they are probably real surface features and not noise in the imagery or processing artifacts can be seen by averaging the two images of the Face together as was done to enhance the "eyeball" (Figure 6).

Instead of trying to explain the teeth and other details seen in the Face, Michael Malin, the Principal Investigator for the Mars Global Surveyor Camera, states that the teeth are nothing more than noise in the imagery that has been excessivily enhanced. The location of Malin's "teeth" are indicated in Figure 7. But as noted by McDaniel, they are not the ones presently under study. Malin's "teeth" are on the right side of the Face and are seen in only one of the images (70A13) while the features under discussion are on the left side and can be seen in both images.

Conclusion

I f the Face is the product of differential erosion as claimed by most planetary geologists, how does one account for the presence of these details? One would expect that they would have been obliterated by erosional processes over time. But they are there. Instead of trying to understand what natural forces could conspire to create such features, the mystery is being side-stepped by certain individuals who maintain that the details are not real—

that they are noise in the imagery enhanced by image processing. If that is the case, then why are these details seen in more than one image? That they can, in fact, be seen in multiple images strongly suggests they are real, whatever they are.

BIOGRAPHICAL NOTE

> Mark Carlotto received a Ph.D. degree in Electrical Engineering from Carnegie-Mellon University in 1981. His book, *The Martian Enigmas*, summarizes over ten years of research on the Face and other objects using advanced digital image processing techniques

The Three-Dimensional Shape of the Face Calculated from Two Viking Images

BY DR. BRIAN O'LEARY

We are fortunate to have two Viking photographs of the Mars "face" viewed from above and at two different sun angles, 10 and 27 degrees above the horizon. For a number of well-established observations of Mars, we can safely assume that the dusty surface texture of the face is an idealized diffusely reflecting material called a "Lambert surface." (The opposite is called specular reflection, as in a mirror.) In the absence of extensive shadows, which are unlikely on virtu-

Isometric plot of the 3-D reconstruction obtained using the single image shape-from-shading algorithm on NASA Viking frame 70A13. A similar result was obtained for frame 35A72.

ally all of the illuminated side of the face, it then becomes possible in principle to derive the three-dimensional structure.

In an article for *Applied Optics,* Dr. Mark J. Carlotto used this approach to formulate the three-dimensional structure of the face. In the work I published in the *Journal of the British Interplatary Society,* I assumed his approach was valid. I then attempted to solve the inverse problem of artificially illuminating his 3-D surface to recover original two-dimensional images at the observed sun angles and directions. Because images of the face at two different illuminations do exist, it is possible to simulate the two dimensional image of one frame from the 3-D surface of the other and then compare them to the original image.

This would be something like taking a model of the face and shining a flashlight on it at the two angles, taking a photograph in each case, and then comparing it to the original photograph. (This has actually been done with a sculptured model by the artist Kynthia, which confirmed the results reported here). We are also fortunate that the two angles of 10 degrees (Viking photo 35A72) and 27 degrees (photo 70A13) show very different illuminations. The artificial illuminations resulting from this process are strikingly similar to the actual photos. We must conclude that Carlotto's 3-D model is almost certainly a valid representation.

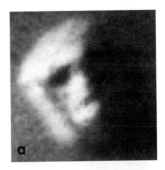

a

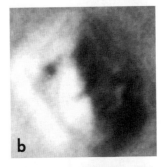

b

c

Cross-check of single image shape from shading results. Top: original images of NASA Viking Frames 35A72 (a) and 70A13 (b). Bottom: synthetic images of the 3-D surface estimated from 35A72 and viewed under lighting conditions of both 35A72 (c) and 70A13 (d). Similar results were obtained using images of the 3-D surface estimated from 70A13 and viewed under lighting conditions of 35A72 and 70A13. (Images regenerated from scan of the original 1988 article.)

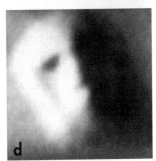

d

Analyzing Planetary Terrain& Features in 3–D

Dr. Mark J. Carlotto

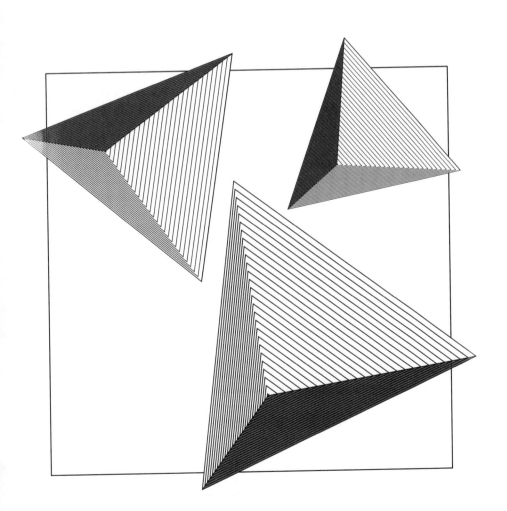

A variety of image processing techniques have been applied to the study of the Viking Orbiter images of the Face and other unusual objects on Mars. They have been used to eliminate noise, enhance contrast, and bring out subtle details in the imagery. Image understanding techniques developed within the artificial intelligence and computer vision communities over the last thirty years go beyond traditional image processing. They can be used to estimate intrinsic properties of the imaged scene such as its shape, reflectance, temperature, and surface material composition. Of particular importance in the investigation of the Martian anomalies has been the use of "shape-from" techniques to estimate the 3-D structure of certain features such as the Face. Once the shape of an object has been determined, questions about how it might appear from other perspectives and under different lighting conditions can be explored even though actual imagery under those conditions do not exist.

Shape-from-stereo (also known as stereoscopy) is the best known of the "shape-from" techniques, using the parallax shift of features on the surface to determine the height of the surface. Terrain elevation over much of the world has been derived using this technique. Unfortunately it is of limited utility in analyzing the Face and the other features in this part of Mars because of the lack of good quality stereo pairs (two images covering the same area taken from two different positions in space).

Shape-from-shading is another way of determining the shape of surfaces. It is based on the relationship between image brightness and the slope of the surface in the direction of the sun. This article explains how shape from shading works and how it can be used to gain new insights about several unusual Martian surface features.

Shape From Shading

Shape-from-shading (also known as photoclinometry) is a method for determining the shape of a surface from a single image. In computer graphics, images are rendered from surfaces. Shape from shading is, in effect, inverse computer graphics, producing surfaces from images.

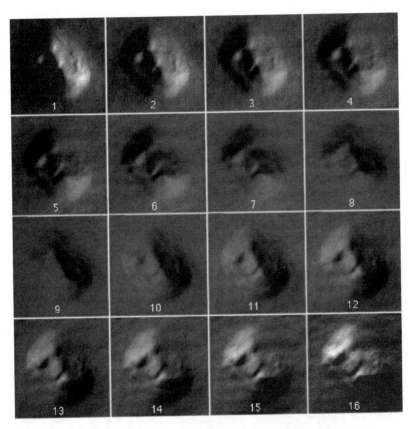

Figure 1   Shaded renditions of the Face under simulated summer lighting conditions.

For a surface of constant color or albedo, the brightness at a point in the image is a function of the component of slope in the direction of the sun. In the computer vision community, this function is known as the reflectance map. Key to shape from shading is the inversion of the reflectance map, that is, in determining slope as a function of brightness instead of brightness as a function of slope.

A variety of methods have been developed for determining slope (and ultimately elevation) from image brightness. A simple method based on some early ideas described by Berthold Horn of MIT is described here that provides satisfactory results in many planetary imaging scenarios.

In general the reflectance map depends on the position of the sun, the observer, and the type of surface material. It can be thought of as a table that gives brightness in terms of slope. For certain types of surfaces that scatter light equally in all directions (Lambertian surfaces), brightness is proportional to the cosine of the angle between the direction perpendicular to the surface and the direction of the sun. In other words, if the surface points directly toward the sun, it is brightest. Surfaces sloped away from the sun are less bright, and those either obscured by other surfaces or facing away from sun are in shadow. If the angle between the direction of the sun and the direction of the observer are more than 30 degrees apart and the surface is not too rough, it can be

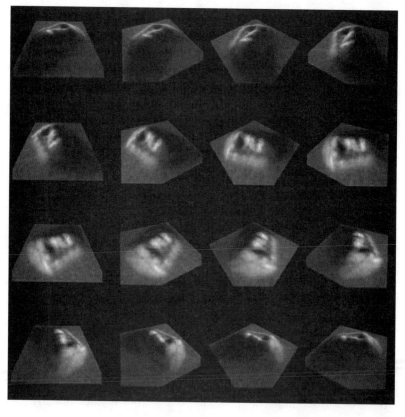

Figure 2   Synthetic image with the sun overhead (left) and the elevation surface computed by shape from shading

shown that image brightness is a linear function of the slope in the direction of the sun. This leads to the following algorithm for computing an elevation image from a brightness image:

1. Rotate the brightness image so that the sun is to the left;
2. For each row in the brightness image compute the average value of all pixels in the row and subtract that value from each pixel in the row;
3. Set the left-most pixel in each row of the elevation image to zero;
4. Moving left to right one pixel at a time, compute the elevation at each pixel by adding the values computed in Step 2 to the elevation value of the previous pixel to the left;
5. Repeat Step 4 for all rows;
6. For each row in the image compute the average elevation value of all pixels in the row and subtract that value from each pixel in the elevation image.

The elevation image produced by this algorithm is an approximation to the true surface topography, and is reasonably accurate to within a constant scale factor and offset provided the sun is near the horizon and the image used was taken from almost directly overhead.

Analysis of the Face

Shape from shading was first applied to the Face in order to determine if its appearance is an optical illusion as claimed by NASA. In order to test their claim, shape from shading was used to determine the 3-D structure of the Face from 35A72 and 70A13. Cross-checks were performed to verify the accuracy of the reconstructed surface. Computer graphics techniques were then used to predict how the surface would appear under different lighting conditions (Figure 1) and from other perspectives (Figure 2). Results of this analysis demonstrated that the impression of facial features is not a transient phenomena—that facial features seen in the Viking imagery are also present in the underlying topography and produce the visual impression of a face over a wide range of illumination conditions and perspectives.

3-D Views of the Tholus

R ecently, shape from shading has provided new information about other features on Mars. The Tholus is one of several larger mound-like objects southeast of the City and Face. Like the Face and several other nearby objects, the Tholus contains strange details, including what appears to be two sets of grooves on either side of the object. 3-D analysis (Figure 3) reveals that these grooves actually wind half-way up the side of the mound, and that one leads to a circular pit on its southeastern side. Could this be an opening into the Tholus? And if so, what could be inside?

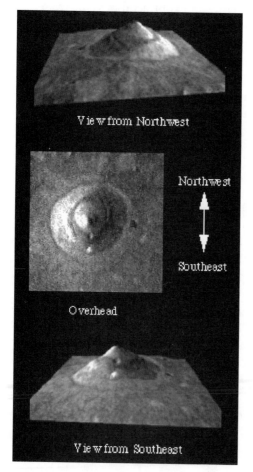

View from Northwest

Northwest

Southeast

Overhead

View from Southeast

Figure 3

Overhead view of the Tholus from 35A74 along with two perspective views generated from its elevation image produced by shape from shading.

Tunnel into the D&M Pyramid?

E ast of the D&M Pyramid, at its base, is a dark circular feature that most believe to be a deep crater (Figure 4). Some have speculated that the impact which caused the crater is responsible for the present condition of the D&M-a five-sided object that seems to have been damaged on the eastern side. 3-D analysis suggests another intriguing possibility. A simulated perspective view looking west toward the shadowed side of the D&M

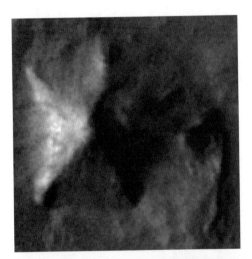

Figure 4

Overhead view of D&M Pyramid from 70A13.

Figure 5   Simulated perspective view of the D&M Pyramid from the east.

Pyramid (Figure 5) shows that what had been believed to be a crater or hole at the base of the formation appears instead to be an opening in its side. Where the other sides are relatively smooth and flat, the east side rises slightly in the middle. In 3-D one gets the distinct impression that the opening might be the entrance to a tunnel leading into the center of the D&M Pyramid. And like the Tholus, one wonders what might be inside.

Conclusion

As additional tests are applied to the Face and nearby objects in Cydonia, they become more and more interesting. New results presented in this article suggest possible subsurface features in the Tholus and D&M Pyramid. No natural explanation has yet to be offered. One has to hope that NASA will soon be given resources to send archaeologists and anthropologists to investigate this extraordinary collection of anomalies on the surface of Mars.

How Shape From Shading Works

BY DR. MARK J. CARLOTTO

To illustrate how shape from shading works, and to understand under what conditions it works well, consider the following example using synthetic data. Figure 1 (left) is the surface of a cone depicted as an elevation image where brightness represents height. The image on the right is a shaded rendition of the cone viewed from the south (azimuth angle = 180°) at zenith angle of 70° (or 20° above the horizon). The sun is illuminating the cone from the west at an azimuth of 270° and a zenith angle of 45°.

Figure 1

Conical elevation surface (left) and shaded rendition from the side (right).

Figure 2's left image shows a synthetic image of the conical surface in Figure 1 as it would appear from above with the sun directly overhead (zenith angle = 0°). The image on the right is the elevation surface estimated from that image using shape from shading. The poor performance of the algorithm is caused by an ambiguity that occurs when the sun is directly overhead, and leads to the confusion experienced by image analysts who do not know whether they are looking at a hill or a crater. Because of this, image analysts prefer imagery collected either in the morning or the afternoon.

Figure 2

Synthetic image with the sun overhead (left) and the elevation surface computed by shape from shading (right).

As the sun moves closer to the horizon, the performance of the shape from shading algorithm improves. Figure 3's left image shows a synthetic image of the same cone from directly overhead except now the solar zenith angle is 30°, i.e., 60° above the horizon. The image on the right is the elevation surface estimated from the image on the left. It is beginning to look more like the elevation image of the cone in Figure 1.

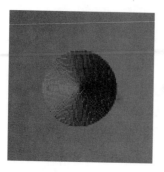 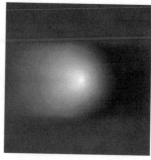

Figure 3

Synthetic image with the sun 60° above the horizon (left) and the elevation surface computed by shape from shading (right).

As the zenith angle continues to increase the true shape of the surface begins to emerge. Figure 4's left image shows a synthetic image of the cone from above generated with the sun 30° above the horizon (zenith angle = 60°). The image on the right is the elevation surface estimated from that image. Figure 5 compares a rendering of the surface computed by shape from shading in Figure 4 with that of the original conical surface.

Figure 4

Synthetic image with the sun 30° above the horizon (left) and the elevation surface computed by shape from shading (right).

As demonstrated above, shape from shading works best when the sun is near the horizon; i.e., in the late afternoon or early morning. Since all of the key Viking Orbiter images over Cydonia were acquired in the afternoon, they are ideally suited for shape from shading.

Figure 5

Actual surface (left) and estimated surface (right) produced by shape from shading algorithm. The slight tilt in the reconstructed surface on the right is an artifact of this type of algorithm.

The North
Kelvinside High
School Project

Chris O'Kane

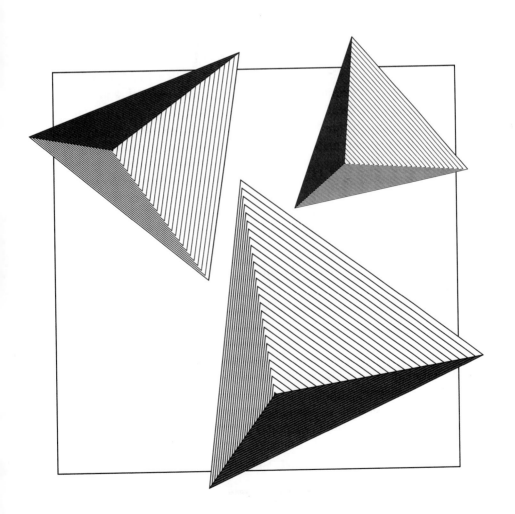

Observe & Question

Doing science requires that you question and learn. In this way, some of the greatest discoveries in science have started with a simple observation. The late physicist Richard Feynman once observed a plate spinning in the dining hall of Cornell University. His curiosity caused him to ask a question about the way that the plate seemed to spin. And this simple little inquiry later led Feynman to the research for which he received of the Noble Prize for physics. If Sir Isaac Newton had observed an apple fall from the tree but had not questioned why, the science of his day would have been grievously damaged.

Likewise, NASA scientist Toby Owen discovered a rock formation on the surface of Mars which seems to resemble a human face. While almost all planetary scientists assumed it was an illusion and never investigated further, Vincent DiPietro, an imaging scientist at Goddard Space Center, asked why. His initial investigation led several open minded scientists to a number of remarkable discoveries regarding the anomalous features of the Cydonia region of Mars. I remember well what a visiting astronomer said to his audience at Glasgow University in 1985 during the Gifford Lectures: "...the only thing you need to ask a question about science is an inquiring mind." The astronomer in question was the late Carl Sagan.

What Else?

It seemed to me from the beginning that there was much to be learned from studying the Viking Orbiter images of Cydonia. My first question regarding the Face was, is there anything else unusual in the surrounding terrain? This to me was a logical question, but the only image I had was the one which NASA published in the August 4 edition of the Viking Mission Bulletin, number 37. This bulletin I had obtained from the Kennedy Space Centre news desk in April, 1981 when I was covering the launch of the Space Shuttle Columbia for a local radio station.

That image of the face stuck in my mind. But I filed away the bulletin and never gave it any serious consideration until I read an article by DiPietro about his further research, which appeared in

OMNI magazine in June, 1982. I decided to obtain Viking image tapes and research the subject myself. I wrote to the National Space Science Data Center (NSSDC) at NASA and requested and received the relevant Viking Orbiter frames. With the help of several colleagues from the Computing Department of the University of Glasgow, I was able to produce reasonable quality images of frames 35A72, 70A11 and 70A13. During this ad hoc study I gathered together a small group of researchers and contacted an organization called The Mars Project in Santa Cruz, California.

It was obvious at this stage that the anomalous features referred to as the Face, D&M pyramid, Tholus, Cliff, City and Fort were clearly real features and not illusions. In short, the data seemed to be good and the results clear. By 1993, Viking Orbiter images were made available in CD-ROM format. This made it easier to conduct image processing routines on the images without needing to purchase expensive mainframe computer time at university.

I began a more in-depth study of the Viking Orbiter frames of Cydonia. NSSDC had supplied me with frames covering most of the images from Viking 1, orbits 3 to 70 along with image processing software written by Ron Baalke at JPL for use on a basic PC. I found it very simple to use the data and the software and could produce good results with little effort. It was during this initial session that I noticed a four-sided pyramid structure on the edge of frame 70a11. This feature later came to be called the NK pyramid, after the North Kelvinside High School in Glasgow, whose role in this study is described below.

A Project Begins

Having spent 10 years in education as an audio visual technician I had an interest in putting this research before young students. I believe that students are more receptive to new ideas and are less bothered by what their peers may think regarding taboo subjects in science. I put a proposal to Mike Turner, head of computing science at North Kelvinside School in Glasgow and Mike thought that a project involving image processing would be very educational for the students. I thought so too.

From February to April, 1996, five students undertook a project to examine 20 Viking Orbiter frames of the Cydonia region. The frames covered the area of the Face and its surrounding terrain and included a total area of over 22,000 sq. miles. Using the data and software supplied by NASA, the team systematically reviewed the surface features of frames 35a68 to 35a74 and frames 70a01 to 70a15. The computer used for this project was a humble 386 PC with a 20 Mhz processor and a math co-processor, 4 megabytes of memory and 40 megabytes of hard disc space. The monitor was a high-resolution 17" with a graphics board. All the equipment was fairly primitive by today's standards and clearly within the operational capabilities of most computer-minded high school students.

On behalf of the group, I contacted Professor Stanley V. McDaniel, author of *The McDaniel Report* on the Martian anomalies, and Mr. Erol Torun, author of "The Geology and Geometry of the D&M Pyramid." Both of these individuals agreed to serve as advisors for the NK student group. During the course of the study they provided valuable input and an international dimension to the student project.

Natural Rotation

The first task set for our budding researchers was to look at the known anomalies such as the Face and the group of structures dubbed "The City." The students noted that frame 35a72 has a lot of noise and data loss from transmission errors. These they cleaned up using a median filter, which replaces all extreme values of pixels in the image with an average grey value based on surrounding pixels. A grey scale histogram

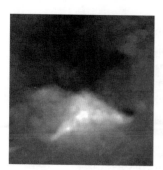

Using simple software and their own determination, the North Kelvinside students rendered very decent images of both the D & M Pyramid and the Mars Face.

revealed that the most useful data was in the 90 to 130 grey scale value. A contrast stretch was performed for viewing the frame. The Face was immediately noticeable among the many other features. As it appeared "upside down" in the image, the students felt compelled to rotate the image through 180 degrees for a more aesthetic viewing angle. We thought it strange that we should want to turn what is supposed to be a random rock formation upside-down, since you would never, for instance, feel the need to turn a photo of a random formation like a mountain upside-down. It is, of course, only our human interpretation that makes us do this, but it is interesting to note that other anomalies are easier to notice when the frame is positioned in this way. One can almost look north, south, east, and west, as if looking at a map.

Observing the Images

It was the opinion of the students that the Face does indeed look like a face and that the crossed symmetrical lines on the forehead, noted by Dr. Mark J. Carlotto, are clear without applying any further processing algorithms. A comparison with frame 70a13 also shows these lines and further detail in the shadowed side of the Face. The students concluded that the face is not symmetrical but that the left side is collapsed, eroded or damaged and does not closely resemble the right side. The Face does however have clear symmetrical markings in the form of lines on the forehead. It was also noted that there is very little noise in frame 70a13 and that features can be clearly made out without cleaning, contrast stretching or sharpening the image.

The shape of the object called the "D&M pyramid" (after DiPietro and Molenaar, its discoverers) cannot be easily discerned from frame 35A72, although the triangular faces of the North and West sides can be seen. However, the images of the D&M pyramid in frames 70A11 and 70A13 clearly show the full outline of the structure and this appears to be five-sided with a collapsed, eroded or damaged section on the eastern side.

A dark circular feature next to the eastern side of the structure is very unusual in that it does not resemble any other crater in the region which was studied. It seems to be a deep, dark hole which the sunlight does not illuminate. We could see the bottom of all craters in this region but we could not see the bottom of this feature. It was also noted that the axis of symmetry of the D&M Pyramid points North to intersect the Face.

The "City" is most prominent in frame 35a72 due to the low sun angle which makes the structures stand out against the surface. The Fort is easily the most artificial looking of the group and has a definite architectural look to it. The largest pyramid structure appears to be six-sided and slightly smaller than the D&M pyramid. It was noted that the City is much less distinctive in the high sun angle frame of 70A11. The structures look much more like natural features under these lighting conditions, with the exception of the object called the "Fort" where the walls of the structure are plainly anomalous in relation to the surrounding features.

A Pyramid
to Call One's Own

On the edge of 70A11 is found the NK pyramid. As mentioned earlier, we named this feature after the North Kelvinside high school in Glasgow, where the student project took place. The NK pyramid appears as a very obvious four-sided, square-based pyramidal feature. Each face of the pyramidal formation is approximately 1.4 km and our student team estimated the height (from shadow length) somewhere around 350 meters. This enigmatic structure is visible in frames 70A09, 70A11 and 35A70. It appears to sit on or very near the 40.86 deg. latitude line and is situated some 50 kms due west of the D&M pyramid, that is, on the same line of latitude.

Other features studied included the "Cliff," "Tholus," "Bowl," and other features along with the surrounding terrain covering a total area of over 22,000 sq. Kms. It was noted that there seems to be a marked dichotomy between the north and south of this region. The south seems to be very hilly with lots of broken up mesas and a range of small to large craters. The north seems to be flat and covered with cracks and fissures and has fewer craters. Some of the craters have ejecta ("splash") blankets that resemble mud flows and seem to be exclusive to the northern region. The group surmised that the northern region had the appearance of an ancient dried-up

sea-floor, with a clearly defined shoreline to the south which marks
a sharp progression to a different terrain.

Anomalies are Noted

The group concluded that the structures studied appear to be
somewhat out of character with the overall geomorphology
of the region and stand out quite distinctly with a minimum
of image processing. The group itself has no particular opinion as
to whether the anomalous features are artificial or natural, but
stress that they appear to be highly unusual and thus warrant further investigation.

The results of the NK Mars Project were presented publicly
by myself and Stephen Walker on April 16th, 1996 at the
Edinburgh International Science Festival. The presentation was
warmly received by the audience. Media coverage was nation-
wide and on the whole accurate and responsible. Stephen Walker
closed the presentation by calling for a responsible investigation of
the Cydonia anomalies by the scientific community.

On April 25th, 1996, North Kelvinside School sent an e-mail letter to Dr. Michael Malin of Malin Space Science Systems in
California, who is in charge of the Mars Global Surveyor imaging.
We asked if Dr. Malin would include the NK pyramid on the target
list for hi-resolution photography. Dr. Malin replied on May 9th,
1996, referring to the feature in question as a "...pyramidal mountain" and confirmed its location as "...near 40.7 N, 10.6 W." Dr. Malin
also informed the school, "...we cannot expect to "hit" any specific
target on Mars. Rather we hope to acquire representative images of
many areas, including Cydonia." Dr Malin added, "In any case, the
attributes of these landforms are quite interesting, and we do intend
to observe them during the Mars Global Surveyor Mission."

A New Generation
of Scientists

The NK Mars Project has been very satisfying. It brought us
into contact with many professionals who have applauded
our efforts, and the increased media publicity has helped

raise the profile of the school. The project has also clearly demonstrated that it is not difficult for students to make a responsible contribution to a controversial science subject. Interest among the students continues even though most who worked on the project have now gone on to university and other studies. In the spirit of Newton and Feynman we have started a process in which these students continue to make observations and ask questions, and thereby to become the next generation of scientists.

Acknowledgements

I would like to thank Stephen Walker, Andrew Gow, Ka Ming Chan, Chi Chung Lee, Wing Chun Lee and all the staff of North Kelvinside School for their time and patience in carrying through this project and hope that NASA's scientists will have the courage to resolve the controversy surrounding Cydonia in the coming years.

BIOGRAPHICAL NOTE

Chris O'Kane is the developer of the Vistamorph panoramic photography system, which has won two innovation awards in Scotland. He is a council member of ASTRA, a Scottish astronautics research organization and is also a member of the International Association of Panoramic Photographers (IAPP). He has lectured on astronomy and space science for public educational events since 1986. As an audio visual technician in the educational system, he initiated and organized the student image processing experiment at the North Kelvinside High School described in the proceeding article.

Note for Educators:
Award Winning Website for Students

For teachers wishing to introduce students to information about the Cydonia anomalies, we suggest Stanley McDaniel's website, The McDaniel Report at: http://www.mcdanielreport.com

This site has just been awarded the Study Web Academic Excellence Award, which indicates a highly educational site with material appropriate for students.

Other URLs and published materials on the subject of Mars anomalies are also listed in the back of the book in the Reference section.

Evidence of Alien Artifacts?

Let's say that each of these civilizations sends out one interstellar expedition per year. That means that every star such as our sun, would be visited at least once every million years. In some systems where these beings found life, they would make more frequent visits. There's a strong probability, then, that they visited Earth every few thousand years. It is not out of the question that artifacts of these visits still exist.

— Carl Sagan

Even without The Face, Cydonia would be a place of almost endless fascination to those searching planets for possible signs of extraterrestrial artifacts. There are about two dozen anomalous surface objects shown in the Viking images of Cydonia. There are also several other features from other areas of Mars which show the kinds of coherence which anthropologists, military analysts and archaeologists search for. Why are there no signs of airports, roads, and cities? If the Earth of today were hit by an asteroid like the one that struck in the Yucatan 65 million years ago and wiped out the dinosaurs, the resulting shock waves might eventually erase almost every discernible evidence of human habitation—excepting, quite possibly, the pyramids of Egypt and other great monuments. Is this the case on Mars? We don't yet know, but the scientific studies presented here, we visit the whole range of Martian enigmas, from the "String of Beads" that some have called a "runway," to the puzzling geometric arrangement of similar-sized mounds, to the Face on Mars itself with its wealth of inexplicable detail and symmetry.

Finding Cultural
Features on
Planetary Surfaces

Erol Torun

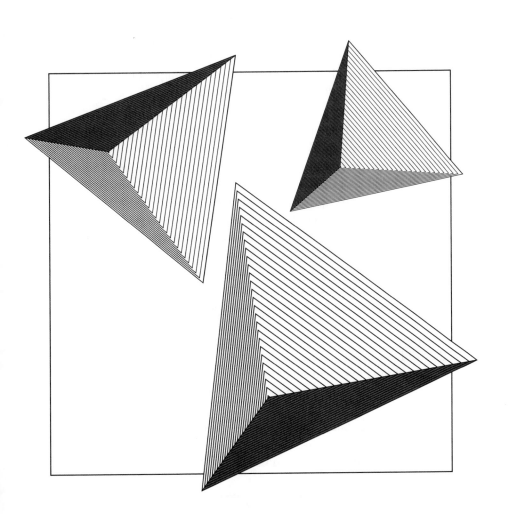

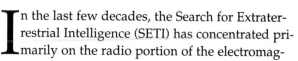

In the last few decades, the Search for Extraterrestrial Intelligence (SETI) has concentrated primarily on the radio portion of the electromagnetic spectrum in a search for intelligent life beyond the Earth. Recent work performed with images of the surface of the planet Mars has effectively extended SETI to include examining a planetary surface for signs of intelligent modification. Planetary SETI presents a set of conditions very similar to the use of aerial photography in archaeology.

Archaeologists have long used aerial photography to simplify the process of site identification and evaluation. Large areas can be examined this way, avoiding the time and expense of unnecessary ground surveys. The advantages of aerial survey are much greater for planetary surfaces other than Earth, since ground survey sadly, is as yet unobtainable, and robotic ground survey will be very expensive and limited to a few select areas. The techniques used in archaeological air photo interpretation can be adapted to the search for intelligent modification of any planetary surface.

Planetary SETI in History

The concept of inspecting a planetary surface for telltale signs of intelligent life has an interesting history. In the nineteenth century, telescopic observation of Mars yielded observations that suggested the presence of linear striations on the surface. In 1877, Italian astronomer Giovanni Schiaparelli claimed to see canali, or "canals" as they were later translated. Much controversy surrounded this claim, as many astronomers were unable to see them.

American astronomer Percival Lowell became intrigued with the controversy. Being independently wealthy, he built an observatory in Arizona to advance the telescopic study of Mars. Lowell also saw the "canals" and produced detailed maps of them. Although they did not show up on time-exposure photographs of Mars, this was attributed to obscuring of the photographic plate by the Earth's atmosphere. Lowell believed the "canals" to be the work of intelligent Martians attempting to deal with diminishing water resources by transporting water from the frozen Martian poles.

The numerous books and articles authored by Lowell did much to popularize the notion that Mars was inhabited. They also

Two pages from Giovanni Schiaparelli's notebook (1877). Schiaparelli saw these lines on the planet and called them "canali" (channels). Only later did they come to be interpreted as "canals" or waterways.

inspired science fiction works, such as H.G. Wells *The War of the Worlds* and a series of adventure novels about Mars written by Edgar Rice Burroughs, the creator of Tarzan. But, in 1965, television images of Mars returned by Mariner 4 showed a barren, cratered terrain that dashed hopes of finding the inhabited Mars of Lowell and Burroughs. The "canals," nowhere to be seen, were assumed to have been optical illusions. Later images from Mariner 9 in 1972 dramatically changed this picture of Mars once again with the discovery of numerous features apparently cut by running water. These are natural erosive features indicating that Mars has had past periods of a warmer, wetter climate.

The discoveries of Mariner 9 put planetary science in an anticipatory mood prior to the launch of the Viking mission. Viking was to place landers on the Martian surface and conduct experiments that might detect the presence of life. At this stage, the search for life on Mars was almost exclusively for microbial life.

Still, during the 1970s, the concept of searching for intelligent life or its ruins on Mars was not entirely abandoned. The astronomy journal *ICARUS*, published a paper entitled "A Search for Life on Earth at 100 Meter Resolution," by Carl Sagan and David Wallace, both at Cornell. This study was performed due to the anticipated availability of new imagery of Mars from Mariner 9 and Viking. The experiment, which utilized several thousand Gemini and Apollo photographs of the earth at 100 meter resolution, found signs of intelligent life, including "rectangular arrays due to human agricultural and urban territoriality, roads, canals, jet contrails, and industrial pollution." False positives, such as dunes, sandbars, and jet stream clouds, were also found, indicating the caution necessary in this type of photo interpretation. The paper closes with the following:

"The anticipated Viking Mars orbiters represent an additional improvement... Thus we conclude that were life on Mars at the same level of detectivity as contemporary life on Earth, it would have a significant prospect of being detected in the next few years. More primitive life would of course elude detection longer."

It is clear from this paper, and from the papers it references, that most planetary scientists regarded intelligent life on Mars, past or present, as an extremely remote possibility. Nevertheless, the concept of examining the surface of a planet other than Earth for the signs of intelligent life was discussed seriously.

The subject of planetary SETI then falls silent, only to resurface in connection with the unusual features in the Cydonia region of Mars, and the independent study of these objects by individuals outside of the planetary sciences community.

Detectability of Artificial Surface Features

The process for distinguishing natural from cultural features is usually not explained rigorously in texts on photo interpretation for the simple reason that photo analysts are very familiar with most artificial structures. Object identification is usually immediate and by direct recognition. When there is some question as to the identity of a cultural feature, photo interpretation keys are available that display examples of less commonly encountered objects that may be compared with the object in question.

There are no absolute criteria for object identification—the process involves probabilities and is highly contextual. The Manual of Photo Interpretation published by the American Society of Photogrammetry offers the following advice: "In order to identify objects he has not seen before, or to understand the meaning of objects once identified, the photo interpreter exploits the principle of convergence of evidence... There may be many clues to the identity of an unknown object. None of the clues is infallible by itself; but if all or most of the clues point to the same conclusion, the conclusion is probably correct. Photo interpretation, then, is actually an art of probabilities. Few things are perfectly certain in photo interpretation in the way that one and one certainly make two; but many interpretations are so probable, when all visible evidence has been considered, that they may be safely regarded as correct. The difficult part of photo interpretation consists in judgment of degrees of probability."

With geological formations recognized and noted, the process of identifying cultural features is one of locating shapes, structures, and geometric patterns that are not easily explained by the surface geology. When using aerial photography in archaeology, cultural features can often be recognized by "...their greater coherence and more precise outlines," whereas geological patterns are likely to be "...blurred, meandering, or incomplete." (D. R. Wilson, *Air Photo Interpretation* for *Archaeologists* (1982))

In extending this process to planetary SETI, it is important to be aware of the geological characteristics of the planet's surface. Some geological features have enough geometric regularity that they can be mistaken for cultural features. In the case of Mars, pyramidal landforms and patterned ground are fairly common, and the photointerpreter must be familiar with these and the geomorphological processes that form them.

A special problem exists for detecting artificial structures on another planetary surface. We cannot assume the features with which we are familiar will exist on another planet. To ask questions such as "where are the roads?" is meaningless. Instead, we must strip the photo interpretive process down to its elemental core. Having done this, we are left with searching for objects and patterns having geometric shapes that are inconsistent with the geology of the planetary surface in question.

This requirement was recognized in the mid-1960s in a National Academy of Sciences report dealing with life on Mars: "An open-air theatre, a housing development or an airport are readily identifiable in high-resolution photographs of the Earth. The discovery of similar well-ordered geometrical patterns on Mars would certainly be provocative, but by no means could we be sure of their identification. *Yet the detection of highly ordered structures on the Martian surface would certainly pinpoint areas deserving closer study.*" (emphasis added)

Imagery analysis of the Cydonia region of Mars has pin-pointed objects that are inconsistent with the local geology, and have enough geometric regularity to warrant the "closer study" recommended by the National Academy of Sciences report. Detailed description of this research is beyond the scope of this article but has been published in various forms and places

Two examples of the unusual objects under study in this region of Mars are an angular formation nicknamed the "Fort" from Viking frame 35A72, and a pyramidal form from frame 70A13 that has been called the "D & M Pyramid" after its discoverers, Vincent DiPietro and Gregory Molenaar.

Searching for Additional Sites

Earlier we saw quotations from the planetary science community's literature in which the search for signs of intelligent life on Mars was openly discussed. Neither the philosophy of science nor the laws of physics have changed in thirty years. Thus, the scientific community of today should not have any logical objection to searching Mars or other planetary surfaces for signs of intelligent modification. In air-photo archaeology, it is not feasible to use random high-resolution imagery in the hopes of discovering new sites. Instead, search criteria must be developed to pre-select likely sites for closer scrutiny. High-resolution imagery of

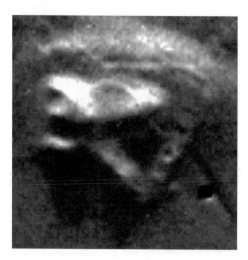

This unusual angular feature from NASA Viking frame 35A72 has been referred to as "The Fort." Its actual nature is unknown.

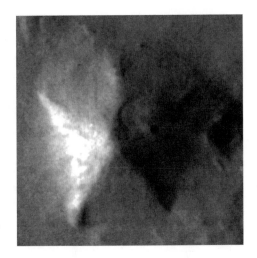

This object, sometimes called the "D & M Pyramid," may have once been symmetrically five-sided. There is evidence of damage on the right side, possibly due to meteor impact.

these locations may then be examined for signs of activity.

Search criteria are especially important for other planetary surfaces. Planetary imaging missions are limited as to the number of images that may be obtained, and many years may pass before another mission is attempted. In the case of Mars, there is only one natural resource whose distribution is known well enough to use as a global search criterion, and that is water. Even a highly advanced civilization would find it far easier to use naturally occurring water than to mechanically extract water from hydrated rock or clay.

Mars currently has no surface water. Considerable quantities of water exist frozen in the polar ice caps and perhaps underground as permafrost. *(See the chapter Mars as an Abode of Life on page 123.)* Future missions with radar sensors would be desirable for pinpointing underground water deposits.

Drainage channels are visible on Mars, and most geologists believe that they were caused by running water. Some of these channels appear to be heavily eroded over time and may have originally been cut by water from permafrost melted by very ancient volcanic activity. Others are much more sharply cut and hence may be relatively more recent, perhaps produced by a warmer, wetter climate in the past. Many areas in the northern hemisphere of Mars show signs of having once held shallow, standing water. The Cydonia anomalies are located near just such an area—possibly the shoreline of an ancient sea.

A recommendation for future imaging missions to Mars is to concentrate on those areas that show signs of once having been adjacent to water. Such areas are also likely places to search for fossilized primitive life. Thus this imagery would serve the dual purpose of looking for intelligent modification and performing site selection for landing robotic equipment to search for fossils.

BIOGRAPHICAL NOTE

Erol Torun is a cartographer with a background in geology. His paper "The Geomorphology and Geometry of the D & M Pyramid" was one of the early studies of the Cydonian feature (1988). An updated version is available at http://www.well.com/user/etorun/

The Mounds of Mars:
ET Artifacts or
Elegant Geology

Professor Stanley V. McDaniel
Dr. Horace W. Crater

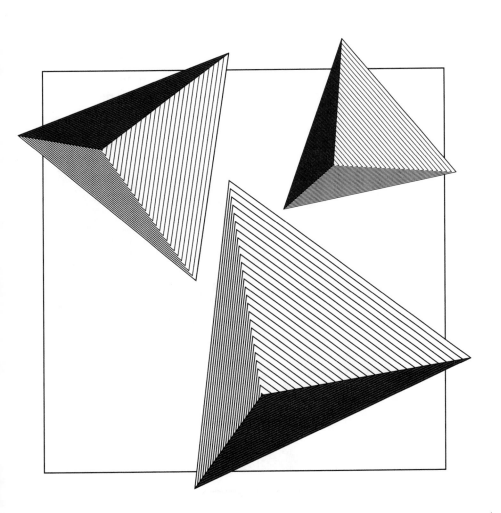

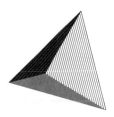

The Aftermath
of Mars Observer

After the mysterious loss of the Mars Observer spacecraft in August 1993, scientists pursuing the Search for Extra-terrestrial Artifacts (SETA) were faced with the possibility that no new images of the Cydonia region might be obtained for some time to come. With no new data forthcoming, it would be necessary to explore previously overlooked, or only partially investigated, features. Several avenues of approach were employed. Among them is the geometric analysis reported here, which identified a striking anomaly in the arrangement of certain small features west of the well-known "Face on Mars."

Here, on the Martian Cydonia Plain, lies a cluster of large formations that has been called the "City" (no one claims it actually is a city). This group is shown in the left center area of the images below. The larger objects are about one mile across, arranged in a roughly pentagonal pattern. The strange object just to the right of top center is also considered part of the "City" and has been nicknamed the "Fort" because of its resemblance to a walled enclosure.

Mounds have been highlighted and lettered in this image. The mounds making up the "City Square" in the central area are not lettered due to lack of space. The area enclosed by the four "City Square" mounds was designated "mound S."

The area of the "City" at Cydonia on Mars. These images are for illustration only and should not be used for research purposes.

Within the "City" and on the open plain to the south, there are several relatively small features about 300-700 feet in diameter and perhaps 100 feet high that have been called "mounds." These stand out distinctly from their surroundings because they are fairly uniform in size and brightness, and are much smaller than the surrounding land forms. Except for a group of four in the center of the "City," they are not tightly clustered but are separated in some cases by as much as 3 kilometers. All told there are not very many of them. We identify about sixteen. For research purposes we have assigned letters to most of these as shown.

In 1992, science writer Richard C. Hoagland reported that three of these mounds-those lettered A, E, and D-appear to form an almost perfect isosceles triangle (a triangle having two sides of equal length). Of course, finding one symmetrical triangle among various scattered formations is of no particular interest. But when Dr. Horace W. Crater of the University of Tennessee Space Institute made careful measurements of the angles in this triangle, he discovered an odd coincidence. The angles, within very close tolerances, matched those in the cross-section of a tetrahedron.

Tetrahedron

The cross-section AED is labeled to match the corresponding mounds. Line EX is the geometric axis of the tetrahedron running from the apex to the center of face AZY. All the angles in the cross-section and its regular geometric divisions are simple linear functions of pi and the tetrahedral constant t = 19.5 degrees.]

Richard C. Hoagland had also noticed that mounds AEG appeared to form a right triangle. Crater measured this triangle and again there was a surprise. The angles in this right triangle (within very close tolerances) match one division of the cross-section of a tetrahedron, having the same angles as triangle AEX in the figure on the previous page. Furthermore, if the cross-section is divided exactly in half by an altitude drawn from its apex (D), the angles again match those of AEG. There was apparently some kind of geometric correspondence between the isosceles triangle marked out by mounds AED and the right triangle suggested by mounds AEG.

Pressing further, Crater measured yet a third triangle, AGD. It turned out to have the same angles as AEG. The odd regularity was beginning to repeat itself. Crater then performed a fascinating experiment. Using analytic geometry, he identified the angles that would have to exist in an ideal figure consisting of one isosceles and two right triangles connected in the manner found in mounds ADEG. The result was tantalizing. All internal angles of this four-sided polygon are either the right angle (90 degrees) or can be expressed by means of the right angle and one particular angle, 19.5 degrees. Comparing this with the geometry of the tetrahedron, it was found that the same is true of all regular geometric divisions of the tetrahedral cross-section. Crater labeled this "tetrahedral constant" angle of 19.5 degrees by the lower-case letter t.

The mystery: why was this tetrahedral angle t showing up so consistently in this figure?

A Trend Develops

Crater next brought the single mound to the south, mound B, into consideration as shown on the following page. Measurement showed that the triangles formed by mounds ADB and EAB contain the same angles as that formed by mounds AEG and AGD. There was an apparent trend toward repetition of a particular set of angles: The angles within the ten internal triangles created by lines drawn between the five mounds GABDE are all simple functions of the 90 degree angle and the tetrahedral constant angle t. Crater christened these five mounds the "pentad."

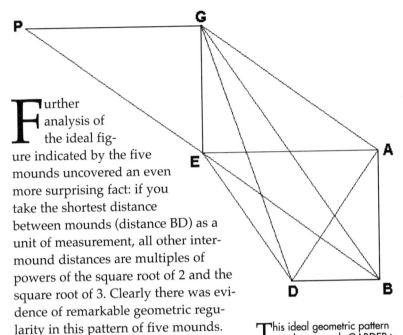

urther analysis of the ideal figure indicated by the five mounds uncovered an even more surprising fact: if you take the shortest distance between mounds (distance BD) as a unit of measurement, all other inter-mound distances are multiples of powers of the square root of 2 and the square root of 3. Clearly there was evidence of remarkable geometric regularity in this pattern of five mounds. What is the probability that such a configuration might occur by chance?

Crater used three different methods, including 200 million computer simulations of random distributions, for calculating the probability that the pentad formation is consistent with chance as might be expected of natural geological features. A test of the reliability of this method was conducted by comparison with the distribution of 4,000 other natural objects on Mars. The net result: the probability that the pattern of five mounds are random is less than one in 200 million.

While this extremely low probability does not prove that the mound pattern is a product of intentional design, it clearly identifies the pattern as a radical anomaly calling for explanation.

This ideal geometric pattern matches mounds GABDEP to tolerances of less than 1.5 pixels. As is the case with the tetrahedral cross-section, All internal angles in this ideal figure are simple linear functions of pi and the tetrahedral constant t = 19.5 degrees.]

At this point we have a five-sided figure, defined by the pentad of mounds GABDE, which exhibits a remarkable degree of geometric regularity. The angles in the figure reference the geometry of the tetrahedron, and the chances of this orderliness being a product of random placement are practically zero. Crater described this situation as indicating a "quasi-predictable phenomenon."

If some nonrandom mechanism of formation were at work here it would be possible that a study of the remaining eleven mounds in the area would show a similar geometry. Acting on the prediction that this might be the case, Crater extended his study to the remaining mounds.

Exploring the Mound Terrain

The last mound that lies outside the "City" boundaries is mound P to the west of mound G. Upon measurement it became evident that again we have an example of a right triangle with angles the same as those found earlier. And not only the same angles: Within measurement error, triangle EGP is the same size and contains the same angles as triangles EGA and EAB, both of which are within the original pentad. These three identical triangles are easily seen in the figure shown on the previous page.

Could this be merely the result of "fudging" about with angular measurements until a mound is located that matches some regular pattern? Not possible. Mound P, like the earlier five mounds, lies in an isolated position. There are no other mounds scattered about that might offer "choices" and create an arbitrary selection.

Of the probabilities involved in this hexad, Crater says that the likelihood of this being a random formation "is obviously less than that of the pentad by at least a factor of 1000" (Less than one in 200 billion).

Turning his attention to the rest of the mounds, which are scattered apparently at random within the area of the "City," Crater realized that four of these mounds near the center of the "City" area, are too close together to allow for meaningful angular measurements. Temporarily eliminating these four mounds (one of which is only borderline under our definition of a "mound"), Crater devised a new test.

With so many mounds involved, the method of computer modeling would be next to impossible to carry out - it would use far too much computer time. Instead, Crater tested all the remaining twelve mounds (six already accounted for and the remaining six within the "City") for the frequency of occurrence of the two types of triangles that seemed to be the basis for the earlier figures. These were, you recall, the isosceles tetrahedral cross-section ADE and the right triangle AGE that was a division of the cross-section.

This was a comparative test that checked the frequency of occurrence against that of an entire range of right and isosceles triangles, treating the angle *t* as a variable and running through all its values from 0 to 90 degrees. The outcome was startling. Crater reports: "The results show in the clearest possible terms a geometrical anomaly." The frequency of occurrence when *t* equaled the tetrahedral value of 19.5 degrees yielded a z-score, or number of standard deviations from the mean, of 5.48, compared to z-scores of about -1 to +1 for all other values. This result is important because it includes twelve of the sixteen mounds in the area (excluding only those four too close together to obtain meaningful measurements), and because it is an independent test of the earlier results obtained by computer modeling.

What about those remaining four mounds? This group has been called the "City Square" because the four objects are arranged in an approximate square. There also appears to be a smaller structure at the very center of this square. Early in the investigation of this area, attention had been drawn to this arrangement because of its evident symmetry.

Rather than try to make measurements of the angles between the four mounds, Crater chose instead the area they enclose. This area is about the same size as the largest mounds. This small area was then factored into the z-score analysis as if it were another mound, which we called "mound S." Once again the result was contrary to chance expectation. Instead of lowering the z-score in the direction of the average curve, as should be expected if the placement was random, the z-score increased from 5.48 to 6.38.

Archaeological
Confirmation

By several independent tests, the pattern of the mounds had been established as non-random by a large margin. When he heard of Crater's results, archaeologist Dr. James F. Strange of the University of South Florida became intrigued. He knew of a different test for random distribution. This test is used in archaeology to evaluate whether an area might be worthy of further investigation. It is called the Kolgorov-Smirnov test.

The Kolgorov-Smirnov test is based upon measurements of the distances between objects rather than on their angular relationships. Strange independently measured the distances between the mounds. His result: "we can say that normal distribution is a poor fit for the data, that is, the distribution of the mound distances is with high probability not normal and therefore with high probability not random."

We find, therefore, that the determination that the mounds are not distributed randomly is confirmed by an independent statistical test based on distance measurements rather than on frequency of triangles containing specific angles

A Cascade
of Evidence

In *The McDaniel Report* by Professor Stanley V. McDaniel, it was pointed out that the object called the "Face on Mars" has gone through an exhaustive series of tests. *(See the chapter Tests "The Face" Might Have Failed on page 249.)* Each of these tests had the capacity to turn up negative results, which would weaken the hypothesis that the Face may be an artificial construction. The striking thing about these tests is that not a single one has turned up negative results. Instead of weakening the hypothesis, the tests, one by one, added to the probability that the Face may be an ET artifact.

In a similar fashion, a series of tests have been performed on the mound distribution in the area of the "City." Crater used three different methods of evaluating the odds against random arrangement. All yielded positive results, and all were consistent with one another. As Crater extended his research progressively until finally all mounds in the area were included, instead of the odds for non-random distribution decreasing, they continued to increase. Finally, the result of the Kolgorov-Smirnov test applied by Dr. James F. Strange could potentially have contradicted Crater's results. Instead they once again indicated non-random distribution.

The fact that the Face, with its constellation of anomalous features, is in the same vicinity as the mounds, provides a context of anomalies that surely should command the active attention of NASA and other space-faring nations. At this moment NASA's latest spacecraft, the Mars Global Surveyor, is slowly settling into final orbit around Mars with a high priority assigned for re-imaging the Face and obtaining high-resolution images of the area of the mounds and other Cydonia anomalies. We may find the truth very soon.

BIOGRAPHICAL NOTE

Professor Horace W. Crater is the President of the Society for Planetary SETI Research (SPSR) and physics professor at the University of Tennessee Space Institute.

Nonrandom Distribution of Angles

BY PROFESSOR STANLEY V. MCDANIEL

The accompanying graph is a dramatic representation of the "signal in the noise" that, among other evidence, has convinced SPSR scientists that the Cydonia area deserves high priority for investigation by NASA. Studying the Cydonia mound configuration, Horace Crater first noticed that among the four mounds GADE there appeared to be an isosceles triangle (ADE) and two right triangles (GEA and GDA), with the odd circumstance that each of the two right triangles, in angles, amounted to just one-half the isosceles. In other words, if you split the isosceles triangle exactly in half, you would get two right triangles having the same angles as the two right triangles found among these four mounds.

By using analytic geometry, Crater determined that a figure of this sort was geometrically unique. Just how unique, and whether the same pattern would be reflected among the remaining mounds in the area, remained to be determined. The question: How many right and associated isosceles triangles, where the right triangles are equal (in angles) to exactly one-half the related isosceles, can occur in a carefully coordinated fit among all twelve mounds at Cydonia? Further, what is the relation of the number of actual occurrences to chance distribution? (Although there are sixteen mounds in the area, four of them are so close together in relation to their size that angular relations between them allow too much freedom for interpreta-

(cont. next page)

tion. Crater therefore restricted the procedure to twelve mounds, but takes the four proximate mounds into consideration elsewhere).

To avoid possible bias toward any particular pair of triangles, or toward any particular angle, Crater examined the set of all right and associated isosceles triangles by allowing a defining angle, *t*, to vary in 1/2 degree intervals from 0 to 90 degrees. As this angle *t* was varied, the corresponding right and isosceles triangles would change. In this way all sets of associated right and isosceles triangles would be tested.

First the number of occurrences, among the actual mounds, of all such sets of triangles was calculated (by computer). For high precision Crater required angles that agree with the ideal within less than two-tenths of a degree. Next, a second curve was produced by a procedure identifying the number of occurrences to be expected as a result of chance, this curve could then be compared with the actual count. If the mound configuration was a result of chance, the two curves should have

matched fairly well. Instead, at one particular value of *t*, the curve for the actual mounds shot up far beyond the level expected by chance.

Finally, from the comparison of the two curves, the z-score, representing the standard deviations, was derived for the two-tenths degree precision. The z-score plot, shown in the accompanying graph, vividly demonstrates the anomaly. Random geology would expect a z-score in magnitude no greater than 2 or, to be conservative, 3, for this particular site. Instead we have a sharp peak, representing a z-score of 7.42 precisely when the angle *t* equals 19.5 degrees, representing one particular set of isosceles and right triangles. It turns out that this particular set is the one containing the same angles as those measured among mounds GADE. Thus the prediction was fulfilled that, if the angles from GADE were significant, the number of times these angles appear among the remaining mound angles would be far beyond chance. The z-score of those angles is so high as to rule out chance as playing any significant part whatsoever in the distribution of the actual mounds.

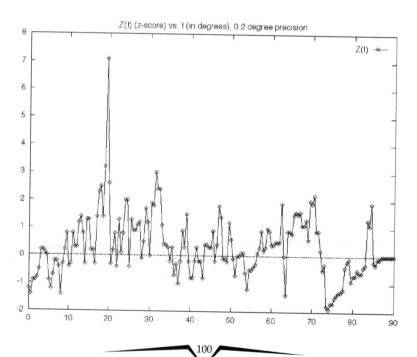

Cydonian
Mound Geometry

Professor Stanley V. McDaniel

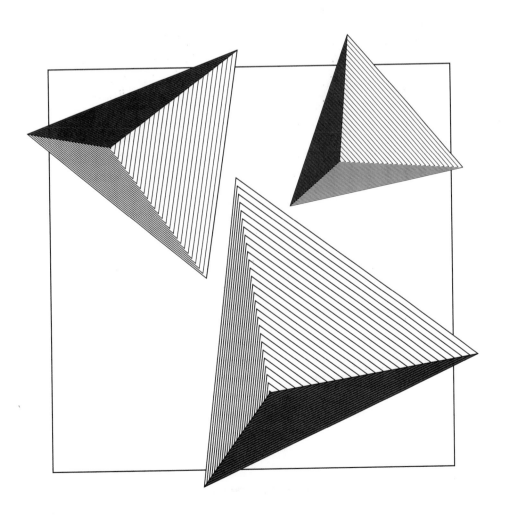

Geometry and Culture

Elsewhere we have described Dr. Horace W. Crater's analysis of the mound distribution at Cydonia on Mars. *(See The Mounds of Mars on page 91.)* Dr. Crater found that the frequency of appearance for two particular types of triangular relationships between mounds was far beyond chance expectation.

If the distribution of mounds at Cydonia is not random, there appear to be just two possible explanations. Either we are seeing some previously unknown geological process, or the "mounds" are intelligently designed structures laid out according to a rational pattern. Perhaps on a closer look we can make some sense of this "Cydonian Geometry" and get some perspective on the question "Is the mound formation a freak of geology, or an artificial construction?"

The Rectangular Grid

In February 1995, while studying Crater's results, I realized that the pattern formed by five of the Cydonia mounds appeared to imply a rectangle, even though two corners of that rectangle were "missing." Using the geometric analysis performed by Crater, the proportions of that implied rectangle were 1:1.414, or one to the square root of two. (This first rectangle constitutes the lower right-hand quadrant of Figure 1 and is outlined by the mounds GABDE.)

Was this implied rectangle merely an accident? One way to test this would be to see whether other mounds in the area might somehow be involved in the same pattern. We extended the original rectangle by doubling its size, and discovered that mound P, to the west, lies on one corner of the extended grid outlined by six mounds GABDEP (lower half of Figure 1).

This could be written off as a further accident, but mound P is an isolated mound, as are the five mounds that outline the original grid. The Mounds define the geometry themselves without any need to force a fit. Furthermore Dr. Crater had already determined by different methods that the chances for the six mounds being distributed randomly were almost infinitesimal. Thus the

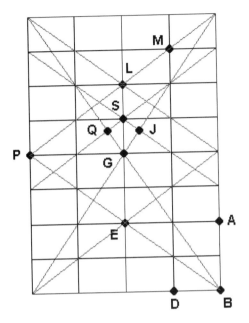

Figure 1

Positions of coordinated fit points for eleven mounds, superimposed on an expanded grid of proportions 1 to square root 2. Nine of the eleven mound fit points fall on regular horizontal/vertical grid locations. Note the symmetrical pattern formed by mounds EGSLQJ. "Mound" S is the central area enclosed by the four tightly clustered mounds sometimes referred to as the "City Square." *(See The Mounds of Mars on page 91.)*

positioning of mound P at one corner of an extended rectangle having the same proportions as the original seemed encouraging.

Studying the geometry of this rectangle, we discovered that it has a unique property. It repeats its own proportions when divided in half along its width. This suggested a rectangular unit implied by mounds ABDE, which can be seen occupying the lower right-hand octant of Figure 1. The position of mound D is at the mid-point on one side of the rectangle, so we took the corners and side mid-points of the rectangular unit as the primary divisions of the grid.

Somewhat like a fisherman casting a net, Dr. Crater then expanded the grid to eight such units. The result was the grid as seen in Figures 1 and 2. In Figure 2, the regular divisions of the grid are numbered (1 to 24) along the perimeter to provide a set of reference coordinates.

Because the grid is "anchored" by the positions of mounds A, B, D and E, we could not move the grid about. Nevertheless seven more "fish" were caught in this experimental net—accounting for all the remaining mounds. (There are actually sixteen identifiable mounds, but four of them are clustered so tightly together that the area they enclose is about equal to that of a single mound. We counted this area as our "thirteenth mound," labeled mound "S.")

The Coordinated
Fit Points

arlier, Dr. Crater had tested all the mounds in the area for
the frequency of occurrence of two specific types of triangles. In measuring the triangular relationships among the
mounds, he applied a very stringent rule. Only one point could be
used within each mound. Thus if several triangles were to use the
same mound as a vertex, this would not be counted unless they all
used the exact same point on that mound. Crater called these common vertices on each mound the "coordinated fit points."

Crater had, therefore, already defined a set of points, one
point within each mound. Yet when the inferred grid was
expanded to cover all 13 mounds, these points all fell at significant positions on the grid. This correlation between the predetermined coordinated fit points and the expanded grid came as a
complete surprise.

Figure 1 illustrates the locations of the coordinated fit points
for eleven of the mounds in relation to the grid. The grid positions
of the fit points for the remaining two mounds are shown in
Figure 2. Keep in mind that although the positions are of the fit
points and not the entire areas of the mounds, these fit points
were not chosen to suit the grid, but were determined in advance
of the grid by an entirely different procedure.

Of the eleven mounds, nine of the coordinated fit points fall
on regular horizontal-vertical grid intersections (MLSGPEABD).
Mounds EGSL are all aligned along the central axis, while mounds
PLM and PEB lie along the upper and lower half-diagonals. The
fit points for mounds Q and J lie equidistant from the central axis
and share the full diagonals with mound G plus a short diagonal
with mound S. The diagonal lines are all drawn from grid unit
mid-point locations. Of particular interest from the point of view
of symmetry is the group GQSJ, which form a symmetrical kite- or
cross-like formation.

In Figure 2 we see that the remaining two mounds, O and K,
also fall on the intersections of lines drawn between the grid unit
mid-points. Mound O lies at the intersection of vertical 2–16 and
diagonal 13–19 (referring to the coordinate numbers along the
perimeter of the figure), while mound K lies at the common intersection of no fewer than five diagonals.

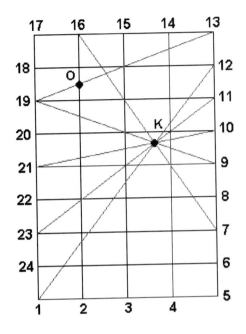

Figure 2

The remaining two mound fit points are also located at grid intersections. Mound O lies at the intersection of vertical 2-16 and diagonal 13-19 (referring to the coordinate numbers along the perimeter of the figure), while mound K lies at the common intersection of no fewer than five diagonals.

It is true that with a total of 24 grid reference points the number of possible intersections is quite high——somewhat over 4,000. If we were referring to the total areas of the mounds, it would be inevitable that multiple grid intersections would fall within each mound area (although even in that case the positions of the mounds in relation to the grid would seem significant). But in this case, the coordinated fit locations are dimensionless points. It is extremely unlikely that thirteen randomly chosen dimensionless points would fall by chance at grid intersections, especially in this partially symmetrical pattern and with nine of the thirteen points located at horizontal-vertical intersections.

Lest there be any misunderstanding, the fact that the mound distribution is far from random is not dependent on the apparent conformity of the mounds to the grid. The nonrandom distribution of the mounds was determined independently by several tests, which are discussed in the chaper "The Mounds of Mars." (*See page 91.*) Their distribution according to the square root two rectangular grid is what we might call "icing on the cake." It suggests some particular geometric orderliness beyond mere nonrandom distribution that may have cultural implications.

Cultural Affinities
of the Rectangular Grid

In his book *The Geometry of Art and Life*, Matila Ghyka identifies the "square root 2 rectangle" as a geometric form that plays a significant role in "Greek and Gothic Canons of Proportion" (Ghyka 1946, Chapter VIII). The ratios derived by dividing the rectangle into regular segments and by drawing lines between nodes were considered within this tradition to be "dynamic" proportions as compared to the proportions, for example, of a rectangle of sides 1:2, which were "static."

Significance was also attached to the simple geometric derivability of the square root 2 rectangle from the square (the diagonal of a square = square root 2) and the series of square root rectangles (2, 3, 5) that could be generated from the square as a starting point. In his investigation of a possible ground plan for the layout of the three pyramids at Gizeh in Egypt, John A. R. Legon demonstrates that the structures conform to a rectangle having the proportions square root 2 × square root 3, with its diagonal being square root 5, measured in cubits × 1000 (Legon 1988).

Legon argues that these values were probably derived by first constructing a square measuring 1000 cubits on a side, then taking the diagonal of that square for the square root 2 value, then constructing a square root 2 rectangle and taking its diagonal for the square root 5 value, "so that the overall dimensions along the two axes of the plan are readily constructed from the square of side 1000 cubits."

In this terrestrial tradition, then, we find that the square root 2 rectangle was referred to as an element in a system of aesthetics, specifically the aesthetics of proportion and symmetry in architecture and art. If the mounds at Cydonia are artificial constructions they were certainly a phenomenon of architecture. The conclusion to be drawn from this is not that the layout of the mounds at Cydonia are therefore artificial—at this stage we cannot know that—but rather that their conformity to a grid based on the square root 2 rectangle has a possible cultural significance over and beyond its purely geometric richness and uniqueness.

Other
Cydonia
Anomalies

Daniel Drasin

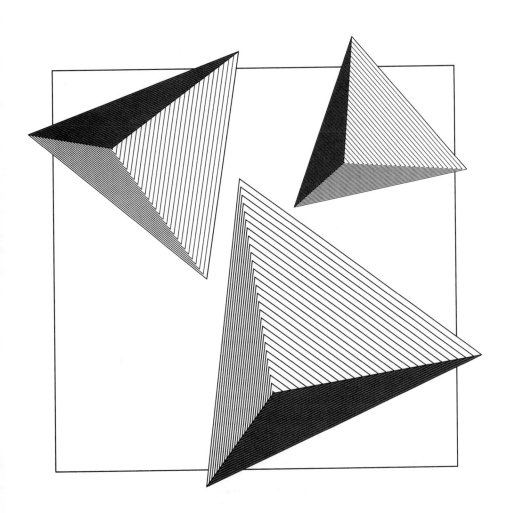

The Face is Not Alone

The Face on Mars has captured the imagination of a generation of inquiring minds, while those of a less inquisitive bent have vigorously dismissed it as a "trick of light" or an "anthropomorphic projection" unworthy of scientific inquiry. Less well known, yet more difficult to dismiss as illusions and projections, are over two dozen Martian landforms at Cydonia and elsewhere that appear to be at least as anomalous as the great Face itself. These formations share the following characteristics:

- To the eye they appear distinctly out of character, virtually popping out of the landscape in NASA's Viking images.
- They seem to defy conventional geomorphological explanation.
- When subjected to fractal analysis some of them display a high degree of fractal model-fit error, which indicates that they are less likely than neighboring formations to be of purely natural origin.
- They all fall within a limited size range: about 1-4 km in their longest dimensions. Such a constraint is entirely uncharacteristic of natural landforms.
- Finally, each is a dominant feature in a grouping of associated anomalies.

In this article we will take a closer look at three of these "forgotten" anomalies, code-named the "Cliff," the "Crater Pyramid" and the "String of Beads."

The Cliff

The Cliff, so called because of its cliff-like western escarpment, is a 2 km-long mesa that rises about 30 meters above a pancake-like crater pedestal, located northeast of the Face in Cydonia Mensae. (Such pedestals, or ejecta blankets, form when the Martian permafrost is melted and ejected during large meteorite impacts.)

The Cliff's outlines, surface texture and internal structure differ markedly from that of the surrounding ejecta, indicating that its formation post-dated that of the crater itself. Geomorphologists point out that had the Cliff pre-dated the impact, ejecta material

The Cliff (left), situated on the ejecta blanket of a large impact crater at Cydonia. From NASA Viking frame 35A74. Image processing by Dr. Mark J. Carlotto.

would have been dammed up on its eastern side-if not burying or destroying the Cliff entirely. The exact opposite, however, seems to have occurred. The terrain on the Cliff's eastern side, rather than being heaped up, appears instead to have been somehow hollowed-out, with this hollow area displaying an unnaturally crisp outline. From this concavity, an unbroken path climbs in a north-westerly direction to the top of the cliff where it makes a hairpin turn southward along the Cliff's ridgeline and finally turns northward to terminate at the Cliff's northwestern extremity.

Another striking aspect of the Cliff's surroundings is the striated or "plowed-field" texture of the ejecta between the Cliff and the crater. Researchers have speculated that if the Cliff is artificial, this may constitute evidence of the quarrying of material for the Cliff's construction.

The Crater Pyramid

Deuteronilius Mensae lies about 800 km northeast of Cydonia along the southern edge of Acidalia Planitia. Here, in three of the first four frames of its forty-third orbit, Viking imaged a four-sided pyramidal formation, also situated on the ejecta blanket of a large impact crater. Whereas the Cliff is separate and distinct from its crater, the Crater Pyramid actually intersects its crater's rim. Like the Cliff, it lacks the expected impact damage or surrounding ejecta flows. Over a kilometer square at its base and at least 600 meters high, the Crater Pyramid is the tallest object within a 100km radius. (For comparison, the Great Pyramid at Giza was 147 meters high when built.)

Associated with the Crater Pyramid is an adjacent crater of nearly equal size whose ejecta blanket displays a unique, somewhat rectilinear arrangement of furrows. Unlike natural erosion channels, these do not seem to branch out radially in fractal fashion but originate in a straight line running tangent to the crater's bowl. No conventional geomorphological explanation has been proposed to account for these furrows.

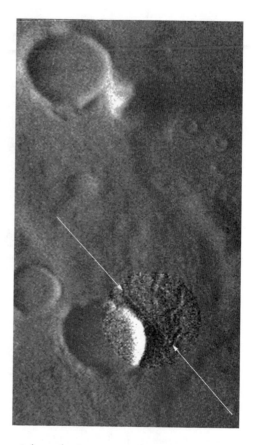

Above, the Crater Pyramid at Deuteronillus Mensae, from NASA Viking frame 43A01. Below, enhanced area with arrows indicates anomalous furrow running tangent to crater's bow. Image processing by author.

The String of Beads

Halfway around Mars in the Utopia Planitia region, at the base of the ancient volcano Hecates Tholus, lies one of the most puzzling features observed to date on Mars. Discovered by researchers John Brandenburg and Vincent DiPietro in the early 1980s, it was originally dubbed the "Runway" due to its appearance as a tiny, ruler-straight line in Viking frame 86A08. Upon magnification it turned out to be a four-kilometer-long string of mounds or pyramids, apparently linked by an off-center shaft. The structure seems to be emerging progressively from beneath gently sloping terrain and appears to be surrounded by vestiges of a shallow basin.

Adjacent to this formation lies another, more clearly defined, basin surrounding a "bow-tie" arrangement of three unnaturally smooth structures about two kilometers in overall length. At the edge of the adjoining mesa, a curious oval formation encloses an apparent grid-like, cellular structure.

According to its discoverers, the String of Beads was located by tracing the course of an ancient water channel called Hrad Vallis to its source at the base of Hecates Tholus. The concept underlying this search was to find a location on Mars which, like

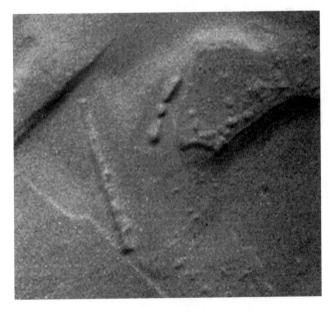

The "String of Beads" and nearby structures.

the Cydonia area, included mesas bordering what once may have been a large bay or lake.

Will We Get
a Closer Look?

Although the forthcoming Mars Global Surveyor mission is designed to map the planet at a resolution lower than that of Viking, it is capable of targeting specific areas at a resolution almost five times greater than that of Viking. However, due to various uncertainties the successful acquisition of high-resolution images of the Martian anomalies cannot be taken for granted at this time.

Fortunately the 1976 Viking image archive remains fertile ground for further investigation by knowledgeable image-processing specialists and geomorphologists with an eye for the anomalous. Although curious structures have turned up in many of the Viking frames studied to date, these represent only a small fraction of Viking's 40,000 digital images, whose examination was limited to only a cursory evaluation of one-fourth of the images due to NASA budget cuts.

BIOGRAPHICAL NOTE

> Dan Drasin is a long-time associate of, and principal photographic consultant to the independent Mars investigations. A writer, designer and award-winning cinematographer, he was educated at Pratt Institute, Harvard University and the New School. He was editorial and graphic consultant on Mark Carlotto's *The Martian Enigmas* and Stanley McDaniel's *The McDaniel Report*. Dan is currently the Director of Production at New Dimensions Radio.

Frame 70A11:
Cydonia's Overlooked
Treasure Trove?

Ananda Sirisena

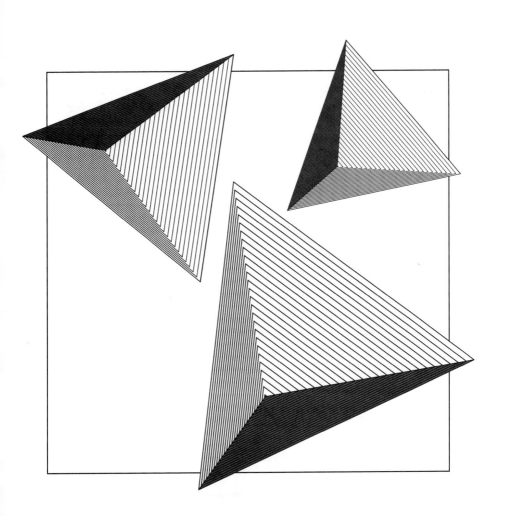

R esearch on the anomalies of Mars has focused on "The Face," the "City," the "D&M Pyramid" and the "Mound Configuration" in the published literature. Presented here are four other unusual formations from a nearby region in the Cydonia area of Mars, demanding pressing study. Each of these has been chosen for a different reason and each represents a mystery from an areological point of view (areology is the study Martian geology).

One of the first Viking frames I analyzed was frame 70A11, which is the eleventh image taken during orbit 70 of Viking orbiter A in 1976. This frame had been taken 8.96 seconds before the now-famous frame 70A13, which had been unearthed in NASA files by image processing engineer Vincent DiPietro. By providing a second perspective, frame 70A13 had established that "The Face on Mars" was not an illusion of lighting.

Frame 70A11 was of interest to me because I was curious about what lay to the west and north of the object called the "D&M Pyramid" and the other anomalous features associated with the "Face." Studying the frame, I noticed that there was what appeared to be another face-like feature in the top left quadrant— more eroded to be sure—yet there seemed to be an eye staring back at me and the outline of a face. This second object, similar to the one originally discovered, later came to be called "The Secondary Face," whilst the original on frame 70A13 is the "Primary Face."

Just to the right of this Secondary Face was a large mesa, which threw a dark and distinct shadow. The reference print I had received from NASA's Goddard Space Flight Centre could not show me what might be lurking within the shadow. NASA reference prints have a high degree of contrast because the grey levels of the pixels constituting the image are 'stretched' to fill out all of the possible 256 level-spectrum. In such an image, what the human eye perceives as impenetrable shadows may contain much unseen information. This information can be brought into view by careful enhancement procedures. But frame 70A11 had apparently not been enhanced during the early years of pioneering work. In Figure A we see a portion of the frame with the "Secondary Face" at the far left and the dark shadows thrown by the nearby mesa.

Figure B shows the same area, adjusted for contrast and brightness. After adjustment, features within the shadow became apparent. It was obvious that the mesa immediately to the right of this possible "face" contained a few surprises. At its edge was a deep square-shaped indentation, which I called "The Quadrangle." This feature was later referred to by Professor Stanley V. McDaniel as "The Sirisena Quadrangle." What lay inside "The Quadrangle" intrigued me. None of it looked like the result of natural erosion.

The four unusual features seen in Figure B are as follows, starting on the left:

(i) the Secondary Face
(ii) the Quadrangle
(iii) three 'mounds' which form a right-triangle
(iv) the NK pyramid, a four-sided pyramidal formation.

The Secondary Face

At first I had been inclined to reject "The Secondary Face." It appears highly eroded and it is not independent, being part of the shelf emerging from the top left corner of the frame. Three facts about this feature however convinced me that I should retain it on the list of "unexplaineds." The first is the size: It is almost exactly the same size as the Primary Face, a few miles to the east. Second, the two "faces" are aligned at almost the same angle with respect to North. And third, the approximate distance of the Second Face from the D&M Pyramid is just twice the distance of the Primary Face from the D&M.

The Quadrangle

The Quadrangle itself is also very peculiar. To the left is a circular 'hole,' a clean-cut, vertical opening (Figure D). Regular markings around the rim almost suggest a 'manufactured' tunnel entrance. This feature I have now dubbed "Crater's Cave," in honor of Dr. Horace W. Crater of the University of Tennessee Space Institute, who performed the mathematical analysis of the layout of the mounds within Cydonia and showed a high degree of statistical anomaly in their pattern. To the right of "Crater's Cave" is the Quadrangle proper, or the "harbor," as some have

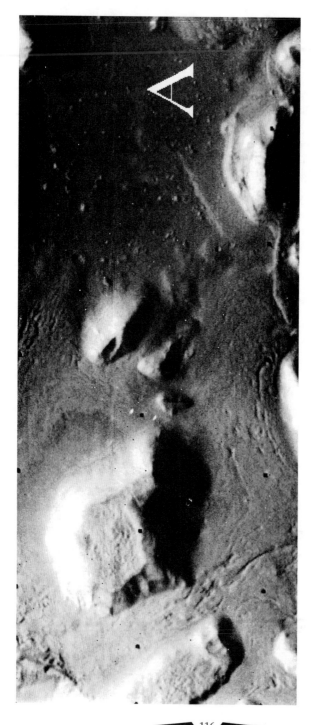

Part of NASA Viking frame 70A11, prior to contrast and brightness adjustments. (Compare to the image on the next page.)

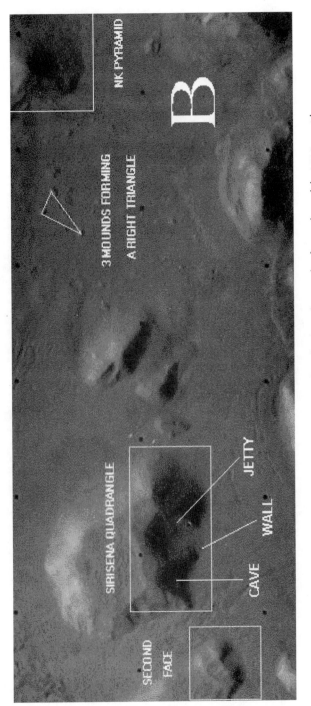

Evidence of Alien Artifacts?

The same area after adjustment showing the Secondary Face, the Quadrangle, the right triangle of mounds, and the NK Pyramid.

117

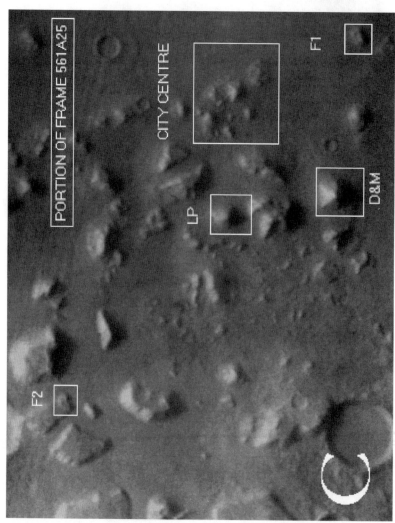

PORTION OF FRAME 561 A25

CITY CENTRE

F1

LP

D&M

F2

F igure C shows Viking frame 561A25, taken from a much greater height than orbits 35 or 70. This frame includes both "Faces" and shows their relation to the other objects of interest. The two "Faces" do appear to be of similar size and orientation.

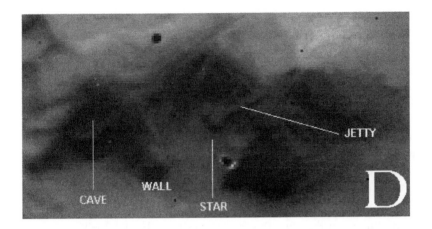

CAVE WALL STAR JETTY D

Quadrangle and Cave from NASA Viking frame 70A11, enlarged and enhanced to bring out detail.

called it because of its resemblance to an ancient ship basin and jetty. It is an enclosure with a stepped wall on the left and a straight ledge on the right that terminates in a symmetrical, star-shaped structure with five radiating "arms."

The Triangle of Mounds

The three mounds nearby form a right-triangle, and are similar in size to the mounds studied by Dr. Crater, mentioned above. Initial measurements suggest these may have some relation-ship to the grid of mounds based on the square root of 2, which Professor Stanley V. McDaniel discovered from "visualizing" the mound pattern. Research on this aspect of the mounds is ongoing.

The NK Pyramid

Whilst studying frame 70A11, I had noticed that there was a four-sided, square-based pyramid along the top edge of the frame, partly cropped out of view. I made a note of it, resolving to study it later, in particular the surrounding frames which were likely to show it in its entirety. As it transpired, fate took a hand in further study of this interesting object. I had written a letter to a news magazine informing them that there was a "Secondary Face" in Cydonia. The magazine published my letter in June 1993. A geography student at Aberdeen University had seen my letter and upon contact, informed me that there was another researcher in Glasgow, Chris O'Kane, who had been interested in the Martian anomalies.

Mr. O'Kane worked at the North Kelvinside school in Glasgow, Scotland. A group of pupils at the school, under O'Kane's tutelage, had completed a project to analyze the Cydonia images. They had concluded that some of the objects in Cydonia were probably not natural and had made measurements of the same 4-sided pyramid I had noticed in frame 70A11. Together we decided to call it the "NK Pyramid" after the school, North Kelvinside. The group of students presented their findings at the Edinburgh Science Festival in 1996.

All in all, frame 70A11 had turned up quite a few surprises. Considering the fact that it includes the earlier identified anomalies as well as the four curious objects discussed above, it represents a piece of 'real estate' on Mars which is likely to become the target for much more study and eventual exploration by humans, as we crawl our way through interplanetary space and attempt to spread our influence toward the larger planets of our home Solar System.

Roughly halfway between the two faces is another conical hill, which I have called "Lookout Point," simply because if one were to ascend this hill, one would have a superb view of both faces in opposite directions. Perhaps one day travelers to Mars will stand upon that very hill and report back to us the true nature of the faces, the quadrangle, and the other anomalies discovered by Viking.

BIOGRAPHICAL NOTE

Ananda Sirisena is a computer consultant with a background in Information Technology training. He has been studying the Martian anomalies for many years. His discovery of a second possible "Face" on Mars and the anomalous object known as "The Sirisena Quadrangle" was reported in his article "Intelligent Faces on Mars?"

Old Mars: Alive & Green?

In the distant past Mars may have been as green as Earth—a warm, wet bed of life for billions of years. It seems thoroughly, chillingly dead now; but evidence from NASA's Mars Pathfinder and Global Surveyor suggests a former Mars well suited for life. The most recent findings hint at a great ocean, larger than our own Pacific, once covering what are now its arid northern plains; a surface warmed long ago by an insulating layer of frozen carbon dioxide high in the upper atmosphere; and plenty of oxygen and water to fuel the cycle of life.

There are no guarantees that this scenario is accurate: Final conclusions await future NASA missions. Yet NASA's study of meteorites, known to have come from Mars, shows that deeply buried in these chips of Martian rock there are what appear to be fossilized microorganisms—the remains of ancient Martian life. Did that life evolve as it did on the Earth? It is our expectation that teams of space scientists including biologists, archaeologists, planetary scientists and geologists will eventually walk those frozen plains in the not-too-distant future and discover final evidence of the life (and death) cycle of our nearest planetary neighbor.

Mars as an
Abode of Life

Dr. Mitchell Swartz

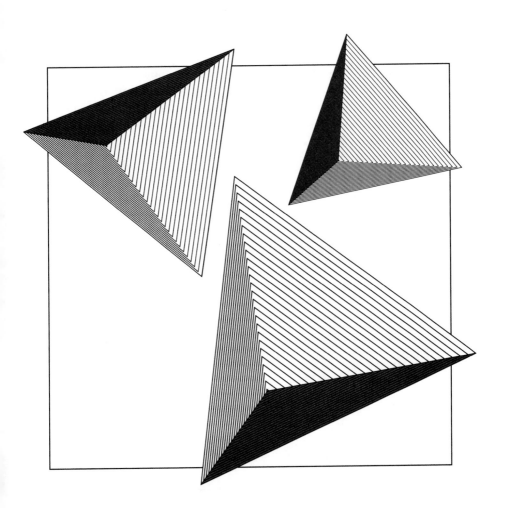

NASA's 1996 announcement that meteorites, apparently originating on Mars, contained evidence of possible ancient Martian life again raises anew the question of the unresolved features at Cydonia on Mars, which some scientists believe may be the ruins of a former Martian civilization. Given these events, and the increasing interest in colonizing Mars, the question can no longer be only "Is (or was) there life on Mars?" but, "Where and how might life find a home on Mars?"

Water on Mars

Water is the primal medium in which organisms can thrive and develop. It is generally believed that ancient Mars (about 2 billion years ago) had a denser atmosphere, with free water producing geologic formations that can be seen to this day. Teardrop-shaped "islands" and other streamlined features, including branching valley networks with tributaries, suggest substantial fluid flow. There is even evidence of subsurface water drainage, water-ice erosion, and geologic structures consistent with ancient shorelines, gorges, and islands.

What about more recently? There is water on Mars. In May 1979, the Viking 2 Lander photographed a thin white layer of water-ice coating the rocky terrain. In the northern hemisphere, some of the meteorite craters are surrounded by water-ice pushed up from below the surface by the impact. Beneath the surface lies permafrost, estimated to be several hundred meters thick at the equator and many kilometers near the poles. Some estimates sug-

Scanning electron microscope image from Martian meteorite shows cylindrical structures smaller than terrestrial fossils but still of considerable biological interest. [NASA S9612609]

Water ice observed by the Viking 2 Lander. In May 1979, a thin white layer of water ice appeared as frost a few microns thick, coating the rocky surface.

gest that the Martian crust holds the equivalent of a layer of water one-half kilometer thick. The meteoric impacts have probably released only 10 to 20 percent of this amount.

Today, Martian air has 0.03% as much water content as Earth. Because the atmospheric pressure is so low, below 40 degrees latitude, all water-ice sublimes (passes directly from solid to gaseous state). Water vapor is most abundant during the summer at the edge of the north polar cap heralded by clouds and early morning fog. By the fall, the peak water concentration decreases by a third as it moves toward the equator creating cyclones. Finally, there is possible evidence of an active water spout on Mars, discovered in 1980 by Dr. Leonard Martin of the Lowell Observatory in Flagstaff, Arizona. *(See Mars: Planet of Mysteries on page 23.)*

Oxygen on Mars

Life requires oxygen, or another "sink" for the electrons of metabolism, required in the burning of fuel. Primitive life on Earth is believed to have begun and evolved under very low oxygen levels. Only as the oxygen level rose to several percent of its present level was there sufficient metabolic energy for organisms to make fibrous tissue required for locomotion (and coinci-

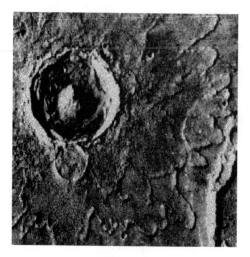

Crater Yuty, Chryse Planitia region, Mars. This 18 km diameter crater is surrounded by rounded ejecta lobes indicating viscous flow. The thin ejected flow covers part of an older crater. Such features could enable the lifesaving harvesting of water-ice from the ejecta. [NASA Viking Orbiter 003A07]

dentally to leave fossils). Today the Martian surface, where sampled, is a mixture of iron-rich clays, magnesium sulfate, and iron oxides. The soil has been found to release oxygen when wet. Therefore, it is likely that oxygen was available in the Martian distant past, as was water, volcanic action, and adequate temperature—all required to support, or spawn, life. But although early Mars may have been similar to early Earth, something caused the history of the two planets to diverge.

What Went Wrong on Mars?

Several things brought about this divergence, including the depletion of atmosphere and the failure of the carbon dioxide "greenhouse system" due to cold temperatures. Another factors is the relatively low Martian mass. Mars is a tenth the mass of the Earth, and has only a third of Earth's gravity. Because of the low gravity, Mars has slowly been losing its precious atmosphere and water content, and underwent its own unique change.

The absence of Martian tectonic plates (slow-moving crustal features) keeps all the hot lava-producing spots beneath the same crustal area on the unmoving surface. This, combined with the low gravity, has produced the largest volcanoes known to exist in the Solar System. The largest of these volcanoes are located upon huge uplifted domes 4,000 kilometers wide. The volcanoes (in the Tharsis region) are up to one hundred times larger than those on Earth.

Olympus Mons, the largest, is 24 kilometers higher than the surrounding plain. In comparison the Hawaiian volcano Mauna Loa is but 9 kilometers high and is only a quarter of Olympus Mons' width.

The enormous growth of the Tharsis volcano system with its massive bulge, all located on one side of Mars, may have actually caused the Martian rotational axis to tumble. The resulting great obliquity (the tilt of Mars' axis at 22 degrees; range 11-38 degrees) may have profoundly impacted Mars by dropping the southern pole temperature below the freezing point of the "greenhouse gas" carbon dioxide, thus causing it to condense into dry ice. As the loss of the greenhouse effect cooled the planet, the remaining Martian water would be locked up as permafrost and ice. This catastrophic event may mark the border in time between the ancient Martian oceans and the more recent desiccated red planet.

Conditions on Mars Today

The current Martian atmospheric pressure is almost 1% that of Earth. What remains of the atmosphere is mainly carbon dioxide (95.32%), with nitrogen, argon, oxygen, water, and neon making up the remainder. Because of the low gravity, however, the atmosphere is thick enough to support dust storms. The temperatures on Mars vary widely. The average temperature on Mars is -63 degrees C (-81 degrees F), with a maximum recorded temperature of 20 degrees C (68 degrees F). There is a daily variation of 35 to 50 degrees C. The Viking lander 1 recorded temperatures as high as 7 degrees F and as low as -107 degrees F. At the northern landing site (Viking lander 2) predawn temperatures reached a low of -184 degrees F, close to the freezing point of carbon dioxide. If the average Martian temperature increased to -28 degrees C, this would enable the occasional appearance of ordinary water. An average of 0 degrees C would restore what is left of the early Martian oceans. (*See Mars: The New Earth on page 208.*)

The Impact of Carbon Dioxide

Unlike the Earth's circular orbit around the sun, Mars' orbit is an ellipse (eccentricity 0.0934). At perihelion (closest approach to the Sun) it is summer at the Martian South pole, but it is a very short hot summer. Mars moves very quickly through this portion of its orbit. As a result the Southern spring and summer are 52 and 25 days shorter than they are in the Northern Martian hemisphere. The result is that although the two Martian polar caps are each about 10 degrees wide (like Earth's), the composition and climates of the two Martian polar caps are very different (unlike Earth's). The North polar cap, with its layered sediments, is mostly water-ice and is 4 to 6 kilometers thick. In contrast, the South polar cap is mostly dry ice (frozen carbon dioxide 1 to 2 km thick).

In the Southern spring, there is massive out-gassing from dry ice sublimation as the carbon dioxide passes from a solid to a gaseous state. This sudden sublimation drives the dust storms that can engulf Mars for months. So great is volume of out-gassing, that it changes the Martian atmospheric pressure. The Viking 1 Lander revealed that when the southern carbon dioxide cap was the largest, the mean pressure was about 6.8 millibars; this increased to a high of 9.0 millibars as the southern seasonal cap vanished.

Carbon dioxide from the sublimating Southern pole riding on the Martian storm winds could be relatively poisonous to life as we know it because it might lead to acidosis (and possibly cell death). On the positive side the increased carbon dioxide could create greenhouse effects as far away as the North pole producing at least a 5 degree additional warming. It may produce even more, and may be implicated in the creation of a band in the northern hemisphere where conditions may be relatively favorable for life.

The Viking Experiments

The Viking lander conducted three biologic experiments looking for life. The Gas Exchange Experiment added Martian soil to a "nutritionally rich" solution containing 19 amino acids, growth factors, and salts. A gas chromatograph looked for H_2, N_2, O_2, CO_2, or CH_4 which might be given up by a living system. A steady increase of CO_2 occurred over months. Oxygen was released if water was added. These were labeled as "false positive" because of the rapidity of the reaction, and because it took place in the dark and continued even after heating to 145 Centigrade (3.5 hr), seeming to rule out the presence of living organisms.

Furthermore, experiment organizer Gil Levin has argued emphatically over the past few years, that the test, in fact, was not just a false positive but quite possibly confirmed life on Mars.

The Labeled Release Experiment mixed a solution of radioactive carbon compounds with the Martian soil. Over months, there was a loss of radioactive gas which was inhibited by heating to 160 degrees Centigrade. This is consistent with a positive response, but because highly reactive materials exist on the Martian surface, this too was labeled as a "false positive." These experiments were limited in scope and in location, and, as we shall see, they do not definitely rule out life, either ancient or present, on Mars.

Where and How
Might Life Exist on Mars Today?

The Archaea are a diverse group of microorganisms undreamed of at the time of the Viking missions. Our current knowledge of such microorganisms may indicate a need to revaluate of the Viking results. Archea are neither bacteria nor eucaryotes (plants, fungi, protozoa, or animals), but cousins of both. The organisms are divided into the methanogens (which produce methane), the extreme halophiles (capable of living on salt), and the extreme thermophiles (heat loving). The upper temperature limit of life is not known, but Archaea thermophiles like subterranean heats of 176 to 194 degrees F (80 to 90 degrees C). Some estimates indicate subsurface terrestrial microorganisms can survive 135 degrees C, at least for a limited time. Thus the fact that reaction continued in the gas exchange experiment even after heating to 145 degrees C. does not necessarily rule out life as a cause of the reaction.

ALH84001 is the famous meteorite of probable Martian origin, composed of igneous orthopyroxrites, and containing what appears to be structures consistent with Martian microfossils. Therefore, there is renewed interest in examining Mars for life. Based upon Earth's surviving Precambrian fossils, NASA's contractors are currently targeting certain Martian mineral beds, where hot thermal springs are potential sources of heat and water. Although we agree that these should be targeted, along with other Martian broad outflow channels, there are two additional areas (one a volume actually) based upon the above discussion to which targeting should be addressed.

The Martian "biosurface" is in the Northern hemisphere. Factoring in the current Martian axial tilt, the relative stinging cold from the dry ice on the south pole, the permafrost-held water ice on the northern pole, the sublimation of water ice below 40 degrees N, and the greenhouse effect of clouds over the polar cap, we can conclude that life as we know it would be limited to a band of latitudes in the range of 55 degrees (+/- about 15) degrees north latitude. This band defines a Martian surface sector with maximal likelihood of bioactivity when considering the issues discussed above. Peak targets of interest include the Northern Cydonia plain (52 degrees N; 357 degrees Longitude, Elevation: 1 to 2 km) and the Ismenius Lacus Quadrangle (44 degrees N; 333 degrees Longitude).

The Martian "biovolume" is a shell located in the Northern hemisphere. Unlike the surface sector of possible ancient Martian life in the northern hemisphere, existing Martian life may actually encompass this kilometer-thick shell located beneath the upper Martian permafrost. Even at depths more than several kilometers below the Earth's surface, extremophilic microorganisms and bacteria (e.g. Bacillus infernus) have been found which are poisoned

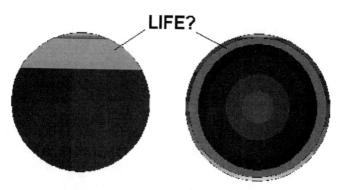

Mars as an Abode of Life

Both fossilized and presently existing life may be found on Mars. Fossils should be sought in areas including the northern water-ice Region (lighter area, left). Present life should be sought in this area and also in the zone beneath the regolith (light grey area, right). Life forms may exist to a depth of several kilometers, insulated by layers of water-ice and permafrost.

by oxygen and which can metabolize diverse hydrocarbons. Some bacteria live deep within the Earth on igneous deposits of basalt. Some synthesize carbon from carbon dioxide using hydrogen as the energy source. Considering such cases, one cannot rule out the possibility that life may exist now deep within the Martian regolith (the upper soil).

The depth of possible Martian life depends upon the upper temperature limit of life, and the rate of increase of temperature with depth. With a conservative estimate of 100 degrees C as an upper limit for Martian biosystems, Martian life would be possible to a depth of several kilometers. Where permafrost is present, organisms may have ample water upon which to draw. Furthermore, that water would liberate oxygen as shown from the Viking probe. This possible deep shell of extant life would be thermally protected from freezing by the water-ice thermal insulation in the upper few hundred meters of permafrost and regolith.

Final Speculative Considerations

Given the past or even current life on Mars, it is important to consider the possibility of former intelligent life. Various tests (many of them described in this book) point to an area of anomalies in the Cydonia region, which lies within the optimal zone defined above. In this region, near the controversial "Face," are features which in a perhaps fanciful (but possible) biomedical/geological interpretation, appear consistent with mining and excavation for water ice. One of these features is the so-called "Cliff" (really a raised ridge). This object lies tangent to a crater east of the "Face" and atop the crater's ejecta blanket (the water ice material "splashed" out upon impact). It has been considered a mystery that there is no sign of the expected build-up of ejecta on the crater side of the "Cliff," which should have occurred if the "Cliff" predated the impact. On that side, instead of piled-up material, there appears to be a deep and unexplained trench or excavation.

Ancient Martian permafrost-held water ice, released by meteor impact in the form of ejecta in the upper Northern hemisphere, may have enabled the lifesaving harvesting of water ice from the ejecta after Mars lost part of its atmosphere and water content. In this scenario, the trench in the ejecta blanket by the "Cliff" would be consistent with a culture facing bleak conditions and forced to harvest precious water by excavation.

Also possibly consistent with this potential mining of water ice, in the western Utopia Planitia region (45 degrees N, 270 degrees longitude), there is large field of possibly coalesced lake bases, which contain oval to circular pits of size 300 to 1000 meters across, with steep scalloped edges and inner benches. Internal flow is one hypothesis for the cause of these (Viking orbiter 2 frame 466B895). Internal flow and dust hypotheses have also been proposed for the findings at Cydonia.

For hypothetical past intelligent life on Mars, the relative absence of a magnetic field would have limited accurate surface navigation. An imaginative, but conceivable, hypothesis regarding the"Face" is that it may have served "in part" as a landmark for surface navigation during the harvest of the water ice ejecta at the "Cliff." The "Face" lies directly between the "harvest area" and the area to the west, on the edge of what appears to be an ancient ocean, that has been singled out as a possible habitation site. As such, the "Face" could function as landmark for navigation in the event of a dust storm, because it is in proper profile only when viewed directly along the correct path between the mines and the harvest site.

The Overview

The Martian climate, composition, and other unique features do not definitely rule out past or even present life there. Mars' extreme surface diversity suggests that when targeting possible abodes of life there, consideration should be given to a strip in the northern hemisphere above 40N, because of the potential availability of water ice. Given that Earth organisms can survive temperature extremes initially thought to be sterilizing in the Viking bioprobes, and have been found to be capable of taking their energy sources from other than sunlight, the routine assignment of "false positives" in all of the Viking tests should be reconsidered.

Mars appears to be inhospitable by Earth standards in recent times. But given that organisms can metabolize a variety of energy sources, and can synthesize organic compounds from atmospheric carbon dioxide, it must be considered that life forms on Mars could conceivably exist now. They could survive at depths of kilometers beneath the permafrost in the Northern Hemisphere because the water ice permafrosts would be capable of shielding organisms from the cold, and would supply both water and oxygen. Finally, for eventual colonization of Mars the northern hemisphere's life-optimal band at 55 degrees plus or minus 15 degrees should be seriously considered.

BIOGRAPHICAL NOTE:

Mitchell R. Swartz has four degrees in electrical engineering from MIT including an ScD, and an MD from Harvard. His background includes biomedical engineering, the interaction of radiation and materials, and imaging systems, including pattern recognition, positron emission scanning, and radiographic imaging processing.

Martian Update
Since Pathfinder's Landing at Ares

BY DR. MITCHELL SWARTZ

Magnetized Dust in a
Slightly Warmer Atmosphere

Since the arrival of the Mars Pathfinder and the Sojourner Rover in July 1997 with fifteen bounces and a roll, more predictions by SPSR appear to have been partly confirmed. These include more evidence for slightly warmer Martian temperatures because of Martian dust's minor augmentation by of the CO_2 "greenhouse" effect, more evidence of Martian water, and the increasingly important focus on whether Mars was, or is, a possible abode of life.

The planned Pathfinder landing site was at the junction of the Tiu and Ares flood plains. There, Mars was actually found to have a slightly warmer, moderately dusty atmosphere (Table 1). The landed cameras snapped images of a pale pink sky with thin blue clouds (water ice) and local atmospheric haze (opacity ~0.5).

So much bright red Martian dust was airborne that it created dust devils which were regularly observed in the early Martian afternoons. The dust was found to be magnetized (4 ampere-sq.meters/kg) and composed of clay-like aggregates containing ferric oxide (Fe_2O_3) and maghemite (γ-Fe_2O_3). It settled out of the atmosphere at a rate of about ~3 micrograms per square centimeter per day.

Although the Martian atmospheric temperature profiles were similar to those of the previous Viking probes, important differences were found. Even though Pathfinder's Ares landing site was similar to the 21 year-earlier Viking Lander-1 site in latitude, altitude and season, the cold Martian nights were about 12 degrees warmer and days 10 degrees warmer than expected. During initial atmospheric entry, beginning with readings at about 50 kilometers, the descending probe found a temperature profile 20 degrees warmer than expected. One conclusion of the warmer than expected surface temperatures is that Mars is a much more likely abode for life than previously thought.

Soil Like Viking, Rocks Like Earth

The surface at the Ares site was covered mainly with rounded pebbles, fine debris and dust-like red deposits. All these were found in high concentrations across the depositional plain and they were even found in the larger sedimentary rocks. The rounded pebbles are important because they demonstrate that running water existed on the surface of Mars. These conglomerates, some arranged with directional consis-

Selected Results from Pathfinder and the Minirover Soujourner

Mission Background	
Surface Landing	July 4, 1997, after seven month cruise
Last Sucessful Communication	Sept. 27, 1997
Number of Temperature, Pressure, and Wind Measurements	8.5 million measurements
Information Returned	2.6 gigabits
Images Returned	16,000 from lander, >500 from rover
Distance Rover Transversed	52 meters (~200 sq. meters of surface)
Number of Movement Commands Sent	114 Commands
Mission Findings	
Mars Core	Central metallic core (1300–2000 km radius)
Ares Soil	Composition similar to Viking soil
Ares Rocks	Composition similar to terrestrial andesites
Water	Evidence of erosion, weathering and water during and prior to Ares flood plain deposits
Atmosphere	10+ degrees warmer than expected, dusty

tency, semirounding and perched positions, are also important because not only do they show that some Martian rocks are not of volcanic origin but they have also strongly indicate that water existed on the surface of Mars, over a period of several epochs. The smoothed pebbles are likely evidence of an Ares flood. The conglomerates suggest evidence of water activity even prior to its being flooded. In addition, weathering of the rocks may have also contributed to the polish, flutes and grooves on their surfaces.

The Pathfinder's mobile alpha proton x-ray spectrometer was able to examine five rocks and six samples of soils before contact was lost with the Martian probe. The soil was similar to the Viking missions. The rocks were all similar to each other, and although high in silica and potassium, they were low in magnesium. This constitution of the Ares rocks is unlike any other known Martian soil or even the presumed Martian meteorites. Surprisingly, the rocks were similar to terrestrial andesites and very similar to the mean composition of the Earth's crust. More on the findings on Pathfinder and Sojourner's findings have been published in *Science*, volume 278, pages 1734-1774.

In summary, the actual observed Martian surface temperature being slightly warmer than expected indicates that Mars is even more likely to be a possible abode of life. The presence of vast amounts of sand and dust size particles, rounded pebbles, and high-silica rocks are further evidence of Martian water in several epochs. Based upon Pathfinder findings, it is less clear that we know definitively the composition of Mars, and therefore a closer look at the supposed Martian meteorites would be worthwhile. Also based upon the findings, of the two possible Martian biozones, we revise our estimate of the upper zone, located in the Northern hemisphere to 50 degrees plus or minus 17 degrees. The estimates of the depth of second Martian "biovolume," located below, and possibly within the buried Martian permafrost in the Northern hemisphere remain relatively unchanged.

Newly Discovered
Mars Meteorites
Suggest Long-Term Life

by
Dr. John E. Brandenburg

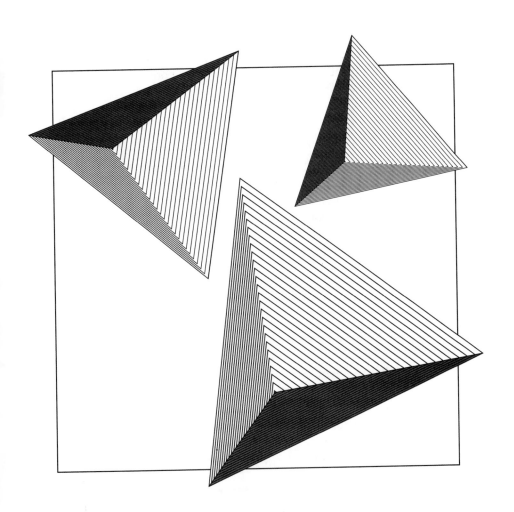

A Turning Point

The NASA announcement that signs of life were found in Mars meteorite ALH84001 has brought about a sea change in human thought. Though it is not discernible now, in coming years that moment will be widely recognized as a turning point in humanity's understanding of its place in universe.

After that press conference in August, 1996 at which NASA revealed that signs of primordial Martian biology had been discovered, we can now no longer think of ourselves as alone in the Cosmos. It has been my privilege to play a part in the adventure of the great end game of human aloneness. When you've heard this story, you'll know why NASA's announcement was anticlimactic for me. You will also have some insight into how the United States government manages great discoveries that may profoundly disrupt the world views of its people, and which inevitably creates conflict between the ideas of responsible government and of representative democracy.

The Cydonian Hypothesis

My adventure began with the Cydonia investigation. The Cydonian Hypothesis (originally suggested by myself and Vincent DiPietro in 1991), says that Mars once was the home of an indigenous humanoid intelligence. This hypothesis, however, was later criticized by astronomer Carl Sagan, who claimed that there were two problems with the hypothesis; first, that no life had been found on Mars; and, second, if life had existed, it had not lasted long enough to evolve anything like humanity.

These were scholarly objections. In response I determined to rebut these two objections if evidence warranted it, by determining whether Mars had once had life, and whether that life had persisted under Earthlike conditions for a long time.

The latter problem was easier to attack, so I began going to scientific conferences and presenting papers showing the evidence for Mars' past climate being warm and wet. At one such conference I ran into a British researcher who was one of the authors of an article reporting organic matter in a Mars meteorite. I asked him why he had not reported any more organic matter. "If you found one trace there must be more," I suggested. He replied he was, "...scared to find more." Imagine that! Faced with potentially the greatest discovery of the century, and he was too timid to look!

I was furious and told him, "It takes courage to discover things." It was obvious to me then that researchers were finding things in Mars meteorites that they were *afraid* to report. They were finding evidence of biology. As someone who had experienced a lot of criticism about my Cydonia research and survived, I regarded this scientist and his collaborators as holding up scientific progress. So I determined to "smoke out" these reluctant heroes in the best possible fashion: I planned to preempt them.

In Carl Sagan's early book, *Intelligent Life in the Universe*, co-authored with the Russian I. S. Shklovskii, I read their report that microfossils had been found in meteorites. This made me wonder if those particular meteorites were from Mars. If so, then the issue of Martian microfossils and organic matter may have already been broached. One only had to determine if the meteorites mentioned by Sagan and Shklovskii were from Mars, publish this fact, and the matter of life on Mars would be settled in one stroke.

Looking for Meteorites

I began tracking down the original articles about these meteorites—an extremely exotic type called CI (the carbonaceous chondrites). I began poring over books and articles on meteorites. Meteorites, I soon learned, had their own classification of types, most of which are of a group called chondrites. Chondrites consist mostly of shock welded rock fragments called chondrules. A second class of meteorites is the achondrites, which resemble lava rock from Earth. The already recognized Mars meteorites were achondrites. The CI, on the other hand, are an exotic type because they are rare and while they are classed as chondrites, they have no chondrules. They actually resemble dried clay.

The clay in the CI is full of a tarry substance called kerogen, similar to that found in terrestrial oil shale. On Earth, kerogen is considered to be of biological origin. It was in this kerogen that Bartholomew Nagy, in 1962, reported finding large numbers of what appeared to be bacterial microfossils. He was severely criticized for this report, but warmed to the fight and defended his work ably. Finally, in 1975, he published a large volume on his findings titled *Carbonaceous Meteorites*. He was still alive when I began my research on CIs, but had moved into the field of paleo-microbiology, looking at microfossils in old Earth rocks.

As I devoured articles on Mars meteorites, trying to find what made a meteorite Martian, I found there were numerous chemical indicators, all having to do with lava chemistry. However, there were two tests which were the most crucial. One was the isotopic composition of trapped noble gases, and the other was isotopic composition of the oxygen bound chemically in the rock itself.

The most important test was for oxygen isotopes. Oxygen has three isotopes, and oxygen combines with almost every element. Most of the substance of rock is actually oxygen (49.2% by weight is the element oxygen and its compounds). When the proportions of the three isotopes in a rock are measured, they can be plotted on a graph. The proportions of all three isotopes in Earth rocks lie on a single straight line on this type of graph, thus producing what is known as the terrestrial fractionation line. Moon rocks and some strange meteorites called aubrites lie on this same line, too. From this we can recognize that the Moon, and aubrites, come from the same cloud of material that formed the Earth.

But meteorites from Mars and the minerals within them lie on a different line above and parallel to the terrestrial fractionation line. The Mars fraction line is not as well defined as the terrestrial line because we have so few samples from Mars. But, while somewhat fuzzier, it appears to be nearly as long as the terrestrial line. When I looked at a book that discussed oxygen isotopes and meteorites, I was frustrated to find that it had a graph showing the Mars line and the terrestrial line and all the other meteorites except the CI! Where did the CI lie on the graph? When I turned the page, my heart leaped for joy—the CI line was not on the same line as the terrestrial fractionation line. On the next page the scale was much expanded, there were the CI, way up the terrestrial line and just slightly above it. They were on the Mars line!

My guess had been right. The CI were Martian.

Moreover, they were very ancient—4.6 billion years old—and they were loaded with organics and microfossils. Now life on early Mars could be proved. But first I would have to publish this discovery.

Guerrilla Science

Vince DiPietro and I were doing our usual bit of "Guerrilla Science"—showing up at conferences and presenting papers on Mars that would undermine opposition to Cydonia. We had been doing this since 1984. It was my own theory that if Cydonia, as it appeared to be, was the site for evidence of a past primitive civilization and thus, most likely, an indigenous culture, then Mars would have had a terrestrial climate for most of its history. This meant subtle signs should be everywhere in the growing body of Mars data for such a past.

This, in fact, turned out to be the case; so Vince and I were busy. We began laying groundwork for what we believed would eventually be a revolution in Mars science. Our paper was going to be on the effects of the Lyot crater impact, a massive event in the history of the planet, on the climate of Mars. I decided to submit a second paper, on the CI, and to our delight both papers were accepted for the American Geophysical Union meeting in June, 1995. I also prepared a paper for publication in a widely read journal for new and important geophysical research letters. We presented our papers and they were well received, but the conference was not frequented by the planetary crowd, so our work was ignored by them.

Vince was particularly entranced by the pictures of bacterial fossils in Nagy's book, and showed them to Dan Goldin, Administrator of NASA, during a visit Goldin made to Goddard Space Center. Goldin seemed impressed. This was the summer of 1995.

Conversely, I found the task of getting my additional work about the CI from Mars accepted for publication very difficult. It seemed to create an emotional reaction second only to the Face at Cydonia. The primary reason for this is obvious in retrospect. Both works placed life on Mars, and by doing so shattered the paradigm of human aloneness, for it was freely acknowledged to me by several scientists that if the CIs came from Mars then life on early Mars was demonstrated. The secondary reason for opposition was that CI meteorites had been the most heavily studied of all meteorites, and were considered almost as "Rosetta Stones" of meteorites, little more than primal cosmic dust, and, as such, the key to understanding the early solar system. Although many of the best and brightest minds of meteoritics had abandoned this view, (noting as they did that the CI had spent a long time in some wet, warm place unlike space at all), the view of the CIs as the most primordial of the known meteorites was still strong in the general space community. To many, the CIs couldn't possibly be from such a mundane place as Mars, since Mars, it was recognized, was a lot like Earth.

The CI Meteorites Go To Press

I took the criticisms of my referees to heart. Many of them made solid objections. So, I sharpened my arguments, marshaled more data and I resubmitted the article. More rejection followed. But this time the criticism were fewer and more focused. As more revisions were made, my case grew stronger, even exhaustive. The final referees discarded their usual anonymity and wrote me openly, scolding me about how could I, "place these cherished stones on so mean a place as Mars?" Finally they admitted they had run out of objections and the article was accepted for publication.

In the middle of my battle with referees, when I realized they had no substantive objections to the CI being from Mars, I was emboldened to try and tell Barthalomew Nagy himself of my discovery. After much searching I tracked him down at the University of Arizona at Tuscon. I got him on the phone in the late summer of 1995 and told him, "Bart, you are the discoverer of life on Mars. You found microfossils in the CI and I have found that the CI come from Mars." He responded in a low key way. "Is that so? Can you send me your article?" When I called back months later in December, I was told that, sadly, he had died. So, it was that the veteran of a thousand scientific battles concerning the microfossils in the CI, had gone to his rest knowing that the battle was to be rejoined and he was about to be vindicated.

I was serving on a NASA Advisory Board at the time, and at one of its meetings in April, 1996, Dan Goldin was in attendance. After getting the permission of the Chairman of our Board, I approached Goldin and told him about the article and how it had been accepted for publication. I explained that my paper placed large amounts of organic matter on Mars, making Mars biology highly likely, if not certain. I also shared my hope that such discovery would help NASA's budget in Congress. Again Goldin responded with what seemed to be great interest.

My article appeared in May, 1996 and was widely read. Although I got many requests for reprints, I had clearly produced many critics as well. In July, 1996, I gave another paper on the CI meteorites at the meteoritics conference in Berlin, Germany, where I met a British researcher, C. T. Pillinger. I told him that in my opinion, he and his group had actually built a case for Mars biology. At this statement he hushed me and drawing me aside like a conspirator, told me that organic matter in some Mars meteorites was very dense. When I returned home from Germany I told my fellows that life on Mars would soon be an acknowledged reality. Though I thought it would be years, a few weeks later, NASA made its own Earth-shattering announcement: There is evidence of life on Mars.

Announcing: Life on Mars

On the morning of the NASA press conference Vince DiPietro and I sat in NASA headquarters. We were very aware together that this NASA announcement could forever change human thought, by bringing us closer to the truth about Cydonia. Dan Goldin made his great announcement clad in cowboy boots, a John Wayne-like figure courageously throwing the whole weight and prestige of NASA behind this announcement.

Dan Goldin's announcement was also a powerful act of leadership. NASA, unable to mount new initiatives and shorn of great visions or goals, was dying the death of a thousand cuts, its projected budgets for future years indicating a fast trajectory to oblivion. We learned from Goldin's response that he was a gambler, a dynamic leader, whose tactics were not unlike those of General George Washington on the cold night in December, 1776, when, faced with the dissolution of his army due to cold, hunger, defeat and expiring enlistments, Washington rallied his men and struck boldly across the ice-choked Delaware, routing the British and Hessians at Trenton and Princeton, and preserving the revolution. Goldin, for his part, strode boldly in with a Mars rock, and routed Congressional resistance in Washington.

As we milled about in the auditorium after the meeting, Vince and I moved past the podium to speak to scientists about the CIs. Goldin noticed me and made a point of coming down from the podium and wordlessly shaking my hand. In that moment, I was so proud. The announcement created a worldwide sensation—and a quite predictable backlash from the scientific community, since science is actually very conservative.

Rather than accepting great discoveries, scientists often resist them. In retrospect it is clear that the signs of life in the Mars rock were noted years before the announcement, and that the research to investigate them was kept under war-like secrecy. The actual events triggering the NASA announcement apparently came from a combination of leaks at the scientific journal where my paper had been accepted, NASA's desire to gain maximum advantage during budget negotiations with Congress in the coming months, and, finally, the unlikely event of a call girl employed by an advisor to the president spilling the beans to the National Inquirer.

What transpired can only be reconstructed. The meteorite in question, ALH84001, was only recognized as Martian in 1994, and its great age was noted within the year. Since organic matter had been reported in another Mars meteorite, and ALH84001 was ancient, it was probably considered the most likely place to find Mars biology. Thus, one and half years of intensive and secretive research must have followed—research sufficiently thorough to make Goldin confident he could throw all of NASA's weight behind it. At this time those in Houston aware of my work must have viewed developments with some apprehension, and wondered if I might preempt them.

The Speed of Science

Was NASA's reticence a sign of cover up or simply scientific prudence? The shortness of the time from determination of ALH84001's ancient Martian origin and the NASA press conference argues that little more than scientific caution and bureaucratic prudence was involved. One and a half years is not that long in science. The researchers at Houston were surely aware of my work, (some of my referees on the article were from the Houston group), so they knew these ideas were in the air, and if they did not publish, someone else might gain the spotlight ahead of them.

However, they had the backing of NASA, and could afford to marshal their data, proceed carefully, and publish after I did, knowing that more data from the CIs might soon back them up.

Their announcement was far bolder than mine, their finding of life on Mars explicit, mine only implicit, so I had to be content with being merely labeled an iconoclast and an annoying upstart, which, given the rarefied air of the discovery, I still enjoyed immensely. Therefore, we applaud the workers at NASA, who struck out so boldly and effectively. And, it was a rare and wonderful thing to see managers of a major government agency move with such power and imagination.

As for the arguments being advanced by some scientists against the evidence for life in ALH84001, I can comment as a scientist who has reviewed their arguments, that they amount to little but rearguard actions. The attempts to explain the numerous evidences of biology in ALH84001 in nonbiological ways, such as that the rock was contaminated by the miraculous millionfold concentration of the trace organics in the Antarctic ice, or that the carbonate was formed at temperatures hot enough to react carbon dioxide directly with rock while mysteriously leaving small whiskers of magnetite intact in the carbonate, remind one of the original arguments by the religious orders against fossil dinosaurs.

As for the human race, we are now fully cognizant of our situation: We are not alone. Since the evidence of life on ancient Mars argues against the Earth being any special case in the cosmos, our own claim as a uniquely intelligent is equally suspect. We are unique, just as every star is unique, and every person is unique, but the odds are great that we are not alone.

The practical import of the CI are many. They will provide more than additional evidence of Martian biogenesis: They contain more than several percent of organic matter and are rich in microfossils of several types, so, if ALH84001 is the first sign of biogenesis on Mars, then the CI are the mother lode. The fact that they contain so much organic matter shows that Mars was not just alive, it was thriving with life. It also means that colonists on Mars will find rich deposits of kerogen, similar to oilshale on Earth, with which to make Mars hospitable and to use as rocket fuel. Therefore, the CI may well indicate that Mars is a much more hospitable place than it presently appears to be.

But perhaps their greatest role will have been in breaking down the last barriers of caution, and quietly pushing the human race into a great, new day in which we will finally journey to another planet and eventually make it our new home.

BIOGRAPHICAL NOTE

Dr. John E. Brandenburg, co-author of *Unusual Mars Surface Features*, is a plasma physicist who works for a NASA subcontractor, primarily on new rocket propulsion systems and on the theory of magnetic confinement of plasmas for fusion power.

New Mars Global Surveyor and Pathfinder Discoveries Lend Additional Support to the CI Hypothesis

BY DR. JOHN E. BRANDENBURG

The latest results from the Mars Pathfinder and the Mars Global Surveyor offer strong support for the scenario already suggested by the probable Martian origin of the CI (Carbonaceous Chondrite) meteorites. With more and more evidence demonstrating that the CI came from Mars, they essentially complete our set of meteorite samples of the Martian surface. We now have an approximately equal number of very old and very young meteorites from Mars. Taken together, these support the tale told by the pattern of craters on Mars' surface, that Mars' surface is dramatically bimodal—i.e., very young in the North and very old in the South. This tells us that the young parts, full of signs of rivers and seas, date from very recent epochs. In this northern region, the Mars Pathfinder found rounded, water-eroded pebbles, and the orbiting Mars Global Surveyor has discovered beds of sedimentary deposits in the Vallis Marineris almost three times as deep as the Grand Canyon. All the evidence indicates that Mars, in its northern areas, could easily have been much like Earth for a very long period of time.

In addition, University of Chicago researcher Raymond Pierrehumbert has said that measurements indicate Mars may have had an insulating layer of frozen carbon dioxide in its upper atmosphere which would have created a atmospheric "blanket" to hold in solar heat and keep Mars warm enough to maintain vast amounts of unfrozen water on its surface. In fact, Pathfinder geologists' analyses indicate that the plains of Northern Mars may once have been covered by an ocean larger than the Earth's Pacific Ocean.

With evidence for many millions of years of both warm temperatures and plentiful water, it now appears more possible that intelligent life could have evolved on Mars, as it did on Earth. This is the heart of the Cydonian Hypothesis put forward in 1990 by myself and Vincent DiPietro as an explanation of the anomalies at Cydonia. We proposed that the reason we find apparent ruins of an extinct civilization on Mars, as we do in places on Earth, is because Mars used to be much like Earth in climate. The probable Martian origin of the CI, together with the Pathfinder and Global Surveyor findings, now provide important support to the Cydonian Hypothesis, and to the whole idea of Cydonia being perhaps the most important evidence yet discovered in our Search for Extraterrestrial Intelligence.

An Alternative Hypothesis of Cydonia's Formation

Dr. Tom Van Flandern

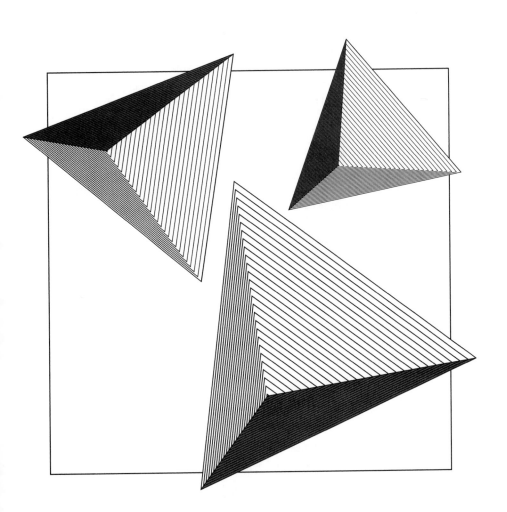

An Asymmetrical Mystery

Mars is extremely asymmetric. Its northern hemispheric crust is rarely more than a few kilometers thick. Yet its southern hemisphere has a thick crust everywhere that exceeds 20 kilometers in places. And the transition from thick to thin crust is strikingly sudden: The southern plateau drops 4-5 kilometers in the span of a few hundred kilometers. Moreover, the boundary between thick and thin crust is close to being a great circle around the planet.

An Alternative Hypothesis

What could cause such a specific type of lopsidedness? The best conventional explanation is a huge impact that blew away the original thick crust of the northern hemisphere. This would have caused a crater the size of a hemisphere that managed to leave a bit of crust behind, but not expose the mantle of the planet—not a very likely scenario. The alternative explanation is that Mars was a moon of a larger planet when the latter exploded. Then exactly one hemisphere of Mars would be buried in debris from the explosion, while the hemisphere facing away would be protected from most impacts from the event. As expected if this model is right, the thick-crust hemisphere of Mars has shoulder-to-shoulder craters everywhere, while the opposite hemisphere is sparsely cratered.

This model of the origin of Mars makes other specific predictions too. One is that much of the original atmosphere of Mars would be blown away by the nearby blast. That too agrees with data showing that Mars once had an atmosphere perhaps 100-1000 times thicker than at present. Also, the explosion impacts would have hit Mars on a hemisphere centered near the equator of Mars. But with so much debris piled up on one side, the rotation of Mars would become unstable, much like a spinning top with a small weight on one side. Mars would have eventually tipped over so that its spin axis again coincided with its axis of symmetry. That would require a nearly 90-degree pole shift. Significantly, areologists (geologists studying Mars) have previously found evidence for precisely that—a former location of the Martian poles that is near the present-day equator of Mars.

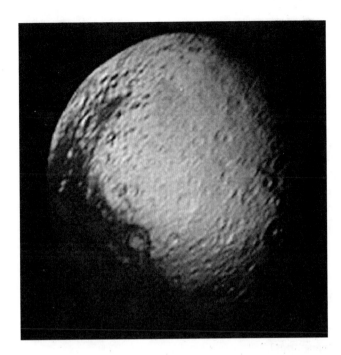

This image is a view of the southern hemisphere of Mars showing the heavy cratering and massive accumulation of surface material not found on the northern hemisphere. A part of the northern hemisphere's relatively undamaged expanse can be seen in the lower left portion of the image.

There is more. Water from a nearby exploding body could have been responsible for the catastrophic, seemingly one-time floods on Mars that left ripple dunes in the sand 4–5 meters high, as recently confirmed by the Mars Pathfinder lander.

But perhaps the best evidence that Mars was exposed to a special cataclysm is the abundance of element Xenon-129, which is nearly triple that found on other bodies where it has been measured. Xenon-129 is a second order nuclear fission by-product, and is not made through natural processes along with other common elements inside stars. It has long been assumed that an ancient supernova was responsible for the presence of that isotope in the solar system. But then why would Mars have an anomalously high amount of it? Proximity to an explosion of its parent planet involving fission is a possible explanation for why Mars is different in this way.

The Exploded Planet Hypothesis, sketched briefly above, appears to have a possible connection with the anomalous objects found in the Cydonia region of Mars, including the enigmatic "Face on Mars." A number of tests for possible artificiality have been undertaken since the area was discovered. These include the findings that the Face has a three-dimensional form, produces a high non-fractal response indicating non-natural structure, occurs in a context of other anomalous formations, has a reasonable amount of bilateral symmetry, and shows detail ("pupil" in the eyesocket, possible "teeth" in the mouth) consistent with a sculptural interpretation.

Additional tests that would add support to the hypothesis of artificiality, but do not at first seem applicable to the Face, would be:

a . to establish whether the Face is at a culturally significant location, such as on the equator or in the lowest valley on the planet (Cydonia, at 41 north latitude, is at an apparently random location);

b. to find a meaningful orientation for the Face such as a polar-aligned north-south axis (The Cydonia "Face" is tilted 22.5 west of north, a seemingly random orientation);

c. some indication of functionality, such as placement for convenient visibility (the "Face" on Mars stares up into space, yet cannot be seen from any other planet, even with our largest telescopes).

That brings us to a year ago when my own opinion was forced to change. Following a discussion of the exploded planet hypothesis by this author on a nationally syndicated radio talk show a listener asked, "Where was the 'Face' on Mars relative to the prior location of the Martian pole?"

This seemed an interesting and logical question. The Martian poles were once located in a different position from that found at the present time. Using information from Schultz (1985) on the most recent stable position of the Martian north pole before its present one, I computed the great circle arc between that former pole position and the "Face" at Cydonia. Imagine my shock when it came out to be 90.1 degrees: Cydonia formerly occupied a location quite close the previous Martian equator. And this passes the "location" test of artificiality.

The orientation test now took on added importance. The computed correction to give the orientation with respect to the old equator shows the "Face" symmetry axis aligned with the old Martian north pole to within the uncertainty of its known position. This passes the orientation test. I cannot express in words how profoundly I was affected by this discovery, because of its implications.

If the exploded planet hypothesis is correct, and Mars was a moon of that planet, then it is very probable that prior to the explosive event, Mars would have kept the same side toward the parent planet, just as Earth's Moon and most other large planetary moons keep the same face toward their parents. So this line of reasoning suggests a previously unimagined cultural purpose for a "Face" to be built on the Martian equator, looking up into space-or down toward the parent planet. It would have been visible to the presumed occupants of the parent planet. This satisfies the functionality test.

At the same time, this hypothesis resolves any difficulties about a technologically advanced civilization evolving on Mars. Instead, that civilization may have evolved on the now-exploded parent body. During the pre-explosion mass ejection phase, which may have lasted weeks or months, the orbital period (rotation) of Mars relative to the parent body could have changed, so that at the moment of explosion the "Face" was no longer oriented directly toward the planet, and in this manner escaped burial by the full explosion mass. (See the more detailed discussion of this at http://www.metaresearch.org, where several technical objections are resolved.)

Thus, if the exploded planet hypothesis is factored into the equation, all proposed tests of an artificial origin of Cydonia are now passed. Even skeptics have nothing to challenge but the data itself, which is all in the public domain and verifiable.

The Mars Global Surveyor spacecraft is now orbiting the Red Planet preparing for a mapping mission. Its cameras can take high resolution pictures of such potential quality that the truth status of the artificiality hypothesis should become clearer to all sometime during 1998 or 1999. In view of the preceding considerations, humankind might be wise to prepare for the possibility of a cultural shock probably unrivaled by any other in our lifetimes.

BIOGRAPHICAL NOTE

Tom Van Flandern, Ph.D., is the former Director of the Celestial Mechanics Branch, Nautical Almanac Office, U.S. Naval Observatory. Currently Head of the MetaResearch Foundation in Chevy Chase, Maryland, USA, he is the author of *Dark Matter, Missing Planets, and New Comets*.

Rhapsodies
on Mars

How wonderful that we have met with a paradox. Now we have some hope of making progress.

—Niels Bohr

It is perplexing. On the one hand, the Cydonia anomalies shouldn't be possible because we have at present no clear scientific rationale for how they could have come to be, hundreds of thousands or perhaps even millions of years ago, on a now-dead planet. On the other, twenty years of research points to there being something decidedly nonrandom on the Cydonia plain. And however you react to the Face, whether with skepticism or downright awe, its anthropomorphic qualities produce strong reactions. That there appear to be many other coherently shaped structures in the same vicinity just adds to the gnawing conclusion that we may be looking at something, whether a trick of geology or a legacy from the past, far outside our present understanding.

In what follows, we share the thoughts of three different social commentators who consider what may happen to our innermost sense of who we are, if we find at Cydonia confirming evidence for the prior existence of another intelligent species in our solar system. Each author approaches it differently. Dr. Michael Zimmerman provides the perspective of a social scientist, philosopher and humanist. Dr. Randolfo Pozos, one of the first to study the Cydonia anomalies, speaks to the issues as a social anthropologist. And finally, as both a dedicated scientist and devoted Christian, Dr. John E. Brandenburg shares with us his thoughts about how Cydonia's implications may fit surprisingly well within the Christian cosmology.

Superior Non-Human Intelligence:
Are We Afraid?

Dr. Michael Zimmerman

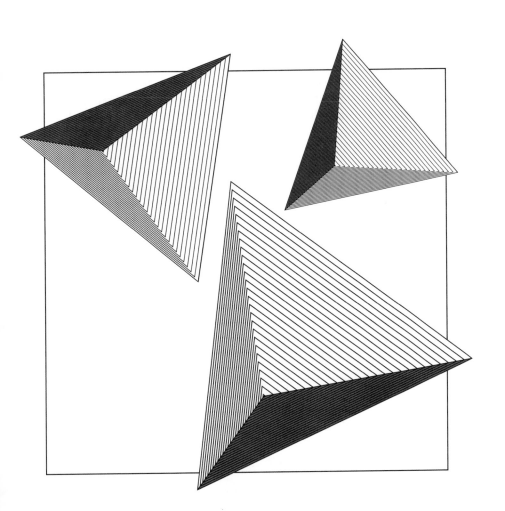

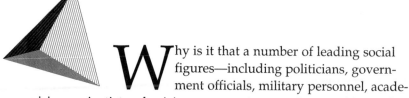

Why is it that a number of leading social figures—including politicians, government officials, military personnel, academicians, scientists, physicians, corporate executives, and journalists—have publicly resisted the very idea of superior non-human intelligence? Most people believe that if UFOs are artificial, since they are evidently capable of accomplishing feats transcending our current technology, they must belong to extraterrestrials whose intelligence is greater than our own.

Two Types
of Resistance

The reasons for resistance to the idea of superior non-human intelligence are complex. There seem to be two types of resistance. Not only does fear of ridicule prevent many people from discussing the idea publicly, but some social leaders, it seems, cannot accept the very possibility of superior non-human intelligence, because the identity of those leaders is tightly bound up with a human-centered world view that would crumble if faced with such intelligence.

Blockbuster films such as *Close Encounters, E.T.,* and *Aliens,* popular television series such as "Alien Nation," and a number of best-sellers have confronted ordinary people and influential social leaders alike with the possibility that non-human intelligent exists, and even that representatives may actually be visiting Earth. Exposure to such ideas has affected popular views. Nevertheless, government agencies have long sought to discourage public discussion of alien intelligence by questioning the veracity, sanity, and stability of those who report UFOs or discuss such phenomena.

In the particular case of the strange formations found in the Cydonia region of Mars, which a growing number of researchers have suggested may be the ruins of a former, if not present, civilization, mainstream science and the media have joined together to establish an atmosphere of ridicule to the point where scientists cannot even get the results of legitimate research considered for American scientific journals.

Opinion polls indicate that the higher the level of education, the more inclined a person is to accept the possibility of extraterrestrial intelligence. For fear of ridicule, however, many educated people will not publicly insist that government and academic agencies should apply themselves seriously to research on either the UFO phenomenon or the Martian anomalies.

Despite lingering hesitation, some government officials, psychotherapists, scientists, military personnel, journalists, and other social leaders are beginning to speak out more forcefully about the need to investigate systematically UFOs and reported alien abductions. Unfortunately this trend has not included an equivalent interest in the Martian anomalies. This is undoubtedly due to the high profile and larger number of individuals involved in UFOlogy.

Cracks in the Resistance

The cracks appearing in the attitudes of many social leaders may be due to several factors. These people have grown up with popular entertainment that dramatically explores the possibility of extraterrestrial intelligence. The end of the Cold War has limited the military's use of "national security" as a reason for discounting UFO sightings witnessed by many reputable citizens. Also the counterculture of the 1960s exposed many contemporary social leaders and opinion makers to "realities" that cannot be squared with the idea of a human-centered universe—sometimes called "anthropocentric humanism." Finally, the growing ecological crisis has convinced many people that despite some positive achievements, anthropocentric humanism is threatening to destroy the conditions necessary for human life, and for much of the rest of life on Earth.

By "anthropocentric humanism" I mean that form of humanism which holds that in a universe that is essentially a mechanism empty of values, "man" is a virtual god, who has the right to use and to determine the worth of all things. Though the arrival of superior non-human intelligence might be a shattering blow to such humanism, it developed, oddly enough, in connection with early modern science, which displaced "man" from the center of the universe defined by the medieval world view.

After Copernicus asserted that the Earth revolves around the Sun (instead of the other way around), other scientists maintained that our planet, far from being unique, is probably only one of many other planets in a vast universe where the laws of nature are everywhere the same.

Any residual conceits about human uniqueness were supposedly smashed a few centuries later by Darwin, who maintained that humans were not specially created, but instead were the products of the same natural, evolutionary processes that gave rise to earlier primates. Soon thereafter, the psychoanalyst Sigmund Freud undermined lingering beliefs in human autonomy by arguing that unconscious instinctual forces explain much of human behavior.

In the course of challenging humanity's assumptions about its own specialness, many scientists and philosophers have argued that extraterrestrial intelligence must surely exist. Destruction of the relatively comfortable medieval world view, and recognition that Earth is but a tiny outpost in a vast universe, led many intellectuals to hope for the discovery of extraterrestrial life, so that human isolation would be overcome. In the post World War II years, continuing debate about this issue was in part responsible for convincing Congress to fund NASA's space exploration as well as (at least temporarily) parts of the SETI program (Search for Extraterrestrial Intelligence).

Yet, contrary to this history, when faced with apparent evidence for possible ruins of a civilization on Mars, NASA has consistently refused even to acknowledge the existence of the research papers done on this subject. One would expect just the opposite. How are we to explain this dogged resistance to the very ideas that gave us one major motivation for space exploration?

Why Does Resistance Persist?

The answer to this question may be found, in part at least, in the paradox of anthropocentric humanism. This type of humanism is paradoxical because it depicts humankind as one animal among others, and simultaneously assigns to humankind the origin of all truth, value, and meaning.

Given the modern scientific view that humans are not the products of a special act of Divine creation, but are members of a lawful universe in which other intelligent life forms have probably evolved; and given the important role played by science in shaping the attitudes of modern societies, one might reasonably expect that such societies would exhibit some humility about humanity's place in the universe, as well as some compassion for non-human sentient life.

Such an expectation, however, would be confounded by the fact that anthropocentric humanism takes for granted that humans, as the most important things in the universe, have the right to use non-human nature however they please in the service of legitimate human ends. The abstract possibility of extraterrestrial intelligence has scarcely hindered modern societies from exploiting non-human nature to such an extent that the very conditions necessary for human existence are now threatened.

Many thinkers of the Enlightenment believed that human reason could make possible the scientific, technological, and political developments necessary for human emancipation, including universal human rights. Many of these same noble thinkers also believed that to become master of our own destiny, "man" would have to learn to dominate nature. Moreover, we had every right to do so, for plants and animals lacked the rational intelligence that was our unique endowment and basis for our special status.

Though apparently accepting modern science's contention that nature should be explained solely in terms of rational and materialistic principles, not in terms of religious revelation, then, anthropocentric humanism retains—in the doctrine that humans possess exceptional rationality—its own secularized version of the Biblical assertion that God gave "man" dominion over Creation.

Many of today's social leaders are agnostics or outright atheists, for whom such anthropocentric humanism poses few problems. Religious leaders may temper their anthropocentrism by conceding that the Creator is infinitely more intelligent and powerful than humankind. Yet even they are generally convinced that only humans are endowed with rational intelligence, a fact that squares with the Biblical claim that only humans are made in God's image. Hence, one can believe in God, while still holding that Creation is little more than the backdrop for the drama of human salvation.

Science's Human "Perspective"

History, at least as traditionally told, tells the story of males, not of females. It was no accident that such leading early modern thinkers as Francis Bacon described nature as a wily female whom "man" would have to seduce in order to control. The history of modern science and society cannot be adequately understood without grasping the extent to which modernity's noble, and purportedly universal, ideals have been distorted by attitudes that make European "man" the standard against which to measure whether someone is truly "human."

Anthropocentric humanism, then, is usually patriarchal. For many patriarchal humanists, the most important kind of liberty is negative liberty, i.e., freedom from control by another. Of course, one does not have to be a patriarchal humanist to resist being subjugated by another person, but many patriarchal males in particular truly dread losing control of their own actions. If such men fear being controlled by another person, they are even more uncomfortable with the idea of being dominated by non-human intelligence.

It is for this reason, I suggest, that at least some leading figures in major institutions discount, debunk, and disparage any phenomena that gives the slightest hint of intelligent alien life. And even if a patriarchal humanist manages to overcome the identity threats posed by the possibility of extraterrestrial intelligence, he or she may fear that public discussion of such a possibility might cost them their reputations and social positions.

Stopping Science to Save the Scientists

In the early 1960s, NASA received a report from the Brookings Institution concerning the implications of peaceful space activity. In one section, "The Implications of a Discovery of Extraterrestrial Life," the authors speculated about the potentially catastrophic social and political consequences of such a discovery, which would drastically challenge the prevailing anthropocentric world view. The report states: "It has been speculated that of all groups, scientists and engineers might be the most devastated by the discovery of relatively superior creatures, since these professions are most clearly associated with the mastery of nature, rather than with the understanding and expression of man[kind]. Advanced understanding of nature might vitiate all our theories at the very least, if not also require a culture and perhaps a brain inaccessible to earth scientists."

Supporters of anthropocentric humanism fear that if enough people conclude that superior alien intelligent beings exist, people will lose confidence not only in scientific rationality, but in related ideals of political tolerance and social progress. But it is not irrational to consider the strong possibility that humans are neither the sole nor the most advanced rational beings in the universe. In recent decades a growing number of scientists have challenged the view that the universe is a lifeless, purposeless, unchanging machine.

Crucial to this challenge has been the claim that the universe itself is not eternal, but rather has its own evolutionary history. Supposedly beginning with the Big Bang, the universe gradually developed galaxies, stars, planets, and life forms. Following chaos theory, cosmologists now speculate that matter-energy involves self-organizing tendencies that gradually produce increasingly complex, self-sustaining, living, and self-conscious forms of matter-energy. Hence, far from being the sheerest of cosmic accidents, the development of life on earth might be an example of what tends to happen on many other planets with appropriate initial conditions.

Today, we are living in a transitional period, in which the verities of anthropocentric humanism are being challenged by dramatic political changes, by socioeconomic difficulties, by religious fundamentalism, by scientific discoveries, and by the growing impact of research into such phenomena as the Martian anomalies, UFOs, and alien abductions. Certainly the scientists, engineers, and other professionals who have had the courage to probe deeply into the mysteries on Mars have made a contribution to this trend, whose full significance is yet to be realized.

BIOGRAPHICAL NOTE

Dr. Michael E. Zimmerman is a professor of philosophy and former Chair of the Department of Philosophy at Tulane University, who has published extensively on environmental and social philosophy.

Encountering Alien Life:
Do We Shake Hands
or Just Shake?

Dr. Randolpho R. Pozos

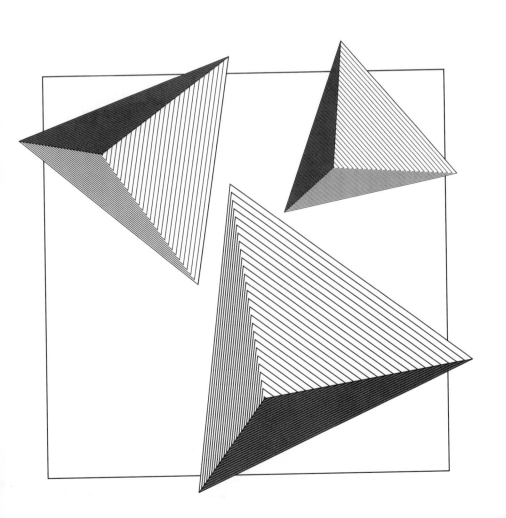

How will we as humans respond to incontrovertible evidence of other intelligent life forms in the universe? The evidence might be as dramatic as a "War of the Worlds" type encounter such as that described by Orson Welles in his famous 1938 radio broadcast. It might be as simple as the discovery of simple life forms in meteors or as hidden as the television sit-coms in which a visitor from another world lives as a guest with a human host or in a human neighborhood. Comedies such as "My Favorite Martian" and "Third Rock" present this notion as a possibility. It might take some other form which is more dramatic, but non-aggressive as well. No matter how and when it happens, the effect will be profound. We as humans will face a challenge to deeply held understandings of ourselves and our place in the universe. Our response may be a simple "Ho hum, we've seen it already in the *National Enquirer*." Or it may be more dramatic, provoking a soul searching evaluation of our most deeply held religious and cultural beliefs and attitudes. Or it might be smoothed over with the impersonal cynicism of contemporary "media think." The first encounter may take place on Earth, but as we continue to explore space, it might also occur on another planet or moon, perhaps even on our sister planet, Mars.

Years of work by a small group of earthbound scientific adventurers pushing the envelop of permitted topics have established that an unusual grid of shapes, pyramids, and a large face in the northern hemisphere of Mars are not tricks of light and shadow, nor are they likely to be exclusive creations of natural forces. As the result of this research, the human species is on the verge of having to develop a new conception of its identity, meaning, and purpose. How this discovery will change our concept of ourselves and our destiny is the focus of these reflections.

The Human Paradigm

The stories we invent in order to create ourselves and our everyday reality are called myths. They lie beyond fact and fiction because they establish the categories by which we classify fact and fiction. Myths not only shape our perceptions but are shaped by them. In other words, they have to explain everyday happenings in ways that make sense according to our basic neurological structure.

In the world of myths, and in the social and behavioral sciences, there is a subset of background stories and plots about the nature and purpose of humanity. These basic types of stories are called paradigms. When we try to estimate the future or imminent impact of a new paradigm of humanity, we have to estimate how it will change our sense of ourselves and our purpose in the cosmos.

The early images from the surface of Mars which showed pyramids and a large face looking heavenward stirred the mythical imagination. However, the more complex scientific imaging work of Dr. Mark J. Carlotto, Vincent DiPietro and Ananda Sirisena, the mathematical models of Dr. Horace W. Crater, in collaboration with Dr. Stanley V. McDaniel and Cesar Sirvent, and the archaeological expertise of Dr. James F. Strange, begin to point toward a change in what we call science fact—a change which will have large ramifications for our concept of ourselves. We must now develop a new Paradigm of Human Existence, in light of its three predecessors, please let me explain.

First Paradigm:
The Epic of Gilgamesh

The First Paradigm is best illustrated in the Epic of Gilgamesh. This story contains its own creation myth in which the universe is the result of the battles and love intrigues of the gods. Creation stories of the First Paradigm are polytheistic. Some are matriarchal, but most are definitely patriarchal and place women clearly subordinate to men. The First Paradigm of Humanity locates men and women as the combination of the basic elements, the union of earth and sky, the beings bridging the animal and the spiritual planes.

Second Paradigm:
The Book of Genesis

The Second Paradigm is contained in the Book of Genesis, which is the creation story for Jews, Christians, and Moslems. The Second Paradigm also focuses on the creation of the universe and humanity, but this time by the transcendent,

One God. Other cultural traditions of the First Paradigm's technologically less developed peoples, focusing on the migration of
heavenly beings or the union of gods with mortals, were pushed
aside by the global expansion and technological development of
Second Paradigm civilizations. Nevertheless, vestiges of these
ancient traditions are still found in the book of Genesis, describing
visitors from the heavens and their intermarriage with humans,
creating very long-lived giants.

One of the most striking examples of the Second Paradigm
is the Deist movement which had such a profound effect in the
17th and 18th centuries on the creation of western institutions
and their imposition through imperialism. In the Deist movement, God creates the universe and humanity and sends it forward in time with its own programming, which can be discerned
by human reason and the scientific method. The amazing scientific and technological developments of the 18th and 19th centuries
which arose from the Second Paradigm's Age of Reason would
eventually lead to its undoing.

Third Paradigm:
Star Trek

Although it seems more reasonable to name Darwin's *The
Origin of Species* or Kant's *Critique of Pure Reason* as emblematic pieces of literature for the Third Paradigm, they are
not pieces of epic literature which define a people and its destiny
and purpose. In the Third Paradigm, human destiny and purpose
derive from organic evolution.

Perhaps the most cogent example of the Third Paradigm is
the television series "Star Trek" and the movies and related series
which have grown from the initial program. Though "Star Trek" is
too young to be classic epic literature, it does have similar characteristics. In "Star Trek," set hundreds of years in the future,
humans have left Earth to explore the universe. Along the way,
they meet other beings and must develop ways to interact with
them, while following the "Prime Directive" of non-interference in
the development of other species and worlds. In some cases the
other species are friendly, in others they are belligerent. Often
there are misunderstandings which require a "cool head" and

rational analysis to defuse. Sometimes, there simply seem to be no alternatives but to fight defensively to protect the intrepid explorers. Through it all, the characters grow in understanding of themselves and of what it is to be human in a larger universe.

Fourth Paradigm:
The InterStellar Origins of the Human Race

The Fourth Paradigm begins on the Plains of Cydonia, in the northern hemisphere of Mars, among looming enigmatic pyramidal shapes and an enormous face looking heavenward through the rosy bitter cold of an eternal sunset. According to Dr. Mark Carlotto's calculation, the last time the alignments of the Face and the City would have "worked" as a ceremonial complex marking the Martian equinox and solstice would have coincided with the rise of Homo Sapiens on Earth.

No longer are we creatures of the gods, in the mythical pre-scientific sense. Nor are we the product of an anonymous planetary evolution. Instead, scientifically, the possibility arises that we are the result of colonization or interstellar grafting. The heavenly origin of the human species is not a new idea in the humanities, literature, and pre-scientific explanations of the origins and purpose of humanity. In fact, it is contained in some of our oldest literature, such as the Epic of Gilgamesh.

Paradigms in Counterpoint

It may seem inconsistent or even offensive to certain sensibilities to link ancient serious religious literature with the lighter weight popular fare of *Star Trek*. However, one of the great ironies of the human quest has been that as we get more serious about our origins, they become more tragicomic.

Douglas Adams' *The Hitchhiker's Guide to the Galaxy* contains a sublimely humorous origins myth. The earth became populated accidentally by cast off consultants in hot tubs, hair dressers, telephone cleaners and other "useless" members of society. This ignoble polyglot outlives its more task oriented parent society, which is wiped out by a virus spread by unclean telephones. In this view,

The Four Paradigms of Humanity and Their Characteristics

BY DR. RANDOLFO POZOS

	First Paradigm	Second Paradigm	Third Paradigm	Fourth Paradigm	Alternative Fourth Paradigm
Story	Epic of Gilgamesh	Book of Genesis	Star Trek	The Hitchhiker's Guide to the Galaxy	2001: A Space Odyssey
Story Type	Polytheistic Creation	Monotheistic Creation	Natural Evolution	Stellar Origins	Alien Intervention in Human Evolution
Species Origination	Conflict Among the Gods	Direct Command of One God	Confluence of Natural Forces	Extraterrestrial Intelligence	Extraterrestrial Intelligence
Significance of the Human Species	Tragic, Caught Between Earth and Stars	The Ungrateful Product of Divine Benevolence	Natural Selection and Scientific Research	One of the Many Sentient Species Without Answers to "The Question"	Specifically Chosen for the Regeneration of the Species
Development Model	Vain Struggle Against Destiny	Following the Law	Ecologically Based Enlightened Self-Interest	The Unfolding of Our Extraterrestrial Heritage	Specific Periodic Interventions Resulting in Human Technological Evolution
Ideal Behavior	Courage, Piety	Obeying Divine Commands	Objective Scientific Inquiry	Finding Our Place in the Cosmos	Accepting Our Fate Through Exploration
Species Purpose	To Live, To Die	To Fulfill the Divine Plan	To Know the Truth	To Explore and Question	To Accept Our Fate

humanity's survival is due to a combination of strategic inaction by consultants, attention to hair and nails, and a predilection for obsessive behavior.

Clearly, this is reading too much into this anti-creation myth. It seems out of place with the gravity of anomalies "unearthed" (if we can use the word) in the Cydonia region of Mars. However, it constitutes a new paradigm for humanity in which there are no answers to the really big questions about "life, the universe, and everything"—beyond, of course, the number "42."

Most serious practitioners of the Future As Religion—science fiction buffs—would probably point out that Arthur Clark's *2001: A Space Odyssey* is much more emblematic of the Fourth Paradigm. Nevertheless, a closer look at *Space Odyssey* and its sequels shows that it has more to do with First Paradigm literature, since it postulates an activist intervention by the "gods" who are never identified, nor is their purpose stated. In Clark's work, humanity is still caught between the Earth and the Stars.

In some respects, the Third Paradigm, the Age of Reason and Exploration, as exemplified by "Star Trek," is a repeat of the last four centuries of North Atlantic history conducted by rational, well-behaved people. It is neat and tidy, with just enough swashbuckle for box office appeal. However, it is intellectually unsatisfying since it leaves unanswered the primary human questions which a semi-military republic needs to answer for its disaffected youth. In many respects, "Star Trek" stops in 1964.

On the other hand, there may be enough evidence on Mars or in life forms beneath the oceans on Jupiter's moon, Europa, to define the Fourth Paradigm as one prefigured in Clark's *2001: A Space Odyssey*. It would be more mysterious and much less absurdist than Adams' *The Hitchhiker's Guide to the Galaxy*.

The reshaping of human art and society which will take place as the result of the discovery of the anomalies on Mars or elsewhere will depend to a great extent on which of the paradigms of humanity is supported by the discoveries. It is unlikely that any one particular paradigm will prevail or that all of the others will be discredited forever. However, the Fourth Paradigm of Stellar Origins will probably be ascendant, since the Martian mysteries will indicate that we have some relationship with beings who are not gods. More than likely, these discoveries, even when they are amplified by actual imaging or site visits to Cydonia, will only pose more questions with unknowable answers.

W e may well greet the news of this discovery with the orthodox belief of our time, which is skepticism, the clarity of our time, which is absurdism, and the fervor of our time, which is detachment. However, much the same could have been said of the 1400s. Maybe people will be unfazed by the new discoveries and will continue about their lives with little or no change occurring. On the other hand, there may be a major social recognition of the need to redefine who we are, resulting in dramatic social changes. Or perhaps the change will occur gradually, starting with small core groups of people who venture out with traditional understandings and discover en route that what they thought was a small world with direct pathways from "here to there" is actually much larger, with new worlds to be discovered and explored between "here" and "there." Such simple discoveries led to the world as we know it today. As a species we have a history of small groups exploring new territories, of questioning the accepted realities and thus bringing new ways of living to birth for the larger community. With the discovery of evidence of intelligent life elsewhere in the universe, human beings may once again be on the brink of this type of transformation, with its accompanying evolution of our myths and image of who we are.

BIOGRAPHICAL NOTE

Randolfo R. Pozos received his Ph.D. in Cultural Anthropology from the University of California at Berkeley in 1980. He is the author of *The Face on Mars* (1986) and the co-organizer of the original Independent Mars Investigation team, 1984-85.

Christianity &
the Coming Shift
in World View

Dr. John E. Brandenburg

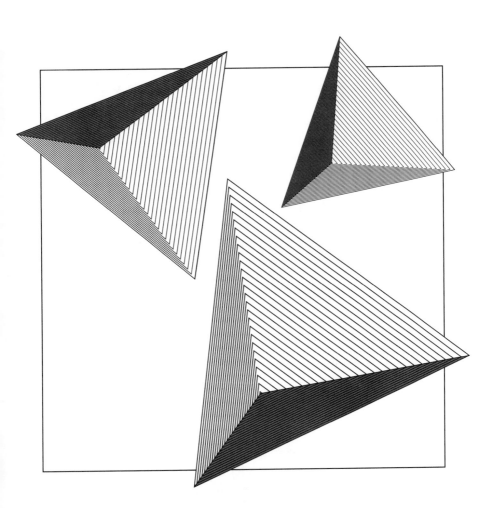

With the arrival of the Mars Global Surveyor at the Red Planet, the Cydonian Hypothesis approaches a moment of truth, and with it, humanity itself. A human-built spacecraft has arrived at Mars knowing exactly the right picture to take of exactly the right portion of that planet, to tell us whether Mars was once the home of people like ourselves. It has taken many probes, many previous pictures, and many years of groping, to bring us to this point. We will ask what we believe is the right question: Does the Mars Face look more like an artifact of intentional design at higher resolution, or less?

On the answer to that question will ride the fate of an hypothesis and of a human world view. The question that should be asked at this point: Is humanity ready to let go of its present world view and embrace another? To let go of Earth as the "whole world" and to embrace the Cosmos? My answer is that as a culture, scientifically and religiously we are ready for a new world view. The reasons for this answer are quite remarkable, but before these are discussed we must understand our present world view and the role of faith and science in it.

If the Cydonian hypothesis is disproved, then the present human world view will survive a little while longer. The present world view is that the Earth is the world, and the rest of the universe is merely a strange distraction from practical concerns. Humanity is the center of the world in our present world view.

This is in increasing conflict with the scientific understanding of the Cosmos and humanity's place in it, which finds the Earth is part and parcel of the Cosmos. We may soon discover that humanity is not alone, that we are probably not even remarkable, and that the rest of the Cosmos can and will affect Earth in ways that are stunning in their practical impact—possibly even dwarfing the importance of humanity.

Unfortunately, the prevailing religious world view, at least in the west, is very much in tune with the Earth as the world, and the human race as the sole intelligent inhabitants of the world. As a practical matter this view (which is not actually Biblical) has not yet caused serious problems. Problems usually occur when a world view has to change. A world view is formed and changed much less often than a scientific hypothesis. The failure of a world view is what destroys cultures; the synthesis of a new one is what saves them. This is, at best, wrenching but unavoidable. Like coming of age, it is essential. This is so because, like a scientific hypothesis, a world view must someday confront truth.

Science is above all the search for truth, and the true scientist must love the truth more dearly than his fondest illusion. For this reason, the true scientist must push ahead boldly, thrusting even his most cherished notions into the harsh inferno of reality, so that only those ideas that survive contact with experimental or observational data are retained. The true scientist must be skeptical even of his or her own ideas, even if believing in them passionately, and cast them aside when they fail in the moment of truth. The testable hypothesis is the only hypothesis worth forming, worth grooming carefully, and then like a child, worth letting loose on the world at large to fail or triumph.

In science, as in life, the only real gain can come through taking risk, the only real success through flirting with failure.

But what if one risks more than mere scholarly reputation? Suppose that in pushing back the unknown one uncovers truth that shakes the foundations of one's culture? Can one be as bold and callous with the beliefs of a people as with one's own? The test of true science is not only that it loves truth but that it *understands faith*.

Faith is not a concept spoken about often in scientific debates, for faith speaks of truths beyond the reach of science, beyond testing, beyond data. However, faith is part of a scientist's life: faith in the existence of truth, faith that truth can be tested, faith that the universe runs on laws that can be found, understood, and trusted. To be a true scientist is to have faith in science and its methods, and to believe that humanity can live and thrive on the truth rather than perish because of it.

As a scientist I know that truth is where life is, but I also know that truth is powerful, that it can cripple and kill unless it is handled wisely. I am also a Christian, and I know from this that faith and hope can sustain life when scientific truth alone cannot. Scientific truth and religious faith have clashed before in this society. Both have suffered because of this. Both have survived. Both are indispensable. Let us hope both sides can do better when the human world view must change again, as change it must.

Whether due to the Global Surveyor images of Cydonia, or the hoped-for discoveries from the SETI project, the human world view will change. No longer will the human race view the Earth as the whole world but rather the human race will view the Cosmos as the world and Earth merely as an important part of it. I consider it my duty as both a scientist and a Christian to help humanity in its transition to this new world view along a good and gentle path. To my delight I have found help in this from a source not many would expect.

Christianity, along with Judaism, is the philosophical foundation of western culture. The Bible is its main wellspring. If Christianity, through a deeper understanding of the Bible, can synthesize a new world view of the Cosmos *as* the world, and humanity still a vital part of it, even if other flesh-and-blood intelligences exist, then the transition to a new world view may not be so traumatic for humanity after all. Religion is the place where people, even scientists, turn when science runs out of answers. It is with God, that great Mystery however conceived, that the great unknowns of life can be confronted. For this reason religious faiths begun millennia ago survive and thrive in the modern and even postmodern age.

The triumph of the West in the Cold War can be interpreted as the triumph of Christianity over scientific atheism, as much as a triumph of freedom over despotism. For this reason, the posture of Christianity toward the impending shift of world view is crucial. Remarkably, it now appears that a Biblical synthesis of a new world view—Cosmos as world, with humanity not lost in it but honored—is easily accomplished. The Bible already contains this world view.

The Bible is remarkable as an ancient document in that its concept of God is completely overarching. The God of Israel is the God of the Cosmos, Creator and supreme ruler of the heavens and the Earth and all the beings who throng those regions, seen and unseen. To a believer in the Bible the God of Israel is the God of the Andromeda Galaxy and all who dwell there as much as the God of Earth. It is God, and not humanity, that is the center of the Biblical world, which is the whole Cosmos. However, humanity is important because God says it is, and who might argue this point with God?

As for extraterrestrial life and intelligence, nowhere in the Bible is life or intelligence or, for that matter, government, power, and sin, ever limited to the Earth, but all are present in the heavens and Earth. For this reason the existence of extraterrestrial life and intelligence, as it is understood by modern science, can be said to be strongly implied in the Old Testament even if it is not mentioned explicitly. It goes without saying that God's covenants with Israel are unchanged by the existence of extraterrestrials. However, it is in the New Testament where the Cosmos as world concept is most dramatic and explicit.

The theme of the New Testament is the redemption of the world through Christ's death on the cross and the "Great Commission" of the church to spread the gospel. Two verses that summarize this are familiar ones: "For God so loved the world that he gave his only begotten son, that whosoever believeth in him should not perish but have everlasting life." (John 3:16) and "Go ye into all the world and preach the Gospel to every creature" (Mark 16:15). The important word in these verses is "world." That word in the original Greek, in these two verses and in countless similar verses, is the word "kosmos."

The Greek word "kosmos" remarkably means exactly the same thing now as it did when it was written: the Cosmos, the ordered universe. Nowhere is the mission of Christ or the Church limited to the Earth in the New Testament. Because the Cosmic nature of these missions is so explicit and is repeated so often, it can be said that the existence of extraterrestrial intelligence is strongly indicated in the New Testament. The heavens are included, in some places explicitly (Col 1:20 and Eph. 3:10), in these missions and yet the redemption on the cross and the gospel that proclaims it are very much matters of flesh and blood. For these reasons, Biblical Christianity is in a remarkably strong position to adopt a new world view of the Cosmos as world. The fact that this world view is inherent in the Bible has been unnoticed simply because until now there has been no need.

Therefore, both Judaism and Christianity, the foundation of western culture, are well equipped to transition to a world view of the Cosmos as the world—even with a Cosmos occupied throughout by other intelligences. The covenants remain, and the Church has the challenge of a truly enlarged mission field. This does not mean the transition will not be traumatic for some; all change is. But the foundations of Biblical belief are more deep-set than anyone suspected, and will hold. This means everything else, fastened to Biblical faith, will hold too.

A s for science and popular culture, it is science's job to be ready for such a development as the discovery of extraterrestrial intelligence and it will certainly not be taken by surprise at this point. In popular culture, science fiction fare has thoroughly saturated the population with the new world view's most important concepts. Some ideas fastened to the view of Earth as the world, of humanity as the center, will collapse, but this is unavoidable. In general, however, the basic structure of the culture seems well-founded. If this matter is handled correctly by the authorities, by being direct but reassuring, it should be absorbed well.

If a discovery of extraterrestrial intelligence is impending, should we of Earth adopt a defensive position, in the military sense? A dead primitive civilization on Mars (according to the Cydonian Hypothesis), or a living civilization many light years distant, present no immediate risk to Earth's security. This means the question of the origin of the UFO phenomenon will probably not be critical at this time. However, in my opinion, the general aspects of defense policy in our world should receive attention. Such public attention by the Defense Department could defuse any immediate popular unease caused by a discovery of extraterrestrial intelligence, on Mars or by SETI signals, which are themselves non-threatening. My thought for this new day is "Good fences make good neighbors." Therefore, I think humanity is ready, at every important level, and I can say this as both a scientist and a Christian. I urge that we move forward without fear, and make whatever discoveries can be made.

Note: This article originally appeared in *The McDaniel Report,* North Atlantic Books, Berkeley CA, 1993. It is reprinted here with permission of the author of *The McDaniel Report.*

Coming
to a Planet
Near You

$\diagdown\!\diagup$

Many images of Mars have captured the public's fancy over the years. It's been called the planet of canals, of little green men, of terrifying monsters bent on invading the Earth, of Edgar Rice Burrough's John Carter and his derring-do. But its reality be may be even more exciting. What would possible confirmation of the Cydonian anomalies as the ruins of magnificent artificial constructions mean for the future of the space program and for all humanity? In this section, five of our authors provide some insight into the possible consequences of a successful opening of the Red Planet to our knowledge and even, perhaps, to our eventual colonization.

Lan Fleming, who works at Johnson Space Flight Center in Houston, points out that confirmation of ruins at Cydonia would vitalize the manned space program as could nothing else imaginable. Humanity's irrepressible curiosity would demand a mission carrying astronauts to Mars to discover the secrets of such ruins. Were they built, as Vincent DiPietro and John Brandenburg suspect, by an indigenous race of Martians? Were they a short-term construction project of an extraterrestrial race just passing through? Or as an incredible revelation, will we discover they were built by our own long-forgotten ancestors among the stars?

In anticipation of such questions, archaeologist James F. Strange writes of the predictions we can make (based on the current level of research) about what possible cultural artifacts we may find on Mars. Dr. Mark Carlotto explores the implications of the Mars Global Surveyor Mission and what it already may have learned. Dr. John E. Brandenburg, taking a dip into the distant past, speculates about what may have destroyed any ancient Martian life. And finally, Baron Johannes von Buttlar describes what may be Mars' eventual redemption—a return to life as a newly terraformed second home for the human race.

Why NASA
Needs Cydonia

Lan Fleming

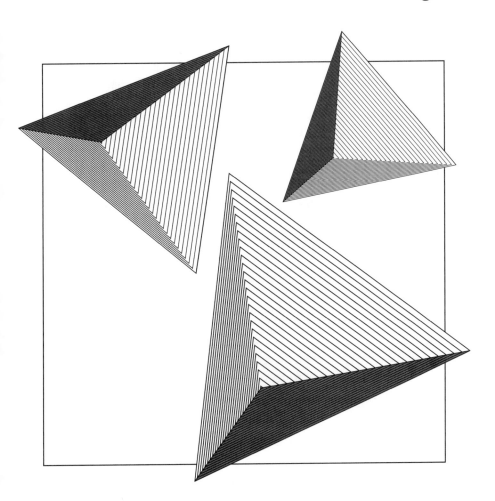

N ASA's Apollo 11 Moon landing in 1969 was humanity's first visit to another world. Unfortunately, this history-making event seems to have been the high-water mark of public enthusiasm for the space program. Despite huge scientific and technological advances that have occurred during the intervening decades, no subsequent space mission has ever equaled its impact on popular imagination. Since the Apollo program was canceled, no human has set foot again on another world. Manned space missions have been confined to low Earth orbit, in large part because the public has been unwilling to pay for the more ambitious programs of human space exploration that had been planned to follow Apollo. With some justification, spaceflight enthusiasts look upon the public's disinterest in space exploration as an indication of a general lack of appreciation for and education in the sciences.

But there is more to the problem than an apathetic public that tires quickly of thrills provided by space exploration. What has often impressed people most about the discoveries of Apollo and the robotic probes to other planets has been the more negative implications of the new knowledge: the dangers posed by killer asteroids obliterating life on Earth or the possibility of a runaway green house effect leaving our planet a hellish inferno similar to Venus if more care is not taken of our environment. It is understandable that further human exploration of this vast wasteland lacks emotional as well as intellectual appeal. So, for the most part, the public seems content with the current program of intermittent, low-cost, and low-risk robotic exploration.

Since Apollo, Mars has offered the only faint hope that the solar system may not always have been as lifeless as it now appears to be. The images returned by the Viking Orbiters in the 1970's showed features strongly resembling meandering rivers. And even skeptical planetary scientists accept that liquid water may have once flowed on the planet in the distant past. NASA's announcement in the summer of 1996 of evidence of possible microfossils in an Antarctic meteorite thought to have originated on Mars has certainly fanned the embers of public interest left glowing dimly by Viking. But has it really caught fire?

The intensity of the current public interest in Mars still seems to fall far short of the enthusiasm for Apollo, fueled as it was by the nationalistic and ideological competitiveness of the Cold War. Even with thirty years of technological advances, the costs of designing and executing a single manned mission to Mars would be much greater now than the costs for all seven Apollo missions thirty years ago.

The smallest straight-line distance from Earth to Mars is 48 million miles when the two planets are closest to each other, nearly 200 times the distance from the Earth to the Moon that had to be crossed by Apollo. Rather than the Apollo capsules' dangerous journeys of a few days' duration, a journey to Mars would require many months in both directions and would be equally, if not more, dangerous.

Rather than carrying nonrenewable supplies of oxygen and food as the Apollo capsules did, a manned spacecraft sent to Mars would require systems that recycle air and water. In addition to chemical recycling, it is envisioned that a spacecraft on a journey of such an extended duration may also need an agricultural section for raising crops to provide a source of food for the human crew and, through photosynthesis, converting some of the carbon dioxide exhaled by the crew back into the oxygen they must breathe.

A Mars-bound spacecraft with a self-contained ecosystem of this sort would bear less resemblance to the Apollo "capsules" than it would to a world in miniature. In size and mass and in the magnitude of the engineering and construction effort required to build it, it would probably be comparable to the International Space Station (ISS) that is intended to function only in low Earth orbit. And the ISS program has itself suffered from much greater technical and administrative problems than anticipated. A manned mission to another planet would require a much greater commitment of resources than what has been allocated to the ISS to date.

It may or may not be true that extraordinary claims require extraordinary evidence, as Dr. Carl Sagan said, but it is certainly true that extraordinary efforts require extraordinary justification. It would take something quite extraordinary to justify to the public the levels of effort needed to realize a manned mission to Mars, something that inspires intense international cooperation rather than the competitiveness that drove the race to the Moon.

Cydonia may be that extraordinary something. If the interpretation of Cydonia as artificially constructed is supported by additional higher-resolution photography from future robotic probes or Mars Global Surveyor, there could be compelling reasons to believe that an intelligent race once lived on a planet other than our own—while still being close enough on the cosmic scale to invite human exploration. If that race existed, then it must have had its own history, with endeavors at least somewhat akin to our own literature, art, and science—endeavors representing values of the highest order in all human cultures.

Most people are probably content to live out their lives without ever knowing the full history of the geology and climate of Mars, but the unfolding story of a long-vanished intelligent race on another planet would be one that most would find irresistible. To piece together that story, a good case can be made that the trained minds, eyes, and hands of human observers present on the scene would be needed to supplement any work done by robotic or remotely operated probes.

Perhaps more important than any rational arguments in justifying a human presence on Mars, there is what could be called a spiritual motivation that could well be the most important factor of all. Given the knowledge that there was once some civilization on Mars, most people would, I think, feel an overwhelming urge to personally walk on that alien terrain where others had lived before, to see first hand the evidence of their existence, to wonder about how they lived, what they thought, what gods they might have worshiped, what they might have feared and hoped for—and how they might have regarded the bright blue star in their evening or morning sky—the star that is our own planet Earth.

Initially, only a select few people may be granted the privilege (and the dangers) of a personal journey to Mars. But those few would carry with them the curiosity and dreams of the entire human race. And should we discover evidence of alien life, humanity, finally, may have the monumental incentive it needs to pay the price to explore other worlds.

BIOGRAPHICAL NOTE

Lan Fleming is an engineer at Johnson Space Center, Houston, Texas.

Predicting the Details:
What We Will
See at Cydonia

Dr. James F. Strange

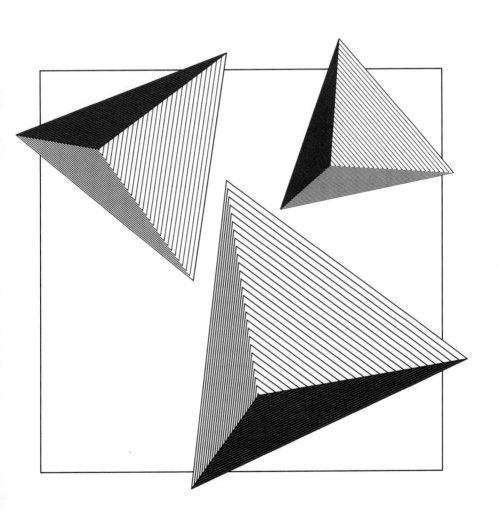

Making predictions is one of the most important features of both the scientific method and scientific research. These predictions should only be generated when the scientist has collected enough data, has made enough observations about that data, and has formed enough hypotheses to then make evidence-based predictions about the behavior or characteristics of the subject studied. These predictions are absolutely necessary since they are then used to test the hypotheses formed from the data.

In the case of the Cydonia anomalies on Mars, after nearly 20 years of research, the independent investigators have mastered the data. Based upon what has been seen so far it should be possible to predict what else one might see.

Usually predictions are about new data, not about the data we already have in hand. For example, if we had formed a hypothesis about Martian soils based on soil samples from the Viking Lander some 20 years ago, then we might have made predictions about Martian soils which could have been tested with new data gathered by the Pathfinder Rover in 1997.

Furthermore, once we have collected the new Rover data, made our exhaustive observations, and formulated our hypotheses about soil characteristics, etc., we would make new predictions. We will be ready for new data from future robotic samplers.

The same is true about making predictions from the well-known Viking frames 35A72, 70A13 and 70A11, which include the "Face," the "City," the "Fort," the small mound configuration and other anomalous features. In this case, our predictions will be based upon our observations and hypotheses about Cydonia as deduced from the Viking digital images.

Specifically, what predictions might be made about Cydonia which can then be tested by analyzing the new imagery taken at higher resolution by cameras aboard Mars Global Surveyor and future Mars missions?

The Data At Present

First, let us recapitulate what we have seen so far at Cydonia.

1. Vincent DiPietro and Gregory Molenaar, and subsequently other researchers, studied a gigantic face-shaped mesa at

Cydonia. It is reasonably bisymmetrical. It has two discernible eye sockets, a nose, a mouth, and is surrounded by
what appears to be a headpiece or helmet (to use human cultural descriptors). There is even a clearly defined "pupil" in
the left eye socket, and a hint of "teeth" in the mouth. The
face is not rendered like a cartoon, but, as measured by
anthropologist James Channon, its shape tends to conform to
humanoid proportions. We also know, by means of more
than one test, that the object is face-like in three dimensions
and not merely an outline. Finally, there is a suggestion of
some possibly decorative markings on the "headpiece." (*See
Enhancing the Subtle Details in the Face on page 53.*)

2. Many researchers have noticed that the face occurs in a context of faceted landforms suggesting pyramids or at least
pyramidal objects. Since this clustering of such landforms
occurred on the shore of an ancient sea, it suggested a "city"
and came to be called "The City." However, to call the clustering a "city" is purely speculative at this point, and not
necessary to the present discussion.

3. DiPietro, Molenaar, Mark J. Carlotto, and Erol Torun among
others have observed that one particular landform at
Cydonia appears to be strikingly pyramidal, and in fact it is
known as the D&M pyramid after DiPietro & Molenaar, who
discovered it. The base of this structure is usually understood to be pentagonal, although there are differences of
opinion on this point. It is not a regular pentagon, though it
may be symmetric around one axis. An adequate determination of its shape awaits higher resolution images.

4. Stanley V. McDaniel and Horace W. Crater have observed a
series of small mounds at Cydonia, all having about the
same diameter and reflectivity (albedo), which appear to be
arranged regularly. Several tests applied by Crater to the
mound data indicate that the mounds lie in a highly nonrandom pattern. Following Crater's results, I applied a different
test, the Kolgorov-Smirnov test based on intermound distances. My result supported the finding of Crater and
McDaniel that the distribution of the mounds is not random.

5. Crater and McDaniel have observed that some of the
mounds lie on the corners or side mid-points of a specific
rectangular grid. The grid is based on the square root of two,

but it is not represented by linear markings in the ground. It must be inferred from the positions of the mounds, which appear to lie at key points on such a grid.

6. Several researchers have observed that the inferred rectangular grid is not based on line of sight considerations. That is, the line of sight from one mound to the next may be interrupted by a landform, but that does not affect the grid.

7. Crater observed that the geometry of the mound arrangement contains multiple examples of an angle that references the internal geometry of a tetrahedron. This angle is 19.5°, and is found in geometric measurements of the cross-section of a tetrahedron as well as in the geometry of a tetrahedron embedded in a sphere. Triangular relationships measured among the mounds also shows a predominance beyond chance of triangles duplicating the shape of the tetrahedral cross-section and geometric divisions of that cross-section.

Predictions Based on the Data

We are a long way from concluding that we are seeing remains of an ancient civilization at Cydonia on Mars, but we know enough to be able to make some predictions. If the landforms, face, and grid at Cydonia are creations of an ancient civilization, what would we be able to say about it? If I were asked to predict what we might find based on my experience and training as an archaeologist, I would reason as follows.

First we turn to the Face as a work of art. If it is a work of art, then we might hypothesize that the Cydonians were roughly humanoid in appearance. More to the point, if they represented themselves in bas-relief, as it were, then we would expect to find more representations of themselves on a smaller scale and perhaps in different mediums. In other words, if we take the Face to be a work of art, then we hypothesize that their art contains their own faces, and we expect to see more faces on a smaller scale and with the same or similar anatomical characteristics as the Face.

Second, if we can see more of the Face at a higher resolution, then we should be able to see more detail. Right now with our current image processing there is reason to believe that there are pupils in the eyes and perhaps even teeth in the mouth, not to mention details on the headpiece. It seems reasonable to predict that we will see more anatomical detail at higher resolution, although erosion of course has to be taken into account. Are there indications of eyelashes, nostrils, or other human-like details?

As interesting as this may be, it is more interesting to make a cultural prediction. At higher resolutions we should be able to see more detail in the headpiece or helmet and conclude one way or the other what it is. If this is what it appears to be, a huge sculpture, then unless erosion has removed all traces of additional detail we should see enough to determine that we are looking at hair or a piece of clothing or armor or other head covering. On the piece itself we may expect details such as one sees in terrestrial artwork suggesting decoration, jewelry, ribbons, seams, an insignia, etc.

To turn to the faceted landforms, if they are artificial, then we expect to see repetition of the geometry of each landform on a smaller scale. In other words, we expect to see small pyramids, not yurts or Quonset huts. Even if they have been battered by erosion or by meteorites, their geometries should be visible and should repeat at least in part what we have observed so far.

Assuming that the D&M Pyramid is a product of this hypothetical culture, we also may expect to see repetitions of its geometry in structures which are too small to be seen in the currently available Viking photographs. There are two main interpretations of the probable original geometry of the D&M, one by cartographer Erol Torun and a more recent one by Rylan Bachman. If Torun's interpretation is correct, we will see angles such as 60°, 120°, 85.3°, 69.4°, 34.7°, and 19.5° (Think of our own fondness for 90° angles in buildings, plots of land, and the lay-out of cities.) If Bachman's interpretation is supported, we will see the angles found in the rectangular grid hypothesized by Crater and McDaniel, since on Bachman's account the D&M geometry is based on that grid.

Speaking of right-angles, it is appropriate to predict that this angle may not occur, or will occur rarely, precisely because we do not see it in the landforms. Although 90 is important in the square root of two grid, one does not see the right angle as part of a structure. It is not present in either of the two main D&M interpretations. One infers a grid only from the arrangement of the mounds and draws that grid on paper or on a computer screen.

But we may expect to see objects on the ground organized in a square root 2 grid pattern, though on a smaller scale. This is because we hypothesize that this grid is an essential part of the "culture" of the Cydonians. Even if that is not the correct explanation, that the grid occurs at all suggests that we should see it again. Culture means standardization and repetition of forms and patterns.

If we do find objects on a smaller scale organized on a square root 2 grid, we would expect also to find that the grid is not constrained by line of sight considerations. This may imply, for example, that other struc- tures are beneath the ground connecting the grid- associated surface objects.

Therefore, even though no one has seen any- thing on the surface of Mars to the degree of detail we would like, we can predict something about what we may expect to see. Even though we cannot say with certainty that we will see such things, it is entirely reasonable to predict that we will see the kinds of features enumerated above. After

Hypothetical Model of the "D&M Pyramid" by cartographer Erol Torun. This is the proposed original shape prior to deformation as a result of erosion. The angles are A = 60°, B = 120°, C = 85.3°, D = 69.4°, E = 34.7°, F = 49.6°, G = 45.1°, H = 55.3°. If the object is a cultural artifact, such angles may be repeated in smaller structures not visible in the Viking images.

all, human beings are remarkably predictable, given enough of them in the sample. So, if they were there at all, then, we hope the same for the ancient Cydonians.

BIOGRAPHICAL NOTE

James F. Strange is a Professor of Religious Studies, former Dean and Former Chair of Religious Studies, at the University of South Florida. He is also the Director of the University of South Florida Archaeological Excavations at Sepphoris, Israel. Author of four books on archaeology, Dr. Strange is also the Secretary of the Society for Planetary SETI Research (SPSR).

Global Surveyor:
Fait Accompli?

Dr. Mark J. Carlotto

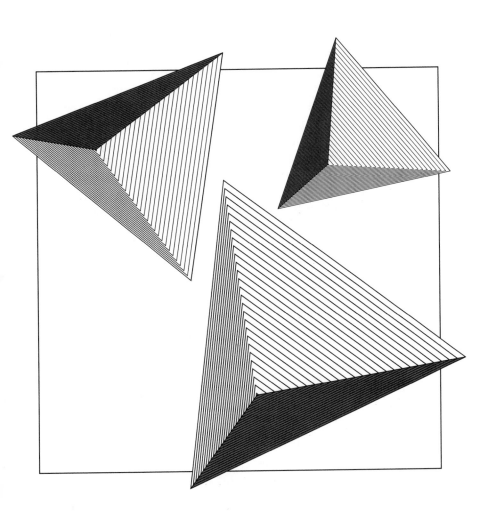

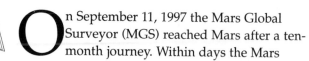

On September 11, 1997 the Mars Global Surveyor (MGS) reached Mars after a ten-month journey. Within days the Mars Orbital Camera (MOC) began taking pictures of the Red Planet. By the beginning of November, well over one hundred images of Mars had been acquired, yet only 6 images (about 5%) had been released to the public.

The MOC was developed and is operated by Malin Space Science Systems (MSSS), a private company under contract to the Jet Propulsion Laboratory (JPL). The trickle of imagery released by MSSS is in stark contrast to the steady stream of Pathfinder images posted over the previous summer. The lack of released MGS imagery is troubling in light of the controversy surrounding the Face and other anomalous objects in Cydonia. MSSS and JPL have stated repeatedly that the MOC narrow angle (high resolution) camera is not likely to image these objects because of its limited field of view and lack of pointing ability. However, examination of the few images released to date suggests that the camera may be more capable than we have been led to believe.

What are the actual capabilities of MGS/MOC? (The term MGS/MOC is used here because, even though the camera itself cannot be steered, the platform to which it is bolted, namely the MGS, can. The two thus function as a system.) Specifically, is MGS/MOC capable of imaging the Face and other objects at Cydonia? Could these objects have been imaged by now? And what are the prospects for imaging them in the future?

In order to evaluate the capabilities of the camera and opportunities to photograph Cydonia, we must first analyze those images that have been released. We can then assess the likelihood that opportunities to image the Cydonia targets have occurred up to this writing and might occur between now and the time the spacecraft reaches its final mapping orbit in 1999.

Analysis of MOC Images to Date

As of November 1, 1997, MSSS had posted 4 images on its web site [Ref. 1]. (Technically there were really six; two are black and white, and two are 2-band color images.) The

Orbit/Image ID	Target	Distance	Camera Angle	Resolution
(P005_03)	Labyrinthus Noctis (4.6 S, 102.6 W)	1600 km	25 deg.	12 m
(P006_05)	Nirgal Vallis (28.5 S, 41.6 W)	800 km	35 deg.	9 m
(P013_01, 02)	Valles Marineris (5-10 S, 73-86 W)	600–1000 km	25 deg.	350–600 m
(P024_01, 02)	Olympus Mons (12-26 N, 126–138 W)	176–310 km	0 deg.	~1km

Table 1   Images Posted on the MSSS Web Site as of November 1, 1997

four images are listed in Table 1. Three were shot during aerobraking. The first two from orbits 5 and 6 were acquired by the narrow angle (high resolution) camera. The third was taken with the wide angle (low resolution) camera. All three were taken with the camera looking east of the terminator—the line on the surface between night and day, which at the time was just below the spacecraft. Later, during orbit 24 after aerobraking had been suspended, an image of the great volcano Olympus Mons was shot looking straight down using the wide angle camera. By this time the terminator had moved to the west so that the ground under the spacecraft was illuminated.

The *attitude* of the craft is the position of the spacecraft relative to the planet and is defined by the three axes of pitch, yaw and roll. In MGS, attitude is controlled using a set of three reaction wheels, not fuel-consuming thrusters. Changing the spin of a reaction wheel changes its angular momentum which in turn causes the spacecraft to rotate around the corresponding axis. Thus, even though the MOC cannot be positioned independently of the spacecraft, the spacecraft itself can be moved with great ease and flexibility without having to use any fuel.

These images reveal that, in fact, MGS is being steered to point the camera toward selected targets. Given this, statements by Michael Malin of MSSS regarding the limited flexibility in pointing the MOC because it is bolted to the MGS are misleading. For example, Malin has stated, "The MOC is body-fixed to the spacecraft," and "The spacecraft has limited pointing control." [Ref. 2].

MSSS states that 132 images were acquired from September 11 to October 28. Of these 58 are low resolution and 74 high resolution. They also state that 28 high resolution and 24 low resolution images were taken after aerobraking was suspended, from October 16 through October 28. On average they seem to be taking about three images per orbit which seems consistent with statements concerning the limited opportunities to take pictures during aerobraking [Ref. 3]. However, the existence of image ID P006_5 suggests that during orbit 6, five or possibly more images were acquired.

The pointing accuracy of the MOC has been a subject of great controversy especially with respect to taking pictures of the Face and other objects in Cydonia. The U. S. Geological Survey (USGS) Mars Mosaiced Digital Image Model (MDIM) is used by MSSS to determine the coordinates of features on the ground. According to Michael Malin, the estimated accuracy of the latitude-longitude grid defined by the MDIM is 5-10 kilometers [Ref. 2], i.e., a given point may actually be up to 5-10 kilometers from where it is thought to be, assuming the position of the camera is precisely known. However, Malin goes on to state that, "There will be a substantial uncertainty in the predicted inertial position of the spacecraft (and hence, the camera)," and gives a value of 7.4 km or more in the crosstrack (lateral) direction at 40 deg. latitude [Ref. 2]. Thus together we are told to expect positional uncertainties in the 12.4 to 17.4 km range.

The MDIM and a subset of Viking Orbiter images that have been registered to the MDIM [Ref. 5] are used by MSSS for target planning. An example output from the planning software showing the Cydonia targets is reproduced in Figure 1.

Figure 2 shows a reduced version of P0005_3 and its corresponding Viking Orbiter context image. Because of the narrow field of view of the high resolution camera, Viking context images provide a visual reference for interpretation, showing the relative location and footprint of the MOC image within a larger area. The correspondence between the MOC image footprint shown in the context image (which is assumed to have been used for targeting as well) and the actual MOC image suggests that the positional errors are far less than 12.4 -17.4 km. P005_03 is about 12 km by 12 km in size. If its corresponding context image was in fact used for targeting, it seems as if the targeting accuracy is far better than we have been led to believe. Comparing this to Figure 1, one would conclude that, given the opportunity, MGS/MOC could probably acquire a high resolution image of the Face or City from the current orbit.

Could Cydonia
Have Been Imaged by Now?

Could Cydonia have been imaged during the initial aerobraking phase that began on September 15 (orbit 3) lasting to the suspension of aerobraking on October 6 (orbit 15)?
Aerobraking occurs at periapsis (the point in a satellite's orbit closest to the planet) when the spacecraft dips into and is slowed down by the atmosphere. According to MSSS, following periapsis, a roll-out maneuver from the aerobraking to array-spin normal orientation occurs. It is only at this point in the orbit, shortly after periapsis, that the camera can be used. Since images can be acquired just after periapsis, imaging opportunities would have been severely limited. It is thus unlikely that MGS had the opportunity to image Cydonia during this initial aerobraking phase because Cydonia was too far to the north. However during the course of the aerobraking maneuver the periapsis latitude will shift toward the north. It is thus possible that MGS may be able to image Cydonia during aerobraking later on in the mission.
In mid October one of MGS's solar panels was damaged during aerobraking. Caused by a significantly higher atmospheric density than expected, aerobraking was suspended for over a month while the problem was examined. Free from the attitude constraints imposed by aerobraking was it possible that during the aerobraking hiatus there might have been greater flexibility in

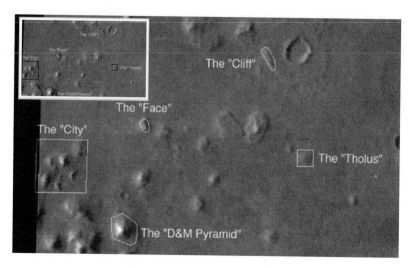

Figure 1   Portion of screen from planning software showing Cydonia targets from MOC target database [Ref. 4]. This portion shows the Viking Orbiter context image. Inset is the image reduced to the same scale as that of the Viking Orbiter context image in Figure 2 (next page) for comparison. (Malin Space Science Systems, Inc.)

changing the attitude of the spacecraft and more opportunities to aim the camera at Cydonia?

A rough "back of the envelope" calculation suggests there was. The orbital period at this point in the mission was about 35 hours. The orbit thus precessed about 154 degrees in longitude to the east each revolution. For example, if the first orbit passed over the equator at some longitude, say zero degrees, the longitudes for that and the following seven orbits would be 0°, 154°, 308°, 102°, 256°, 50°, 204° and 358°. Putting these into ascending order, 0°, 50°, 102°, 154°, 204°, 256°, 308° and 358°, we see that during the aerobraking hiatus, MGS passed within about 26 degrees of longitude of any point on Mars. Since the operation of the camera was not limited to the roll out maneuver, it could have, in theory, imaged just about any point on the surface to within the accuracy of the targeting software (provided the surface was illuminated at the time).

Given the ability to move the camera up to 35 degrees off nadir, which is evident in the four images reported thus far, one would have to conclude that the MGS was being tasked by MSSS to point the MOC toward a predetermined set of targets of interest. That the Face and objects in Cydonia could have been one of

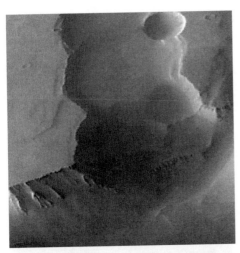

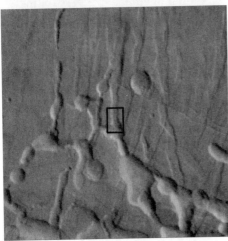

Figure 2

Reduced versions of P0005_3 (top) and its corresponding Viking Orbiter context image (below). (Malin Space Science Systems, Inc.)

these targets is a possibility, and it is almost certain that MGS could have already acquired images of Cydonia if it was instructed to do so.

In fact, using orbital simulation programs (Microsoft Space Simulator V1.0 and Maris RedShift 2), Peter Nerbun has determined that MGS was in position to have imaged Cydonia on October 29 during the aerobraking hiatus. This can be seen in the MGS/MOLA ground tracks (a portion of which is reproduced in Figure 3). During orbit 30 MGS crossed 40 N latitude to the east of Cydonia at 0 W longitude.

From the orbital simulation programs (Figure 4) Nerbun determined that MGS's closest approach to Cydonia on that date was at 4:56 PM Local Solar Time (LST) at an altitude of 240 kilometers. It was 497 kilometers from Cydonia. At this distance the image resolution would have been about 1.5 meters per pixel. Adequate light for acquiring an image would have been available at this time. This conclusion is supported by viewing MSSS's image at Schiaparelli Crater at 4:50 PM LST and Olympus Mons at 5:30 PM LST.

Future
Imaging Prospects

Aerobraking was resumed on November 7, 1997. Continuing on at a more gradual pace, it will take perhaps as long as 8-12 months to complete, according to MGS Project Manager Glenn Cunningham. Extending aerobraking means that if a sun synchronous orbit is ultimately achieved, it will be one that passes over the equator earlier in the day. This is an exciting prospect. It would permit the Face and other anomalies to be imaged in the morning with the sun coming from the east instead of from the west as in the Viking Orbiter photographs. Cunningham also states that, in a worst case, they could still achieve a 16 hour elliptical orbit.

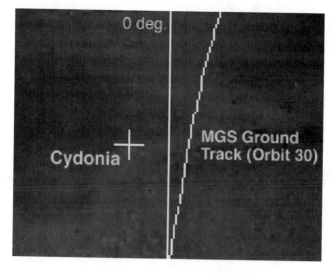

0 deg.

Cydonia +

MGS Ground
Track (Orbit 30)

Figure 3

MGS/MOLA Ground Tracks (NASA)

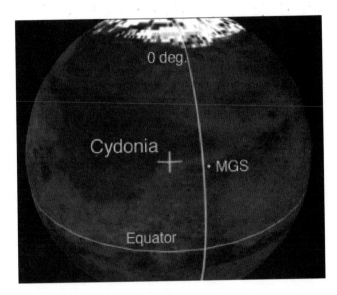

Figure 4

Conditions for October 29 Imaging Opportunity

Although the mapping orbit provides the highest resolution (1.4 meter/pixel), the field of view is so small (3 km crosstrack) that given positional uncertainties of 5 km or more, MSSS cannot guarantee that it will be able to successfully image an isolated target like the Face. However targeting Cydonia from an elliptical orbit—either now during aerobraking, or later from a 16 hour orbit has the advantage of a larger field of view and thus a significantly better chance of imaging the Cydonia targets.

Because of the difference between MGS's orbital period and the length of a Martian day, the longitude at which the orbit passes over the equator will shift from orbit to orbit. Over time MGS will likely fly close to most points on the surface. This combined with the ability to steer the camera should provide opportunities to image Cydonia at lower and, from the standpoint of targeting uncertainties, more forgiving resolutions, like those seen thus far from orbits 5 and 6.

MGS may be the last chance for a long time to verify the possible discovery of ancient ruins on Mars. It is hoped that MSSS and JPL will take advantage of any and all opportunities to image these enigmatic objects as soon as possible.

Internet References

1. http://www.msss.com/mars/global_surveyor/camera/images/index.html

2. http://barsoom.msss.com/education/facepage/face_discussion.html

3. http://www.msss.com/mars/global_surveyor/camera/images/c10/aerobraking.html

4. http://barsoom.msss.com/education/facepage/target_map.gif

5. http://www.msss.com/mars/observer/camera/papers/gds_papers/geodesy/geonav.html

Did a Meteor
Kill Mars?

Dr. John E. Brandenburg

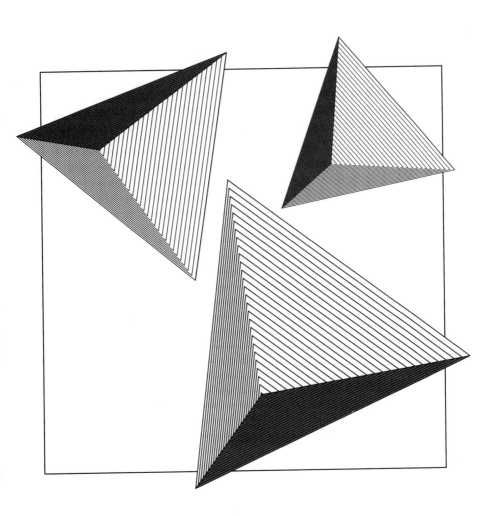

Introduction

To search for signs of extraterrestrial intelligence is an affair of science; however to discover it is an affair of state. As the Mars Global Surveyor approaches its rendezvous with Mars, humanity approaches a crisis. At NASA's Jet Propulsion Lab (JPL) there is mounting tension; and in the halls of government there is indecision.

Humanity is at a delicate stage in its journey of experience. Like an organism that has outgrown one stage of life, it must attempt to leave the protective chrysalis it has constructed for itself, emerging as a new intellectual creature to face a wide New Cosmos. The New Cosmos is a frightening place. It is alive, it is dangerous, and it is heartlessly beautiful. The present world view and the intellectual calculus that supports it is inadequate to address the implications of what we see and so avoids it, as a mild-mannered boy avoids the stare of a bully. The temptation to remain in the old mindset, our old world view, is strong.

Daniel Goldin, the administrator of NASA, has announced that, within the constraints imposed by overall mission objectives, an effort will be made to re-photograph the Face in Cydonia at high resolution. If the effort is successful, the images will be posted on the internet as soon as they are received. But to do so may shatter the operating paradigms of much of humanity, its view of the world, and of itself. So in the halls of government there is ambivalence and fear over this publicly stated intention. Yet humanity must leave its chrysalis, spread its wings boldly, and mount the strange new sky.

This is the origin of the crisis at Mars: that we must move forward, to see, even if we suspect we may see things which may elicit discomfort and even fear. How we reached this place of crisis, how we will pass through it, where we will be when we emerge, is the subject of the present essay.

The Coming Confrontation

On Mars, humanity confronts the nature of the New Cosmos. Mars apparently once lived. It apparently lived a long time. This life was apparently rich and full. And then

Mars died, and in all probability violently. One thus confronts both life and death on Mars.

When one finds apparent archeological ruins at several sites on a planet that cannot support human life one then knows the past climate of that planet, but one also knows much more. One knows in the same instant that humanity is not alone, that it shares the Cosmos with other life similar to itself, and that this intelligent life is probably close by. One also knows in the same instant that death is near also. We are not alone but we are lonely: Not only is humanity lost like a salmon hatchling in the sea, but the sea, it seems, is an indifferent and deadly place.

These realizations are a marked departure from our present world view. Our present world view is that we are the center of the biological Cosmos, and its only and dearest child. The conflict of what is seen on Mars with our present world view is both total and mortal. Thus finding what looks like archeology on Mars, and pressing for a closer look at it, creates a crisis at Mars.

The crisis is one of world view, an inevitable collision between a Cosmos of the mind and a Cosmos of the real. Humanity placed itself on this collision course long ago, when adopted a habit of thought, originated by the Greeks and perfected by the Romans, of breaking down the puzzle we call reality into small solvable problems. This was not a holistic way of understanding everything to be connected and therefore mysterious; it was a mechanistic deduction from observation. Things can be understood if they are separable from each other. If they can be understood they can be solved. This means that, as a problem solver, one continually separates the world into important and understandable things and those things which are either not important or not understandable.

Such a mode of thought is a useful approximation. Certainly everything is connected to everything, by physical law if nothing else, but if one views events as disconnected in the first approximation, then much that is useful can be done. To divide the Cosmos into a region of interest and an outer world that is unimportant, in the first approximation, is to focus attention properly and to define a problem that is solvable. To pick a flower is to disturb a star, yet one can pick spring flowers and bring them home without worrying about the stars. This mode of thought lends itself to much practical problem solving in the selected region of interest. That it might predict or accumulate absurdity in the outer world is not considered important.

This technique of dividing the Cosmos into a region of interest and an outer world that is not of interest lends itself to a specialized intellectual calculus for solving problems. Modes of thought become optimized in a competitive society for analysis of the problems at hand, and those approximations that led to them, and the conditions those approximations place on the outer world are not discussed.

The fact that the intellectual calculus we employ to solve problems is merely a practical subset of a general technique of thought is forgotten—that is, until a problem develops in the outer world.

The intellectual calculus of this age does not handle problems that are unbounded, that contain infinities, or extremes approaching absolutes. Ours is an age that seeks and finds closure, because it exists in a world that is finite, and getting smaller, and is closed. This age seeks analysis, studies, forecasts, and unloads your stock if earnings are below projections. It is averse to risk and dislikes vast unknowns. It seeks dialogue over confrontation, even with the reprehensible. It sneers at bravado and dismisses people who act on impulse and intuition as "cowboys." It is a world of optimization as opposed to exploration.

In short, it is a world that has had no frontiers for some time, nor any desire for them. Confront such a mindset with that which is unbounded, that which is unknown, that which contains infinities and the infinite, and yet must be dealt with, and intellectual retreat and denial is what follows. The intellectual model of this age approaches the crisis at Mars and fails.

Mars:
A New Region of Interest

The heavens have always been important to humanity. In ancient times they were viewed as affecting events on Earth, yet forever beyond our understanding. In more recent times, the reverse: they were understandable, but unimportant in everyday affairs. True to our intellectual heritage we separated the Earth from the rest of the Cosmos, and called it the region of interest, the world of everyday concerns. The rest of the Cosmos we classified as an interesting abstraction: beautiful, orderly, but not important. Now all of this must change. We see this by shifting our focus to Mars. Mars can become a region of interest.

To look on Mars closely is to see a planet whose climate almost certainly once sustained life, but whose conditions have changed so that life as we know it cannot survive. These changes could have occurred slowly, but probably occurred catastrophically.

Conditions that support life are generally those conditions of pressure and temperature allowing liquid water. Evidence from numerous images of Mars' surface is that liquid water flowed in abundance there in the past. Some of these signs are fairly recent, but we can only estimate the age of these water flows. The number of craters gives us clues as to the age of a portion of Mars surface (older terrain = more craters). However, Mars is close to the asteroid belt. This means Mars will be bombarded far more than Earth or the Moon.

Asteroidal debris has impacted Mars at times so violently that rocks were hurled from the Martian surface into space. Some of these rocks, after wandering in space for millions of years, eventually were captured by Earth's gravitational field. Crashing to Earth, the Martian meteorites give us a sampling of conditions on Mars in the distant past. The meteorites can be age-dated by examining their radio isotopic makeup, as would be done for any rock on Earth.

The fact that a meteorite from the primordial period on Mars shows signs of life is not surprising. What is surprising is the time spread. Dating from the oldest of these meteorites to the youngest known (approximately160 million years ago) we find that Mars may have borne life for 4.3 Billion years before it became unable to sustain life on its surface. That is almost as long a period as on Earth. *(See the charts on pages 28 and 29.)* We have good reason to focus our attention now on Mars.

Asteroid Impact!

On Earth over 4.3 billion years, life evolved. Dinosaurs and mammals arose. Some 4.2 billion years after this, a large asteroid struck Earth at Chicxulub in the Yucatan. Earth was afflicted with a mass extinction that wiped out three-quarters of its living species. Warmed by the Sun, soothed by the cleansing rains, the biosphere of Earth eventually recovered from its terrible wound. Earth was changed but lively again. Life headed off in a new direction that produced humanity.

It is now apparent that something similar may have happened on Mars. In a paper presented to the American Geophysical Union in 1995, Vincent DiPietro and this author showed that a combination of evidence from detailed maps of Mars showing the ages of various terrains, particularly those etched by water, plus the data provided by Martian meteorites, led to a stunning hypothesis: Mars had not only probably lived-it had died.

Mars apparently suffered it own Chicxulub event. The impact, relatively late in Mars' history, created the crater called Lyot (pronounced Leo), slightly larger than Chicxulub. After this event, the rate of water erosion on Mars dropped by a factor of thirty and temperatures fell. It is apparent from isotopics of water in the Mars meteorites, that until this event Mars had a working hydrocycle of evaporation and precipitation.

Such a hydrocycle requires an atmospheric "greenhouse" cover of carbon dioxide. Until Lyot, Mars apparently had such a "greenhouse." When the asteroid hit, the atmosphere was filled with such levels of dust that a "asteroid winter" ensued. The carbon dioxide in the atmosphere collapsed into dry ice onto the poles, and the greenhouse effect collapsed along with it. All major life forms would have died. We have termed this the "Thanataster" (Deathstar) scenario. Only a full scale nuclear exchange approaches the magnitude of such an event.

A thousand miles from the Lyot impact basin is Cydonia Mensae, the Cydonia Plain. Cydonia is the name of an ancient port in Crete that was probably named after another larger and older place, Sidon of the Phoenicians. For this reason, Sidonians are mentioned in the Bible. In 1990 Vincent DiPietro, Gregory Molenaar, and I put forward the hypothesis that the Face at Cydonia is an artificial construct built by an indigenously evolved population, which we called the Cydonians. Our hypothesis is known as "The Cydonian Hypothesis."

What were these hypothetical Cydonians like? If we assume that most of the anomalous objects are actually their constructions, we can make certain inferences. They would seem to have built large pyramids, fortifications and edifices, apparently by reshaping preexisting land forms. The work would have been facilitated by the lesser gravity on Mars—one-third that of Earth. And, judging from the Face itself, they would have been similar to humans in appearance and psychology. There is no sign that they attained any technology higher than the Bronze age of the Egyptians when they constructed the Sphinx and the Pyramids.

If the face in Cydonia is what it appears to be, and new close-up images of it are posted on the internet as it has been promised, the separation that humanity has made between the Earth and the heavens will collapse. In a single stroke humanity will realize that it is not God's only child in the Cosmos, and that the Cosmos is not just a giver of life to its inhabitants, but a destroyer of life. It will realize that the issues of Mars are not just "life on Mars" but "life and death on Mars."

Curiously, the people of a previous age may have been far better equipped to deal with this potential crisis that looms before us now. They lived a world that seemed infinite, full of mysteries. The intellectual calculus of that age accepted infinities and dealt with them. Lack of closure was no problem. They took and managed massive risks. They sought to gentle their surroundings but were not intimidated by a wild sea or a howling wilderness. They traversed depths that were fathomless, inhabited by sea monsters, to reach shores occupied by civilizations so alien and exotic, and in some cases vast, that they strained comprehension. It all made for a great tale in the tavern at home.

This was the age of exploration, of the renaissance and of the reformation, of Copernicus and Galileo. Give Sir Francis Drake a primer on modern technology, sit him down and show him the Face in Cydonia: After an outpouring of various oaths, he would be at the palace that same day to petition the Queen for four ships. He would promise her a fourth of all gold recovered from the ruins, and possession for the crown of all lands surveyed. He would then say to all, as preparations were made, "Throw away your annals of Cortez in Mexico, the tales of a coxcomb and mean sailor!"

The advantage Drake had over us was that he lived in an age of faith. To confront what may be found on Mars requires a new form of intellectual calculus to be created, a new world view, a new age of faith. The old modes of thought, with their tidy analysis of well behaved factors in a closed and finite system, must be discarded. To bring these to Mars, and the restricted Cosmos it indicates, would be like launching a yard stick to carry you on a sea voyage. The new intellectual calculus must be able to confront infinities and solve problems in unbounded domains, it must be able to deal with large unknowns. Existential despair can sustain one in the parlor having tea with one's friends, but on the wastes of Mars, it may cause one to languish and surrender to the cold.

To reason in a new way is to stride boldly across the plains of Mars under the cold unblinking stars, seeing and apprehending all. Mourn for Mars as for a lost brother or sister, but then make Mars live again. We may be but a speck of dust, but our future is absolutely in being a speck of dust to be reckoned with.

A New Vision

Without a vision, the people perish. What is necessary now is a vision of the human future fully integrated with the living Cosmos. We need a vision of the human race advanced, enlightened, vigorous, and eager to colonize new worlds empty and open to us. Our vision must include dialogue with other races inhabiting the Cosmos. If Cydonia holds the remains of a dead, primitive civilization, then living, advanced civilizations may be close by. We may be the "third world" in more than one sense of the term—a less advanced civilization on the third planet from an obscure sun. However, in innumerable times and places, portions of the human race, often in the "third world on Earth," have displayed an amazing capacity to adapt and reinvent themselves—to become a new people with a new plan.

The Brookings Institution report to NASA of 1960 argues that widespread social disruption might occur upon the discovery of intelligent extraterrestrial life. That report suggested that the government may wish to withhold such a discovery to prevent panic among various religious groups as well as among establishment scientists. However, by withholding important facts from its people, a government risks its most important tool of governance, which is trust. It is the job of government to ascertain the facts of Mars and make those facts known to the human race, however jarring they may be. This Rubicon must be crossed, if at Mars, so be it.

Today a NASA spacecraft, the Mars Global Surveyor, carries to Mars a camera with greater resolution than those of the 1976 Viking mission. The mission goals now include a clear priority for re-imaging the Face and other objects of interest. The state therefore is the purveyor of knowledge at Cydonia and has an interest in the circumstances of its release. Will the Global Surveyor provide us with the truth about Cydonia? And if the truth is that a civilization once existed on Mars, will the caution of the Brookings Report prevail? Will the government, fearing social dissolution, hold back the truth?

Mars and what it may contain is now an affair of state. The government must take the people into its confidence in this matter, so that we may engage the Cosmos as it is. The people will bear this well, even if it is what it appears to be, even if the artificial nature of the Cydonian objects is dramatically apparent. Although religious beliefs might at first seem an impediment to dealing with Mars, it is in fact a key asset. For the devout, humanity is not the center of the Cosmos, God is. Nor should scientists flinch from the prospect of a new, living Cosmos that could shatter the old calculus of knowledge, for it is the business of science to discover the new and shed the old as the facts come in. Humanity is a rugged, resourceful tribe, descended from a long line of tough customers, and it will do well. Therefore, bring on Mars and all it bears. We were born for it.

The Brookings Institution Report

BY PROFESSOR STANLEY V. MCDANIEL

In 1960, a report titled "Proposed Studies on the Implications of Peaceful Space Activities for Human Affairs" was delivered to the Chairman of NASA's Committee on Long-Range Studies. The report, prepared by the Brookings Institution, Washington, D.C., under contract to NASA, was also delivered to the 87th Congress. In a section on "The Implications of a Discovery of Extraterrestrial Life," the report acknowledges the possibility that "artifacts left at some point in time" by intelligent life forms might be "discovered through our space activities on the Moon, Mars, or Venus."

The Brookings Institution report directly questions the view that the discovery of extraterrestrial intelligence (ETI) would necessarily lead to "an all-out space effort." Instead, the report notes the possibility that society might "disintegrate," or survive only by "paying the price of changes in values and attitudes and behavior." Among the changes that might take place, the report suggests, are threats to political leadership and even revolution. The report states

"The degree of political or social repercussion would probably depend on

(cont. next page)

leadership's interpretation of (1) its own role, (2) threats to that role, and (3) national and personal opportunities to take advantage of the disruption or reinforcement of the attitudes and values of others."

In particular, the reactions of politically influential religious groups, including "fundamentalists," "antiscience sects," and "Buddhists," were a matter for concern. Noting that "Buddhist priests are heavily politically engaged in Ceylon [now Sri Lanka]," the report considered the potential reaction of such groups as an unknown factor that should be researched, in order to weigh the possible social consequences of their actions should an ETI discovery be announced.

Most significantly, the report indicated that the greatest area of concern might be that of the impact upon scientists themselves:

"It has been speculated that of all groups, scientists and engineers might be the most devastated by the discovery of relatively superior creatures, since these professions are most clearly associated with the mastery of nature, rather than with the understanding and expression of man[kind]. Advanced

understanding of nature might vitiate all our theories at the very least, if not also require a culture and perhaps a brain inaccessible to earth scientists."

As a result of these possibilities-that major social upheaval and psychological "devastation" of many scientists might occur (including the implied possibility that antiscience fundamentalist groups could attack scientific institutions and perhaps threaten individual scientists)— the report speaks of the possibility that scientists and other decision makers might interfere with the release of ETI information, even to the extent of withholding it altogether:

"How might such information, under what circumstances, be presented to or withheld from the public for what ends? What might be the role of the discovering scientists and other decision makers regarding release of the fact of discovery?"

It has been speculated that the ongoing reticence of NASA to commit significant priorities to the re-photographing of the anomalies at Cydonia on Mars may be due to the influence of the suggestions contained in this report.

Mars—
The New Earth

Baron Johannes von Buttlar

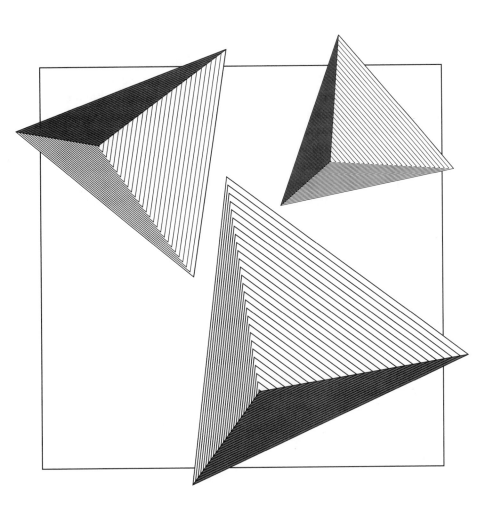

A NASA study entitled "On the Habitability of Mars" indicates that in principle no unsurmountable barriers would rule out the settlement of Mars by human beings—provided the planet is successfully altered by "terraforming" (i.e., engineering the environment to approximate Earthlike conditions). The questions remain as to which methods would be required, and how they would be implemented.

To carry out a plan of such gigantic proportions, certain basic conditions would necessarily have to be maintained:

- The terraforming process must be technologically practicable.
- It must be financially feasible.
- It must take place within a specified time frame.

The key to terraforming a planet lies in the composition of the planet's soil and atmosphere, as well as the characteristics of its poles. The currently existing atmospheres on the planets Mars and Venus consist largely of carbon dioxide that is unsuitable for human life. The presence of water in any form on the planet is a basic requirement for any terraforming process. Permafrost, bound in rocks, or an ice layer at the poles can become a source of water vapor and oxygen. In all these aspects, Mars is an ideal candidate. Although the Red Planet is about half as large as the Earth, it has an almost equally large land mass, and, as we know already, it offers adequate water in frozen form.

Ironically, the "greenhouse" effect of carbon dioxide in the atmosphere, that produces intolerable heat on the planet Venus, would have to be generated artificially on Mars in order to warm the planet. To produce a greenhouse effect on Mars, a "chemical factory" equipped with small nuclear reactors could be built to generate greenhouse gases such as carbon tetrafluoride or sulphur hexafluoride that may be pumped into the Martian atmosphere. In this manner, a "greenhouse gas roof" could be installed on the planet to prevent the stored heat from escaping the Martian atmosphere.

The brilliant white polar caps of Mars consist primarily of frozen water (particularly the northern cap) and reflect 77 percent of the sunlight. If they were slightly darkened, they would absorb more sunlight, and subsequently melt and release steam. Also, the released steam and reduced light reflection would begin to warm the planet.

One suggestion for causing the Martian poles to melt is to cover them with an ultra-thin layer of dust or soot to increase heat retention. This material may not have to be painstakingly transported from Earth to Mars but may be present on the surface of the immediately neighboring planets: The pictures of the two potato-shaped Martian satellites, Phobos and Deimos, taken by Mariner 9 show that they are not only marred by ancient and more recently formed craters but also apparently covered by a thick layer of a black powder. This may be an ideal material for covering the Martian poles and for subsequent heating and melting, so that the ancient dried river beds would again contain water and irrigate the thirsty Martian soil.

Huge sun reflectors in the orbit above the Martian poles would provide another method for melting the polar ice. Blue-green algae specifically created for Mars with genetic technology could be sprayed on the poles. This would produce a vast burst of algae growth as its photosynthesis consumed part of the atmosphere's carbon dioxide and released oxygen.

Over time the atmosphere would become denser, and temperatures would rise. This would initiate a cycle which would increasingly release oxygen, carbon dioxide, nitrogen and water vapor contained in the sandy Martian soil and in the porous rocks. The denser Martian atmosphere would cause the barometric pressure to rise, and after an extended period, to approximate a pres-

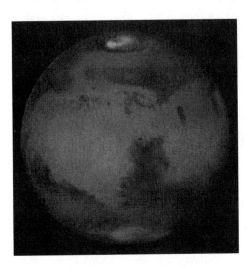

This NASA Hubble Space Telescope (HST) picture of Mars [March 10, 1997] shows the north pole of water-ice at the top, on the last day of Martian spring at the north pole. The seasonal cap there has sublimated and the water-ice cap is visible. Polar frost in the north, and giant water ice clouds are visible at the Hellas impact basin (bottom), and over the Elysium volcanos (right).

sure corresponding to that found at an altitude of approximately 20,000 feet on Earth. In the meantime, the average Martian temperature would have risen to above freezing, and white clouds would float in the Martian sky.

The next phase of terraforming would require building chemical plants to create an artificial ozone layer equivalent and thereby begin to protect Mars from hard shortwave radiation such as ultraviolet radiation. In the equator region, a vegetation similar to that found in Earth's arctic tundra regions could be introduced. Barometric pressure would have continued to rise, and small shallow oceans would have started. Rain could appear at regular intervals.

Simultaneously, increased oxygen release from algae, vegetation and chemical plants would continue uninterrupted. Wooded regions would slowly extend and create organic soil—and it would be time to settle the first animals on the Red Planet.

Before transformation of Mars to a life-sustaining planet was completed, humans would have settled in specifically constructed, domed biospheres. The average temperature would have risen in the interval to eight degrees Celsius (46 degrees Fahrenheit), and the icy, red desert planet would have been transformed into a habitable green world ready to welcome terrestrial pioneers. But what problems would confront us with the implementation of this apparently utopian plan and how could we overcome them?

First, there is the problem of transporting humans, flora, fauna and material from Earth to Mars. The space transporters required for Martian terraforming could use the Moon as a base, thereby saving lift-off energy. The orbiting solar reflectors needed for heating the poles would be built on Mars, where there is enough sodium and magnesium—the materials necessary for manufacturing mirror systems.

Some critics propose that the whole terraforming process on Mars can also be accomplished without manned missions and complex Martian bases. Remote or computer-controlled algae bombs alone could initiate the biological transformation process needed, letting them proceed independently and without further expenditures. But this an absolutely unrealistic view. If one were to rely exclusively on algae photosynthesis processes, Mars would certainly be late in arriving as the lifeboat to save humankind. In this instance, about 150,000 years would be necessary to generate

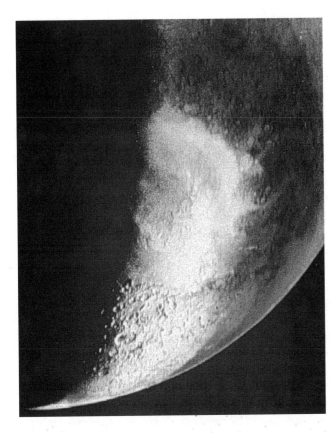

South Polar Cap of dry-ice near its maximum size extending to 45°S, and over Hellas Basin. [NASA Viking Orbiter image]

a Martian atmosphere friendly to humans—even if 25 percent of the planet were covered with algae.

In order to create life sustaining conditions on Mars within a somewhat measurable time frame, it would be necessary to implement the most diverse processes of oxygen generation, for which some manned missions would be indispensable. If it were possible to generate or release sufficient oxygen levels on Mars we still would have an atmosphere which would consist primarily of carbon dioxide and oxygen. But humans on earth are used to a mixture consisting mainly of nitrogen and oxygen. In fact, the Martian atmosphere contains only three percent nitrogen. It is conceivable that Martian pioneers could get used to the carbon dioxide and oxygen mixture on Mars because oxygen does not necessarily have to be mixed with nitrogen for breathing. However, it is suspected that the Martian soil contains nitrogen in the form of nitrates, nitrites and ammonia compounds, and perhaps this nitrogen could be released with the aid of certain bacteria known on Earth.

Another grave problem for early Martian pioneers would be the powerful sandstorms. These, however, would lose much of their strength and frequency as a consequence of terraforming. Melting of the polar ice caps would cause the release of great amounts of water vapor. This, in turn, would cause regular precipitation, minimizing the problem of sandstorms. In the course of these developments, the present reddish hue of the Martian sky would gradually change to our familiar terrestrial blue.

The terraforming of Mars, while basically attainable by means of the existing technologies, would confront humankind with the greatest technological and financial challenges in its history. But even assuming this is accomplished, Mars would not be transformed into a mere copy of Earth. Mars would remain a unique world which, while sustaining human life, would necessarily possess specifically Martian features. With a gravity less than 40 percent of the Earth's, there would be unknown consequences for flora and fauna—including the settlers, who in adapting would eventually become true "Martians."

A difficult problem would be the provisioning of the human vanguard with essential foods. Transportation of water and food to Mars would be very expensive and therefore only possible on a limited scale. Since the advance team, living in insulated domes, would not have a terraformed Mars to rely on, the supply of water and food must be assured. Rations in powder form commonly used by astronauts cannot sustain life for an extended period.

Unfortunately the current soil consistency on Mars is not suitable for planting terrestrial plants. For this reason, the Martian mission vanguard would have to bring small hermetically sealed soil cultures for the first base or biosphere and also seeds genetically cultivated for Mars. Thanks to the composition of the Martian soil, water and oxygen can be extracted by heating. Production of fertilizers would not be difficult since important components such as nitrogen oxides can be released by heating an oxygen/nitrogen mixture.

Hydrogen and oxygen can be generated by hydrolysis of the water frozen from the poles—space fuel, especially for return flights to earth. *(See Newly Discovered Mars Meteorites Suggest Long-*

Artist's conception of ancient Mars when oceans (the dark areas in the image) may have covered the northern lowlands. Cydonia is near the center, Tharsis ridge at extreme left. This image is reproduced in color on the back cover of this book. (Painting by Grace DiPietro, ©1982.)

term Martian Life on page 137.) Since the two Martian satellites, Phobos and Deimos, consist of twenty percent water, they would become additional important water and fuel suppliers. Because of these possibilities, a supply of technical equipment would have priority over provisioning in a first Martian mission.

Envisioning the future of humanity beyond Mars, the boldest, most demanding plan—the ultimate goal—is the development of processes and technologies for transforming other inhospitable planets in a manner that they become habitable for humans. The lessons learned through terraforming Mars will be the first step in this greater endeavor.

BIOGRAPHICAL NOTE

Baron Johannes von Buttlar is the leading science writer in Germany, with 25 pubished books and over 25 million copies of his work sold world-wide. His studies were in psychology, astronomy, physics and mathematics and he is a Fellow of the Royal Astronomic Society in London. Some recent German books include: *Terraforming, The Methusalah Formula* (English & German) and *Lieben auf dem Mars* (*Life on Mars*).

Cydonia, Viking & Pathfinder Geology

550 million hits. That's how many hits at last count NASA's Pathfinder web site had received. Millions and millions of people, seemingly fascinated by the geology of Mars. But was it only geology, or were all those individuals looking for something beyond?

What the Pathfinder Mission achieved certainly captured the public's imagination, but judging from popular culture, that fascination is with life, and not with rocks for their own sake. The fascination is in the possibility that life exists or has existed on other planets; with the possibility of advanced life either similar to our own or inexplicably alien; with evidence of life that implies a living solar system and universe beyond our fragile atmosphere, and even with miniscule, fossilized remnants of life in ancient Martian meteorites.

Here we frame the geology in light of the greater questions. Does the geology imply life or at least past life on Mars? What do the new findings mean for our evaluation of the mysterious objects at Cydonia? Is ours a solitary stand by life in a barren universe or but one node in an almost endless universal web of life?

Cydonia Geology: Enigmas With An Ocean View?

James L. Erjavec

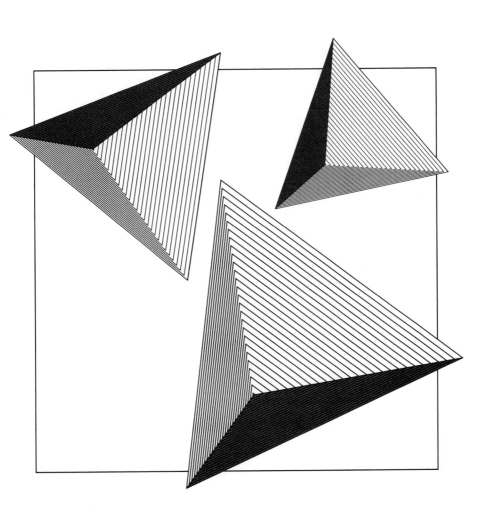

The landforms in the Cydonia region of Mars are often described as nothing more than products of erosion and weathering. But does that answer hold up to a close geologic scrutiny? To address this question, the area (approximately from 40 to 41.5 degrees N latitude and 7 to 11 degrees longitude) was analyzed in detail during a six-month mapping process. Viking images were transferred to a basemap for evaluation. During the mapping process, the landforms were subjected to geologic evaluation and referred to a variety of geologic processes. The results show that it is a simplification to suggest that erosion was the primary means for the development of Cydonian landforms.

More likely, the development of the landforms was the result of a complex interplay of geologic events. These events, as interpreted from the surface features, would include impact cratering, stream erosion, wind erosion, shoreline deposition and erosion, slumping/sliding, mass-wasting and possible liquefaction/venting, local volcanism and subsurface faulting. *(See the Glossary of Geologic Terms on page 228.)*

The geologic findings presented in this article are not just based on observations of the Cydonia area, but are supported by a number of accepted research works on the geology of Mars. What is discussed in this article is a detailed analysis of Cydonia images integrated with the current understanding of Martian geology and geomorphology.

Can Erosion Alone
Explain Cydonia Landforms?

The more or less "official" perspective on the Cydonia landforms is that they are the product of differential erosion. According to this scenario, in Mars' geologic past the Cydonia area was covered with one to two kilometers of soft, erodible overburden (sediment). Over time this "soft" sediment was removed by erosive forces. After a wide-scale erosion of material, what remained were the variety of resistant "knobs" and mesas one sees in Cydonia today. At first glance, this explanation may seem both plausible and supported by the evidence.

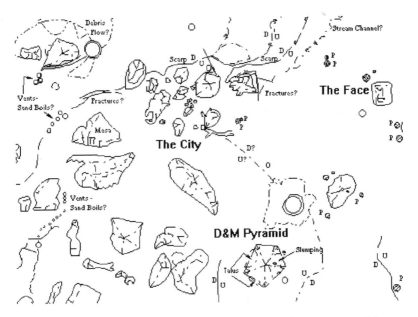

This detail from a much larger Geomorphic Feature Map shows a portion of the Cydonia region. (Copyright James L. Erjavec, 1994)

However, if a one to two kilometer overburden once covered this area, a very large volume of sediment would have to have been removed and deposited somewhere. Since the Mars of today has no liquid oceans or large bodies of water, there is no place for that sediment to 'hide.' The material should be identifiable somewhere on the surface of Mars. The reality is that there appears to be no place on Mars where such a large volume of sediment has been deposited.

Numerous ejecta flows (material thrown out by meteor impact), debris flows and impact-related landslides are evident in Cydonia which provide a means of gauging relative timing of geologic events—for example, which impacts occurred first. Despite an assumed area-wide erosion, it appears that some of these pre-burial sediments (the ejecta flows, for instance) have not only been resistant enough to withstand the erosive event, but still display distinct signs of timing and superposition in relation to other impacts and landforms. If this area were dotted with pedestal craters (craters eroded to a degree where they appear as raised pedestals above the surface) some credence could be placed in large-scale erosion. But Cydonia does not have a large number of pedestal craters. Those that do occur seem to suggest a preexisting surface markedly lower in elevation than the peaks of the larger structures (known as "knobs"). The existing pedestal craters, along with benches and mesas, suggest that this area did not experience as significant an erosion event as is commonly described. Differential erosion is simply too generalized a mechanism and falls short of satisfactorily explaining Cydonian landforms.

On Earth, erosion is a strong factor in the development of landforms. But erosion is not the only factor. Erosion by the Colorado River, for example, is responsible for the Grand Canyon of Arizona, but the whole picture cannot be understood unless the original rock characteristics are taken into consideration, along with the tectonics which have also played a role in how the Grand Canyon appears today. One should not expect anything less on Mars, a planet known to exhibit most earth-shaping processes.

If Not Erosion, Then What?

At Cydonia, since the fabric and compositions of the rock types observed are not known for certain, we must rely upon the visual evidence for answers. Impact craters are prominent features, providing insight into the relative ages of the land surfaces and landforms. A strong unevenness has been noted in the distribution of small impact craters (less than 1 kilometer in diameter) in Cydonia. There are two fairly distinct areas, the Knobby Terrain and the Pediment Surface, separated by a series of winding ridges and scarps which generally trend in a North/South direction. The Pediment Surface is dotted with a large number of small impacts, but the Knobby Terrain is rather devoid of such impacts. It appears likely that some process has been working on the Knobby Terrain which has not been working on the Pediment Surface where small craters are abundant. A possible solution exists in the evidence for an ancient ocean at Cydonia—a position now strongly supported by the JPL/NASA October 2, 1997 announcement that initial Global Surveyor measurements show the plain on Northern Mars to be a far more even surface than previously suspected, making it possible that it was once an ocean bottom covered by a sea greater than Earth's Pacific Ocean.

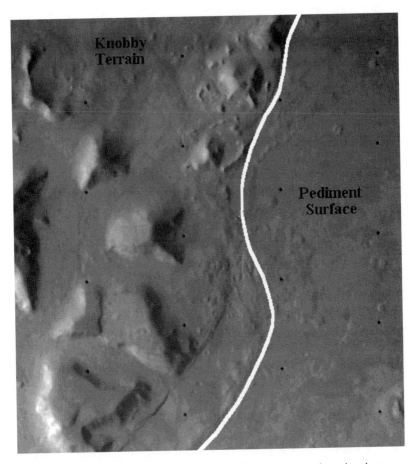

Portion of NASA Viking Image 70A14, showing the approximate boundary between the Knobby Terrain (left) and the Pediment Surface (right).

An Ocean on Mars?

Linear trends of craters on the Pediment Surface, along with landforms and scarps which define the edge of the Knobby Terrain, suggest that perhaps the Pediment Surface was once covered with water - possibly the site of a Martian ocean. If there was an ocean, though, it would not have been influenced by tidal forces nearly as much as earth's oceans because Mars lacks a large, close moon. The ocean would behave more like a large lake. Is there any more supporting evidence?

It has been suggested for some time that the nature of the ejecta of many large impacts seems to indicate that the subsurface of Mars may hold water in the form of ice or an ice-sediment mix. Basically, when a sizable impact occurs, the ice and sediment is thought to "fluidize" from the impact's heat, splashing ejecta out in a lobate (curving) pattern. Mars has many lobate ejecta craters which suggest that water in the subsurface may be widespread. *(See Mars as an Abode of Life on page 123.)* Further evidence suggesting that a large lake once existed at Cydonia is that there are a number of structures along the Knobby Terrain/Pediment Surface boundary which are similar to shoreline features on Earth. These landforms are similar to eroded (wave-cut?) benches, barriers or bars and scarps and cliffs which might be found in a shoreline environment.

Also, there are a number of landslides extending into the Pediment Surface from knobs on the edge of the Knobby Terrain. These landslides could be evidence of shoreline erosion where material may have been undercut by water currents. There is an interesting trend of eroded impacts on the Pediment Surface which generally parallels trends of the westward scarps defining the Knobby Terrain boundary. It could be suggested that these craters are indicative of a lakeshore erosion process where landforms closer to shore are modified more by wave action than those in deeper waters.

Certainly such a scenario is plausible and supportable by the evidence. Still, as with any theory, it should not be regarded as fact, but only as a possible solution. In any event, it seems to be a more realistic approach to the geology of this area than attributing the landforms to a differential erosion process based almost entirely on the presumed existence of an overlying "soft" material which now shows little evidence that it ever existed.

This "ocean" scenario also provides a possible answer to the impact crater distribution puzzle. If the Pediment Surface represented a Martian "ocean," the Knobby Terrain may have been the "continent." If so, the Knobby Terrain would have been subject to greater modification because it was exposed to terrestrial processes. The impact record alone seems to support the probability of more geologic activity occurring in the Knobby Terrain than in the Pediment Surface.

Some Anomalous
Landforms in Cydonia

Anumber of landforms in the Cydonia area have been termed anomalous or enigmatic. It is true that many of them cannot be easily explained by erosive forces alone. Are there other mechanisms to rely on? The object sometimes called the "D&M Pyramid," a large, sharp-angled landform, is difficult to explain in light of known geologic processes, such as volcanism, wind erosion and glacial activity. Though some uniquely Martian process may exist to explain this object and other Cydonian "pyramidal" landforms, current knowledge of Martian geologic processes does not permit more than conjecture. *(See the chapter Finding Cultural Features on Planetary Surfaces on page 83.)*

Another object, called informally the "Cliff" (really a raised ridge), appears to "sit" atop a large impact crater's ejecta blanket. Its position cannot be readily explained. This enigmatic object does not appear to be a product of a volcanic eruption or similar event. Its associated crater is decidedly the result of meteor impact. The timing of the impact in relation to the Cliff's origin is unclear: If the Cliff predated the impact, the ejecta from the meteor impact should have covered, damaged, or obliterated it. But although the ejecta blanket extends for at least a kilometer beyond the landform, there is no evidence to suggest that the ejecta once covered the landform. On the other hand, if the Cliff is a remnant of a larg-

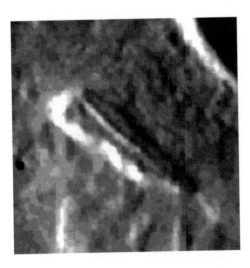

The "Cliff" is an elongated ridge perched on a crater's ejecta "splash."

er preexisting overburden, why is there no other evidence of the overburden in the vicinity of the impact?

The "Face" is another enigmatic object. It has been contended that it is either an optical illusion caused by shadows or a "freak" erosional landform. Analysis of the two images of the "Face" seem to preclude the "illusion" explanation. Thus if the morphology (shape) is real, and from geologic evidence it appears to be real, could it have been formed by erosive processes? Most certainly. But its degree of detail, consistent with a facelike appearance, and its association with a number of other unusual landforms, demand a more serious analysis. To pass this strange object off as an erosional "freak" does not sit well with the scientific process.

At the very least, its origin as a natural feature is unclear and even if the odds of the landform being artificial are still problematic. (See the Statistical Evidence section to learn how such odds are defined), it should still be a prime directive to obtain higher resolution images which could possibly settle the controversy.

The Tholus, a broad nearly circular mound, is very peculiar in form. Its low relief and uniform shape make it difficult to explain as the product of wind erosion, unless the original form was circular as well. It exhibits neither volcanic nor impact affinities. Using the "ocean" scenario of this article, with more evidence it may be possible to explain it as a wave-eroded remnant. Wave activity might provide for more uniform shaping than wind. Still, an apparent "channel" that spirals up the landform is hard to explain in a geologic framework.

Conclusion

It is apparent from the geologic evidence that a generalized erosion scenario does not adequately explain many of the landforms and landform relationships in Cydonia. And despite other more complex interpretations, anomalous characteristics of some of these landforms are not satisfactorily explained.

The goal of this discussion of Cydonian geology is not so much to determine whether the landforms are natural phenomena or artificial structures, but rather to show that in science there should be no closed doors. If a solution has been put forth to explain a set of conditions, one must ask whether everything has been explained to satisfaction, what is the solution based on, and what assumptions have been taken as part of the explanation. In the case of widespread differential erosion, it could be used to describe the development of almost all of the landforms on Earth, but that is not an acceptable explanation in science.

An increase in the resolution of images anticipated from the Mars Global Surveyor, now in orbit around Mars, will hopefully shed new light on the origins of the anomalous Cydonian landforms. Still, there is always the possibility that future images will not resolve the issue, but only create more questions. That is often the way science works. What should be of utmost importance in any study is that generalized statements and assumptions should not lead to premature conclusions without proper investigation.

Ideas and theories have been battered on more than one occasion and will inevitably be battered again. One should take nothing on faith (this writer's conclusions as well). True science should and will strive for the truth and remain open to the wonders being discovered today and those that will be discovered tomorrow.

BIOGRAPHICAL NOTE

James Erjavec holds an M.S. degree in Geology from the University of Arizona and is a specialist in mapping and computer graphics. He has developed a detailed geomorphological feature map of the Cydonia region in order to better understand the landforms in this part of Mars.

Glossary of Terms

geomorphology: The branch of geology dealing with the form of the earth.

liquefaction: The transformation of a substance into a liquid. This occurs from earthquakes on earth . On Mars, liquefaction (if it has occurred) may be marsquake related or impact-induced. Liquefaction features are also called sand blows or sand boils. (This is another mechanism that might have created pseudocraters on Mars.)

mass-wasting: The slow downslope movement of rock debris or sediment.

overburden: Material or sediment which overlies another type of material of interest.

scarp: Cliff or escarpment which extends for some distance along a landform (i.e., a plateau).

subsurface faulting: Relative displacement of rocks along a fracture, e.g., the San Andreas Fault. Subsurface means that there is no surface expression of the actual fault and that the fault's presence is inferred from other geologic features.

tectonics: Deformation of the Earth's crust.

venting: Out-gassing or eruption of volcanic or volcanic-related material (a mechanism of creating pseudocraters on Mars).

Artificial
Linear Features
at Cydonia

Harry Moore

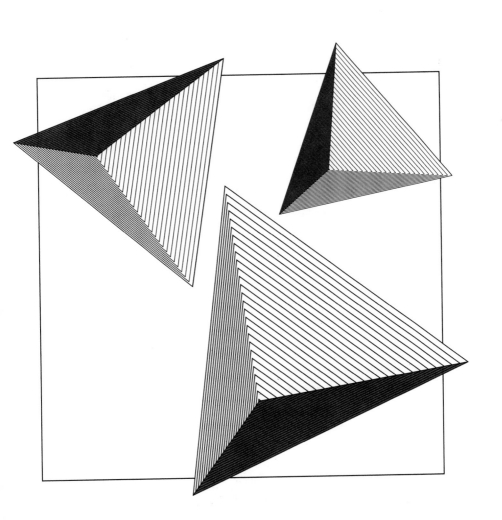

The Martian landscape is currently being studied in greater detail than ever before. New photographic and geologic data has recently been acquired by the NASA Pathfinder which landed on Mars July 4, 1997. Even more information will be returned to Earth via the Mars Global Surveyor orbiter, which will map the entire Martian surface beginning early in 1999.

Before the Pathfinder and the Global Surveyor, the surface of Mars was dramatically photographed in the 1970s by the Viking Orbiters. These remarkable photographs disclosed a number of surface features worthy of continued study, including volcanoes, landslide features, stream channels, and buttes and mesas (both common landforms in the southwestern United States).

Of particular interest are the lineaments, or linear surface features, because these can disclose information about the underlying geology. Surface lineaments are straight or gently curved linear features that may extend up to several kilometers. Topographically these features appear as lines of depressions or relief in the surface. The San Andreas Fault in California, for example, displays a surface lineament easily seen from aerial photographs. Some lineaments certainly express structural geologic features such as faults, zones of intense fracturing or jointing, solution features such as sinkholes aligned along joints, and even aligned volcano vents.

In the northern plains region of Mars called Cydonia, unusual landscape features include "pyramid" shaped or faceted structures, several mesas, including one that looks like a hominid face (and is called the "Face"), and some interesting lineaments. The present discussion details some of the lineaments found in this region and their possible relation to the anomalous surface features in the area.

A total of nine lineaments are identified, with most of those being in the "City" area of roughly pyramidal landforms SW of the "Face" which are seen in the figure on the next page. We express the orientation, or direction, of a lineament by how many degrees east or west of north the lineament bears. For example, a bearing of N25W would indicate a lineament running 25 degrees west of north.

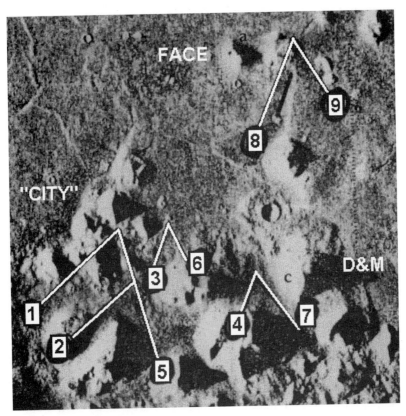

A rea of research surrounding features found on the Viking photograph frame 35A72. The surface lineaments are indicated with white lines and are numbered for reference.

Using this notation, the Cydonia lineaments and their orientations are as follows: Lineament No.1 – N73E; No.2 – N72E; No.3 – N45E; No.4 – N48E; No.5 – N10E; No.6 – N2E; No.7 – N8W; No.8 – N47E; and No.9 – N5W. These fall into two major orientation directions: northeast-southwest and north-north slightly west.

The two orientations result in the intersection of the lineaments, producing an angular feature on the surface. The lineament intersections form three groups of angular features easily observed on the surface. The internal angles formed by these groups of lineaments can be divided into two sets: Set (1) 63–64 degrees and set (2) 45–56 degrees.

a. The angles made by the intersecting lineaments appear to be generally similar in size, and point toward the northeast.

b. Some lineaments (# 1, 2, 3, 4, and 5 in the figure shown) if projected, will align along some of the pyramidal features (i.e., the lineaments will parallel the ridges created by the intersections of the pyramid faces)

c. Lineament 3, if projected to the northeast, will intersect the "Face" structure exactly between the "eye" locations.

As to the origin of these lineaments, it appears that they are related to the geologic structure of the region. Faults, large-scale joints (fractures that are several meters wide and can be traced along the surface for several kilometers), and tectonic rifting (movement of the crust by pulling apart) of the crust appear to be possible candidates.

Two previous studies concerning Mars lineaments and surface mound configurations at Cydonia may be compared with the lineament analysis above. These include "Mound Configurations On The Martian Cydonia Plain: A Geometric and Probabilistic Analysis" by Horace Crater and Stanley V. McDaniel in 1995 and "Analysis Of Tectonic Directional Pattern On Mars: No Indication Of Artificial Structures In The Southern Cydonia Region" by Johannes Fiebag in 1990.

Crater and McDaniel performed a study of geometric relationships of small features, termed "mounds," in the area of the "Face" and "pyramidal" structures. Of particular interest for our present study is the geometric relationship they found among three mounds labeled EAD in their study. The interior angles formed by this triangle of mounds, within measurement error, form a symmetrical isosceles triangle of angles 71, 54.5, 54.5 degrees.

For comparison I undertook a lineament analysis of the Viking photograph used by Crater and McDaniel. I identified a total of 13 surface lineaments and 12 pyramidal structural lineaments and measured their orientations. When compared to the EAD mound triangle, it was found that the line segment formed by mounds A and D (Crater and McDaniel study) is parallel to Lineament No. 6 and the line segment formed by mounds A and E is parallel to Lineament No. 3.

The angle formed by the intersection of Lineaments No. 3 and No. 6 was measured to be approximately 45° in the present study. However, these same lineaments as identified and mea-

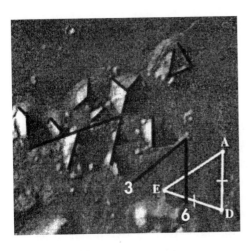

Lineament 3 is roughly parallel to line EA found in the McDaniel-Crater Analysis and lineament 6 is parallel to McDaniel-Crater's line AD.

sured from the Crater and McDaniel photograph was found to be 53.5°. This is almost identical to the angle formed by mounds EAD (53.5° + 2.2°). Further, the EAD angle is very similar to the lineament angles formed by Lineaments No. 4 with No. 7 (56°) and No. 8 with No. 9 (53°).

It is striking that the surface lineaments seem to parallel not only the "pyramid" structure lineaments but also some of the mound geometry as identified by Crater and McDaniel. This may suggest that the mound geometry is in some way influenced by the lineament orientation. If this is the case, there may be some common geological explanation for the lineaments and the mound geometry. But the relationship may simply be coincidence. A more adequate determination will require better images and eventually ground investigation.

J. Fiebag (1990) compiled a comprehensive study and analysis of the tectonic directional pattern on Mars. Fiebag's study was oriented toward tectonic lineaments in the Cydonia Plain and their relationship to the geologic history of the same area. Much of the Fiebag study was directed toward identifying and comparing the tectonic lineaments with the unusual Martian surface features. A result of Fiebag's effort was his development of two maps of the Cydonia Plain area showing the lineaments, impact craters, and ejecta blankets.

I performed orientation analysis of the lineaments identified on Fiebag's maps (taken from Figures 5 and 6 of Fiebag's study in 1990) in the subject "pyramid" area. A total of 22 lineaments were measured from the figure 5 map of Fiebag's study. In addition, I measured a total of 18 surface lineaments from figure 6 of Fiebag's study. The lineament orientations taken from the Fiebag study fall into three groups. All three groups appear to parallel the initial groupings of surface lineament orientations and the lineament orientations derived from the Crater and McDaniel study discussed earlier.

From the foregoing analysis it appears that the natural lineation of the Cydonia Region parallels the lineaments of the "pyramid" structures of the same area. This conclusion coincides with the results of Fiebag (1990) where he shows that all of the bearings connected with the subject structures ("city," "pyramids," etc.) agree with the orientation of the natural lineation of the region.

From this data Fiebag concluded that the pyramidal structures are natural features. This conclusion is based on his assumption that non-natural features would differ in orientation from the lineaments. Although in general this may be the case, it is not a necessary condition for non-natural features that they differ in orientation from the geologic background.

The goal of this study has been to show the parallel relationship between the surface lineaments in the Cydonia Region, the lineaments of the "pyramid" structures (the "city", "fort", etc.), and the geometric relationships of the mound configuration studied by Crater & McDaniel. I have not attempted to identify the origin of the lineaments that were measured during the investigation. However, the lineaments measured in the Fiebag study (1990) were concluded by Fiebag to be of natural geological/tectonic origin.

Perhaps all of the lineaments are of a geologic nature, perhaps not. As additional research reveals new information about the planet Mars, then perhaps the genesis of the lineaments found in the Cydonia region may be better understood. For the moment, however, we cannot conclude from the parallelism between the lineaments and the other features that the latter are necessarily natural in origin.

BIOGRAPHICAL NOTE

Harry Moore took his Bachelors and Masters Degree in Geology from The University of Tennessee, Knoxville (1971, 1974). He is currently the head of the Tennessee Department of Transportation geotechnical office in Knoxville. He is the author of two books on geology as well as numerous technical papers dealing with karst, landslides, and other geotechnical issues.

Pathfinder Geology:
More Support for the
Cydonian Hypothesis

James Erjavec

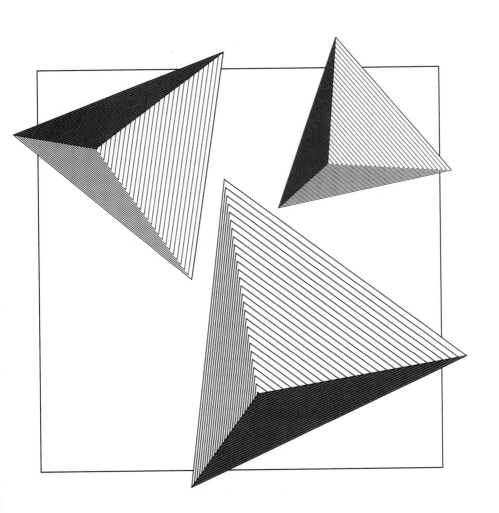

Duricity its short but dramatic existence, the Pathfinder spacecraft has given us data and images that shed much light on the geology of Mars as well as provide us with a more refined interpretation of Martian rocks. In addition, the lander and rover have provided a tantalizing and fresh pictorial view of an area of Mars which appears to have been more geologically active than those of the Viking lander sites. Since this was primarily a geologic mission, we'll have to use geologic terms which at times may seem foreign and difficult to comprehend for those not versed in the geologic sciences. A glossary is provided with this article as a quick-look reference in an attempt to "lighten" those terms.

Piecing together information that has been released to date by NASA and JPL from the Pathfinder Lander and the Sojourner Rover, with a geologic perspective in mind, what have we learned from the Pathfinder mission so far? The mission's main goal was to gather geological information about the rocks, soils and landforms in the Ares Vallis region of Mars because this area was believed (from Viking images) to contain more interesting and illuminating Martian rock types. The Pathfinder craft landed at roughly 19.33 N latitude and 33.55 W longitude in the Ares Vallis, which is an ancient outwash channel that originates in the chaotic terrain on the eastern end of Valles Marineris and empties into the Chryse Basin (Chryse Planitia). Because it is believed that the Ares Vallis was formed during a major episode or episodes of flooding, it was hoped that the waters brought a variety of Martian rocks through the channel and that some of the rocks would represent distinct geologic types and environments (such as those from volcanic areas or sedimentary rocks from lakes, for example). Preliminary analysis of both the images and the geochemical data shows this hypothesis to be basically true. The Pathfinder site is marked by an assortment of Martian rocks which appear to have formed in different geologic environments. More so, Pathfinder has provided enough new information to the Mars database to ask some provocative questions and to speculate about past Martian environments.

Preliminary chemical analyses of five rocks has been reported in the journal *Science* . These rocks are Barnacle Bill, Yogi, Wedge, Shark and Half Dome (see Figures 2 & 3). Assuming that these rocks are volcanic in origin (more on this later) they have been plotted on a standard diagram used for the classification of volcanic rocks (SiO_2 versus Na_2O and K_2O—Figure 1). All five of the rocks basically plot within the fields of andesites and basaltic andesites. It was a surprise to some researchers that the chemical analyses showed that the rocks might be andesites as the difference between basalts (what was expected) and andesites is a critical factor in the evaluation of the geologic history of Mars. Barnacle Bill and Shark are plotted as andesites, Half Dome and Yogi as basaltic andesites and Wedge is on the line between basalts and basaltic andesites.

If these rocks are andesites, as it now appears, it will require much rewriting of Martian geologic history. Finding andesites on

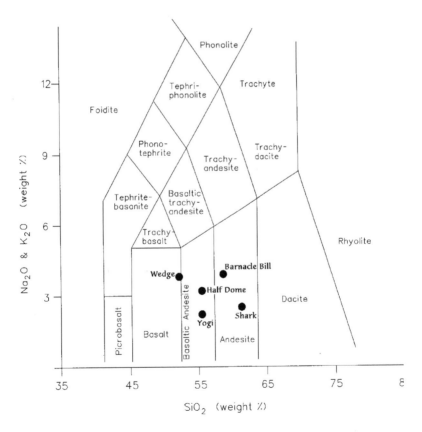

Figure 1 Classification of Pathfinder Rocks based on SiO_2 vs. Na_2O and K_2O. Boundaries for Volcanic Rocks from NASA Web Site, http://mars.primehost.com/ops/science.html; file hap_5.jpg (1997)

Shark   Half Dome

Wedge

Figure 2 (Courtesy NASA and JPL)

Mars would probably be an important revelation because andesites on earth are generally formed from the remelting of basalt in conjunction with a mixing of continental crust. Andesitic lavas are often associated with explosive volcanoes, similar to Mount St. Helens, and they occur in the volcanoes that form the Pacific Ocean's "Ring of Fire," a zone created where oceanic plates crush up against continental margins. Basalts, on the other hand, are associated with "quieter" volcanism, such as that of the Kilauea Volcano on Hawaii.

Andesites would imply that Mars was, for a long time, more earth-like and warmer than previously believed. This conclusion would be more likely since andesites require more "heating" time in order to be created from the remix of basaltic magmas with continental rocks. It would also support the possibility that plate tectonics may have once been active on Mars.

To date no evidence has been found showing that Mars has tectonic plates, but Global Surveyor readings which indicate an erratic magnetic field and the recent discovery that a ring of frozen carbon dioxide may well have made Mars much warmer in the past than it is now both point toward a greater likelihood that a warmer Mars may have been a more techtonically active Mars. However, an

Figure 3 (Courtesy NASA and JPL)

essential bit of information is lacking to resolve the issue, since the Viking orbiters did not carry radar altimeters like the one used to successfully develop topographic maps of Venus. Without altimeter data, it is only guesswork as to how high a mountain is or how deep a canyon. One of the goals of the Mars Global Surveyor, now in orbit around Mars, is to develop a topographic map of the planet where we should be able to definitively tell the highs from the lows with reasonable numeric accuracy. With this added dataset for Mars, it may be possible to see if tectonic plates exist or have existed, and whether there is a differentiation between "continental" crust (silica-rich) and "oceanic" crust (silica-poor). If Martian plate tectonics can be proven, it would indicate that historical Mars was even more earth-like than previously believed. Some questions would follow. How much did tectonics shape the planet? How long did tectonics play an active role? Is there any evidence that tectonic activity is occurring today?

It should be noted that many of the news releases concerning the silica-rich rocks erroneously called them quartz-rich. This little error makes a great difference when it comes to the classification of volcanic rocks and the determination of their origins. Quartz-rich is not the same as silica-rich. If the Martian rocks were quartz-rich and volcanic in origin, they would be classified as rhyolites or dacites for example (see glossary). They would not be basalts or andesites. The more quartz there is in a lava, the higher the viscosity (thickness). Subsequently, the extrusion of such a lava usually requires a greater force and thus a more violent type of volcanic eruption. Rhyolitic lavas are typical of volcanoes that are continental in origin and these volcanoes are some of the most violent during eruption and thus cause major devastation.

Having now completed your short-course in volcanic petrology, you might now be asking if there is anything else of interest in the x-ray analyses? Decidedly, yes, and this brings us back to the volcanic issue for the Pathfinder rocks. Rieder et al (1997) state "However we cannot be certain that these rocks are igneous." In other words, the textures of some of the rocks as shown by Pathfinder and Sojourner images are not necessarily distinctive of volcanic rocks and thus these rocks could be sedimentary or metamorphic as well.

Table 1 shows a breakdown of the oxide components in weight percent of the five Martian rocks as well as some average values for sedimentary rocks on earth.

A JPL press release issued August 27, 1997 states that two distinct type of rocks have been found on the Red Planet, one earth-like and full of silicon, the other inexplicably high in sulfur. As it turns out, not only do all five analyzed Pathfinder rocks have high silicon, several have high sulfur contents as well, Yogi for example. The tested soils are also high in sulfur.

One might ask why are high sulfur contents significant? Part of that answer is based on the role of sulfur in rocks. The three most important sources of sulfur on earth are sulfide minerals such as pyrite (fool's gold—FeS_2), sulfate minerals such as gypsum ($CaSO_4*_2H_2O$) and native sulfur. Sulfide minerals are important sources of metals and occur extensively in igneous rocks as well as in sedimentary rocks. Sulfates are usually associated with sedimentary rocks and native sulfur is often associated with volcanic vents and fumaroles.

Since sulfur can form in a variety of environments, if we can determine where the sulfur on Mars came from (which type of sulfur we're looking at—sulfides, sulfates or native sulfur) we can

	Na_2O	MgO	Al_2O_3	SiO_2	SO_3	K_2O	CaO	TiO_2	FeO
Barnacle Bill[1]	3.2	3.0	10.8	58.6	2.2	0.7	5.3	0.8	12.9
Yogi[1]	1.7	5.9	9.1	55.5	3.9	0.5	6.6	0.9	13.1
Wedge[1]	3.1	4.9	10.0	52.2	2.8	0.7	7.4	1.0	15.4
Shark[1]	2.0	3.0	9.9	61.2	0.7	0.5	7.8	0.7	11.9
Half Dome[1]	2.4	4.9	10.6	55.3	2.6	0.8	6.0	0.9	13.9
Avg. Sed. Rocks[2] (Earth)	1.1	2.7	13.4	58.0	0.5	2.9	5.9	0.6	5.6
Avg. Sed Rocks[3] Russian Platform	0.4	5.6	7.7	34.2	2.1	2.1	21.8	0.4	4.0
Avg. Clays (Earth)[2]	1.3	2.4	15.4	58.1	0.6	3.2	3.1	0.7	6.5
Avg. Clays Russian[3] Platform	0.8	3.3	15.1	50.7	0.6	3.5	7.2	0.8	6.5
Avg. Sands (Earth)[2]	0.5	1.2	4.8	78.6	.07	1.3	5.5	.25	1.4
Avg. Sands Russian[3] Platform	0.6	1.9	8.2	70.0	0.7	2.1	4.3	0.6	4.5

1) Rieder et al, 1997.
2) Clarke with corrections by Mason, 1952.
3) Vinogradov and Ronov, 1956.

Table 1 Compostion of the Five Pathfinder Rocks Compared to Averages for Earth-based Sedimentary Rocks (in weight percent of oxide).

make plausible inferences as to what environments the sulfur formed under. Another possible source of sulfur on Mars could be from meteorite impacts.

The first to consider is that the sulfur at the Pathfinder site is from volcanic processes. On earth, sulfur is often formed near fumaroles and hot springs where sulfur-rich gases are vented and sulfur is deposited. The images from Pathfinder though, do not show landforms which are typical of an active volcanic environment. Because of that, it's unlikely that the sulfur is derived from a nearby volcano.

Since the Martian soils have a higher sulfur content than do the rocks, it's possible that the sulfur in the analyzed rocks is actually from a dust or a weathering rind. It has been suggested (Reider et al, 1997) that the soils are the result of both local rock input and a global redistribution of other weathered rocks. Since Viking soils also contained high sulfur contents, this is a plausible scenario.

The question though is what is the source of the sulfur? Volcanic sulfur would seem unlikely, but sedimentary sulfur sources as well as meteorite sources could provide the sulfur content that is detected in the soils. Of the two, sedimentary input is the most tantalizing as it would reveal much about the geologic history of Mars. Sedimentary sulfur usually takes the form of sulfates or sulfides (i.e. gypsum or pyrite). On earth the sedimentary rocks with which contain the greatest amounts of sulfur are evaporites, which are rocks that were formed in isolated basins where evaporation exceeds recharge into the basin. The result is the precipitation of a variety of minerals (salt being one of them). Evaporite deposits often have sulfur contents in the range of 180,000 ppm (18% by weight). The White Sands area of New Mexico is a classic example of evaporite deposits.

From Table 1 it can be seen that the overall sulfur content in sedimentary rocks on earth is less than that found in the Martian soils and rocks, but individual rock types do contain appreciable amounts of sulfur, most notably, the evaporites. Since the scientific opinion (from the evidence) is that Mars may have had large bodies of water at one time (in fact some suggest a Pacific-ocean sized body of water) could evaporite deposits have been formed in isolated basins? Is it possible that the globally distributed sulfur is sourced by weathered evaporite minerals? Or perhaps some other sedimentary rock types? One method to determine the probable source of the sulfur is through the use of isotope mass spectrometery. A mass spectrometer was not brought to Mars with the Pathfinder, but should be considered for a future mission if feasible. It would be one way to decisively (hopefully) solve the sulfur question.

It has also been considered that meteoritic impacts could bring sulfur-bearing minerals onto the Martian surface. Iron sulfides (particularly troilite, FeS) are often accessory minerals in stony meteorites (chondrites), making up about 10 to 15 weight percent of the meteorite. Chondrites are believed to be the most abundant meteorites that fall on the earth. About 69% of falls are stony, 28 percent irons and about 3% stony-irons.

If meteorites are the source of the sulfur on Mars (or at least part of the source) the apparent lack of nickel at the Pathfinder site seems puzzling. As most meteorites found on earth contain nickel-iron alloys, which is one of the most distinguishing characteristics that a rock is a meteorite, one might expect to find at least some nickel concentration in the rocks and soils on Mars. Still, we can't be certain if Mars has been impacted with the same types of meteorites as has the earth nor what chemical and physical weathering processes may have been active during its past.

The visual observations of the Pathfinder site through the images, suggests that a variety of environments are represented at the site. The apparent bedding planes in some of the rocks and in the Twin Peaks as well as flat-surfaced rocks, seems to suggest a sedimentary environment that may or may not be related to the presumed flooding. If the andesite analyses of some of the rocks holds true and it can be confirmed that they are indeed volcanic in origin, we're looking at a Mars with possible heat flow and mixing mechanisms similar to that of earth. Plate tectonics is not out of the realm of possibilities. Of course, some of the rocks at the site will also undoubtedly be determined to have originated from meteor impacts.

The most interesting of the observed rock types are the "conglomerates" (See Figure 3). For the most part, conglomerates on earth are indicative of stream processes or beach environments. They are rocks which are generally made up of cemented pebbles or clasts. The more rounded the clasts are, the more they have been reworked by water currents. It is thought that Shark and Half Dome are imbricated rocks (embedded by flood-waters). Because of what appear to be conglomeratic pebbles on these two rocks, despite their andesite chemical analyses, they may actually be sedimentary in origin. Is it possible then too that they are outcrops rather than flood deposited? If so, it would be strong evidence that water was flowing in the Ares Valles for a much longer period of time than a catastrophic flood scenario would entail. Even if Shark and Half Dome are flood-deposited, they would likely have had to have formed somewhere else on the planet via more "normal" sedimentation processes. Or perhaps water flow through the Ares Valles was episodic in nature.

Since we don't have definitive age dates yet for Mars, the timing and relations between the various landforms we see on the planet are not fully knowable. Though it appears that liquid water was an early feature of the planet, we can only guess as to how long it remained in that state. Mars seems likely to have once held an atmosphere and environment that was conducive to liquid water. A great amount of water. Pathfinder data seems to offer initial support to that case. The questions remain though, when did it change—and why?

Glossary of Terms:

andesite: Volcanic rock which contains more than 60% light-colored minerals (felsic, but less than 10% quartz). Sodium feldspar predominant. Intermediate in composition between basalt and rhyolite.

basalt: Volcanic rock which contains more than 40% dark-colored minerals (mafic). Oceanic crust is made chiefly of basalt.

conglomerate: Sedimentary rock composed chiefly of rounded fragments of rock or pebbles held together by a mineral cement.

evaporites: Rocks which are often deposited in isolated basins where recharge is less than the evaporation rate. Gypsum and andhydrite are two of the most common evaporites.

dacite: Volcanic rock which contains more than 60% light-colored minerals, but more than 10% quartz. Sodium feldspar predominant.

differential erosion: A process whereby different rocks erode at different rates dependent upon variations in the compostiion of the rock or the intensity of weathering activity. For example, a limestone will normally erode more quickly under the action of water than will a more resistent sandstone.

isotopes: Elements which have an identical number of protons in their nucleus, but a different number of neutrons. Carbon 12 and carbon 14 are two isotopes of carbon.

law of superposition: In a sequence of layered rocks, any layer is older than the layer above it. As in the case of impact craters, any rocks or structures (provided they are not impact-induced) beneath the impact are older than the impact itself.

mass spectrometry: Measurement of chemical isotopes by their difference in mass.

metamorphic: Mechanism whereby rocks are altered to new forms chiefly through pressure and heat.

pediment surface: A broad surface with a low relief or gentle slope, generally located at the base of a surface with a steeper slope.

rhyolite: Volcanic rock which contains more than 60% light-colored minerals, but more than 10% quartz. Calcium feldspar predominant. Fine-grained equivalent to granite.

tectonics: Pertaining to the structure of rocks and landforms formed by the deformation of the earth's crust.

topographic map: Map which represents changes in the relief of the land. Elevation changes usually shown as contours.

Ancient Oceans on Mars—
New Evidence from Global Surveyor

BY JAMES ERJAVEC

An image recently returned from the Mars Global Surveyor presents the strongest evidence yet that Mars had a long period in which liquid water, essential for life, was present on the surface. The extremely clear, high-resolution image shows a spectacular exposed rock face, 3200 feet high, located in the area of the Valles Marineris.

This exposed surface, which, according to NASA's information, represents only about a fifth of the total sedimentation layer, displays no less than eighty generally parallel layers of alternating light and dark colored rock. Such layered or "bedded" features are almost certainly sedimentary in origin (originally deposited in water). Though volcanic eruption of ash does form bedded features, as can lava flows, the apparent regularity of the light and dark layers, the nature of the bedding and the thickness of the rock section indicate that is not the case here.

What kind of sedimentary rocks have we found? The geological question is whether these layers represent sandstone and conglomerates, or limestone and shale. Sandstone and conglomerates are typically formed in stream and river environments, and these do not usually produce a layered feature thousands of feet in thickness. Beach environments, on the other hand, as well as what are called turbidite flows (turbulent deposits in water as a result of a sudden event such as an earthquake) can provide massively thick features of sandstone and other types of sedimentary rocks.

Deposits due to evaporation (evaporites), typical of lakes and isolated marine basins, are also found as thick rock sections and are often associated with interbedded limestones and shales. Evaporites, limestones and shales on Earth are usually indicators of large and sometimes deep bodies of longstanding water, such as oceans or lakes.

Given the evidence to date, it seems probable that these layers in the Valles Marineris rock face were deposited in either a lake or ocean environment. The body of water was likely present on the planet for a very long time—on the order of hundreds of millions of years. Taking a long-shot guess at what the layered rocks were—the most likely is that they were interbedded evaporites and carbonates (limestones, but there are other types of carbonate rocks as well). If this turns out to be true, the geologic history of Mars will have to be entirely rewritten.

What is the significance of the Valles Marineris rock image for the history of Mars? The thickness of the exposed layers can perhaps provide us with an estimate as to how much time may have been necessary for their deposition. The area of the Ouachita Mountains of Arkansas and Oklahoma, as a comparison, contains a very thick section of sedimentary rock and according to Morris (1974) the rate of deposition there for various sedimentary units has been calculated to range from as little as 14.6 feet per million years to as much as 3,000 feet per million. If the 3200 foot sedimentary rock face of the Valles Marineris was deposited at about 14.6 feet per million years, the Martian section might represent some 220 million years of depositional history. At the highest depositional rate it would represent only about a million years of deposition. Using an average rate of deposition for the Ouachita Mountains, the exposed rock face in the Valles Marineris would represent some 12 million years of deposition, but since the rock face appears to be only a small part of more extensive sedimentary layers, we are possibly looking at tens of millions to hundreds of millions of years of

(cont. next page)

deposition—if we use Earth-based analogies, which, of course, brings up some big unknowns. However, these are the best estimates we presently have to work with.

Despite the unknowns, whichever measure turns out to be true, the thick complex-bedded units seen in this new Global Surveyor image point to a much longer period of sedimentation and thus a much longer time in which Mars was Earth-like, potentially a billion years or more. Such a revised time scale for Martian sedimentary processes would result in an overlap with the early period in Earth's history, when life is believed to have originated and evolved. If so, it would not surprise me in the least that one day a space probe or human explorer will collect the first authenticated Martian fossil. The study of Martian paleontology will have begun.

This spectacular high-resolution view of a triangular rocky outcrop on Mars shows about 80 layers of sedimentation probably deposited over many millions of years on the bottom of a Martian lake or ocean environment. (Image courtesy of NASA/ JPL/Cal Tech.)

Statistical Evidence

You could put it in the form of an equation. The importance of gleaning further information on certain Martian objects equals the likelihood of their being products of intelligent manufacture times the importance of that fact if proven true. Now, no matter how small the first number is, as long as it isn't zero, the equation is going to return a sizeable total; because the second number is BIG!

—Joseph P. Kerwin,
former Skylab astronaut (on reading *The McDaniel Report*)

"You can prove anything with statistics," said a skeptic when offered the Cydonia data. But the skeptic was wrong. We depend on statistical analyses in many, many ways for knowledge. Statistics help you to know what medication may save your life, or what habits will likely kill you with cancer or heart disease. Such statistics make your life better and safer than it would be otherwise. Self-interested people who misuse statistics can lie, but the tests of peer-review and critique by scientific peers are an essential part of the scientific process, weeding out the wheat from the chaff. The studies presented here, which calculate the probability of artificial objects at Cydonia using several different methods, have undergone such critique and review.

The convergent results of these independent studies are indeed startling: They clearly indicate that some of these features could very well be the result of intelligent design. If we follow Kerwin's equation, the combined message of these fascinating and original studies is that obtaining further information about the Cydonia enigmas should occupy a position of overriding importance for NASA's Mars exploration program.

Tests "The Face" Might Have Failed

Professor Stanley V. McDaniel

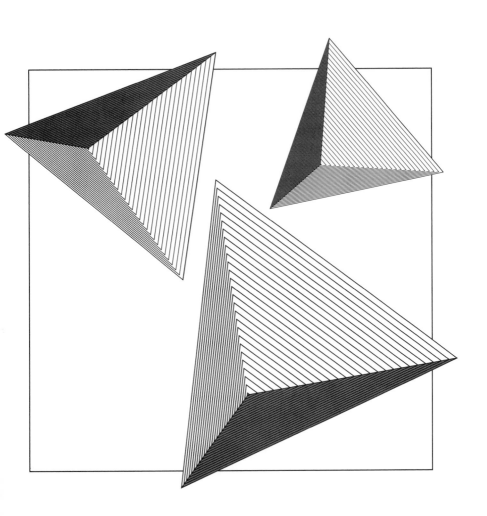

It is often argued that to qualify as a scientific hypothesis, a proposal must be falsifiable — there must be tests that could be failed. Is the hypothesis that the Face on Mars may be artificial falsifiable? Although the final result must await better images or even ground investigation, several tests have already been applied that the Face might have failed. In each case the results favored the hypothesis.

Test 1: The facial appearance should be viewed in other images taken at different sun angles. If the Face "disappears" this will falsify the hypothesis.

Result: The facial appearance is retained over at least a 17 degree difference in sun angle between high-resolution Viking frames 35A72 and 70A13, and is also visible in a lower-resolution frame 561A25. No other frames with sufficient resolution to make out detail exist.

Test 2: Three-dimensional modeling based on computer analysis will show that the structure is not really face-shaped. This will falsify the hypothesis.

Result: Dr. Mark J. Carlotto applied the technique of photoclinometry (the estimation of 3-D shape from levels of brightness). The results were tested by cross-comparison of different frames. The object does have the 3-D structure of a face.

Test 3: It will be possible to construct a model of the surrounding terrain that will show the facial appearance is merely the result of shadows thrown by other nearby objects which are unrelated to one another and do not resemble a face.

Result: There are no nearby objects tall enough to throw any shadows on the Face. A model sculptured in clay and tested by painstaking comparison with actual photos under the same lighting angles shows that only a face-like shape in three dimensions can produce an appearance simultaneously consistent with all Viking images.

Test 4:   Insufficient detail will be found in the structure, proving that the facial appearance is merely a superficial
resemblance that can be accounted for by wind erosion.

Result: Investigators have identified five separate details in the
object, including a "pupil" in the left eye socket, that are
difficult to explain by erosion but are consistent with a
deliberate sculpture.

Test 5:   Quantitative mathematical analysis, using fractal mathematics, will show that the object is no different from
hundreds of other knobby mesas in the area.

Result: Dr. Mark J. Carlotto applied fractal analysis that gave
the opposite result. The Face stood out as quantitatively
unique by a large margin over an area of 15,000 square
kilometers on Mars.

The Beauty of the Martian Mound Geometry

Dr. Horace Crater
Cesar Sirvent

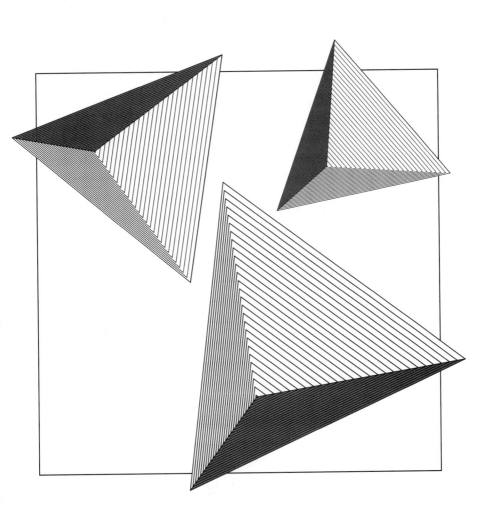

A ll who were inspired by Pythagoras retained an element of ecstatic revelation.

— Bertrand Russell
on the Pythagoreans

Beauty is said to be in the eye of the beholder, but mathematical beauty and elegance is of a special nature, tied together inti-
mately with the universal concepts of number and geometry. The
most compelling feature of the mounds of Mars and their possible
implications for artificiality is the mathematically elegant geometrical configuration with which they appear on the Cydonia plain.

In"The Mounds of Mars, ET Artifacts or Elegant Geology"
(see page 91), McDaniel and Crater present images that specified
the location of the twelve mounds at Cydonia by giving them letter designations, and presented a review of their geometric relationships (Figure 1). Looking first at just the four mounds GADE,
on visual inspection it appeared that one triangle (mounds ADE)
is isosceles while two others (EAG, GAD) are right triangles.
Using analytic geometry, Crater found that in an ideal geometric
figure matching the mound positions, all the angles in these triangles would be expressed in simple terms using only the right
angle (90 degrees) and a particular angle designated *t*, equal to
19.47 degrees. Furthermore, the right triangles are equal (in
angles) to just one-half the isosceles triangle.

Using this unusual relationship of triangles as a clue, Crater
then tested all the mounds in the area for occurrences of right and
isosceles triangles related so that the right triangles are one-half
the isosceles. In these tests he allowed the angle designated t to
vary, so that he checked for occurrences of all possible right and
isosceles triangles having this particular one to one-half relationship. The remarkable result was that when the triangles were
made up of angles determined by the right angle and just that one
particular value of *t* discovered earlier (19.47 degrees), the number
of occurrences of these triangles shot up to a degree far beyond
what chance would allow *(see "Nonrandom Distribution of Angles" on
page 99)*.

Subsequently Cesar Sirvent, working in Spain, proposed that the parallel lines found in the geometry of the five mounds GABDE (referred to by Crater as "the pentad") are even more visually compelling, and perhaps more basic, than the triangles. What struck Sirvent's attention was the remarkable combinations of four sets of parallel lines as indicated in Figure 1. A check by both Crater and Sirvent revealed that for any way you place five points, out of all the possible relative positions, there are only two or three configurations that will yield four sets of parallels—the Martian mound configuration being one of them. As a result, we conclude that the five-mound configuration called the "pentad" represents a uniquely elegant geometric pattern.

Sirvent then asked the question whether the same angles as those found by Crater would follow simply by replacing the assumption that triangle ADE is isosceles with the assumption that the visually apparent parallel lines are actually parallel. A series of careful calculations confirmed the fact: Again all the angles in the figure turned out to be based on the right angle and angle t at 19.47 degrees.

The repetition of this pattern of angles, obtained by two different approaches, is extraordinary. But are we seeing elegant areology or elegant, intentionally constructed geometrical patterns? Clearly we are not seeing the action of entirely random geological forces. Crater's statistical analysis had already proven that. Perhaps we will never be certain of the final origin of this uniquely elegant mound configuration until human explorers walk on the surface of Mars at Cydonia.

In the meantime, however, if mathematical and geometric elegance weigh on the side of an artificial origin, we find that the mound pattern yields even more surprises. In "Cydonian Mound Geometry,"*(see page 101)*, Stanley V. McDaniel describes how he discovered that the pattern formed by the pentad of five mounds GABDE implies a rectangle having the proportions one to the square root of 2, referred to as a "square-root 2 rectangle." Subsequently, investigation by Crater confirmed that all sixteen mounds in the area appear to fall in positions related to an expansion of this square-root 2 grid.

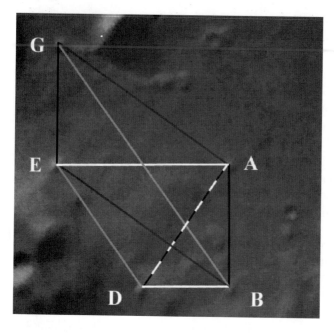

Figure 1

Parallel lines in the pentad formation: GA parallel to EB, GE parallel to AB, EA parallel to DB, parallelogram formed by GABE, and dotted line marking the right angle GAD.

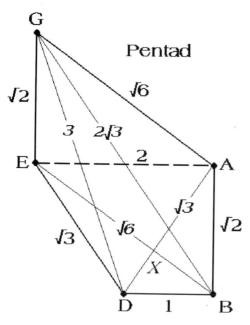

Figure 2

Distance ratios among five mounds are based on the square root of 2 and the square root of three.

Using the geometric results described above, we find that each of the distances between the mounds is a multiple of either square-root (2) or square-root (3), or both. Choosing the distance between mounds DB as our measuring unit, the distance between mound A and E is the square of square-root (2) while the longest distance (between mounds B and G) is twice the square root of 3. Furthermore, one can show that if we choose the area of the smallest triangle (ADB) as our unit of area, all other triangles have an area of 1, 2 or 3. Finally, the area of the four-mound tetrad GADE is four such units, while the area of the five-mound pentad GABDE is five units. Geometrically, in the area ratios of its component triangles, the figure may best be described as self-referential.

Again, one must keep in mind that the above ideals are based on vertex locations that are very accurately represented by the center locations of the mounds in Cydonia, on Mars. The self-referential character of the figure, the uniqueness of expression by means of parallel lines presented in the most economical fashion, and the square root ratios, work together to attract our attention in a directly intelligible way. Without a compelling geological explanation these mathematical qualities argue in favor of intentional construction—particularly when seen in the context of Crater's statistical studies indicating nonrandom distribution.

BIOGRAPHICAL NOTE

Cesar Sirvent-Sempere is a graduate student in Physics at the University of Zaragoza, Spain, is a former director of the science magazine, *Lumen*, and has published several Spanish articles on scientific anomalies.

Why Archeologists Should Explore Cydonia

Dr. James F. Strange

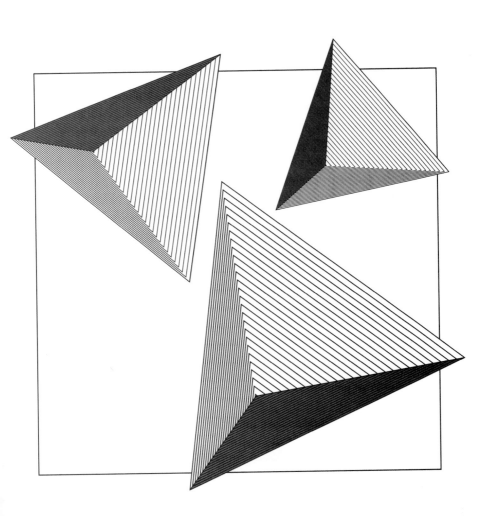

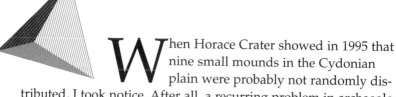

When Horace Crater showed in 1995 that nine small mounds in the Cydonian plain were probably not randomly distributed, I took notice. After all, a recurring problem in archaeology is how to work with data which might turn out to be random. If the data are random, then there is no reason to pursue them archaeologically. For example, if the Nazca Lines in Peru actually turned out to be drawn randomly, that is, with no patterns at all, then there is no reason to waste resources sending archaeologists to examine them further.

It so happens that archaeologists use many statistical methods to calculate the probability that any given set of data scattered across the landscape is random. One that is popular in Europe is called the Kolgomorov-Sminov test for randomness. It seemed that this test, which is simple to understand and use, would be ideal to test the randomness of the mound data.

When we speak of the "mound data" we mean the set of lengths of line segments drawn from mound to mound at Cydonia. If one thinks about it, it seems clear that the mounds themselves could be scattered randomly on the surface of Mars. If so, then the measured distances from mound to mound would also be randomly distributed.

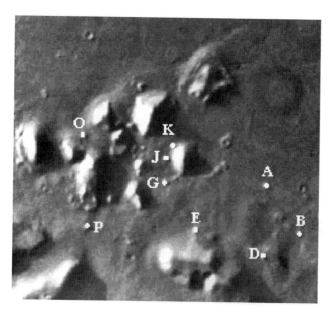

These are the nine mounds used in Horace Crater's 1995 study which when analyzed using the Kolgomorov-Sminov test which show an almost 99% probability that they are not randomly distributed.

	B	D	A	E	G	J	K	P	O
B	0	0.5	0.707	1.225	1.732	1.815	1.823	2.450	2.809
D	0.5	0	0.866	0.866	1.5	1.652	1.708	2.061	2.582
A	0.707	0.866	0	1	1.225	1.224	1.192	2.121	2.238
E	1.225	0.866	1	0	0.707	0.934	1.051	1.225	1.750
G	1.732	1.500	1.225	0.707	0	0.280	0.446	1.	1.086
J	1.815	1.652	1.224	0.934	0.280	0	0.174	1.205	1.013
K	1.823	1.708	1.192	1.051	0.446	0.174	0	1.372	1.069
P	2.450	2.061	2.121	1.225	1	1.205	1.372	0	1.110
O	2.855	2.582	2.238	1.750	1.086	1.013	1.069	1.110	0

Distances between each of the nine mounds (with the distance from A to E established as equal to 1).

In this case I decided to use data for all nine mounds as published by Crater in his paper. For nine mounds there are thirty-six distances between them. The nine mounds are A, B, D, E, G, J, K, P, and O. The distances between them were arranged in a nine by nine matrix so that the distance between A and B, for example, could be seen to be 0.707. In this matrix the reference datum was the distance from A to E, which was set to unity or 1. Obviously the distance between any mound and itself is zero.

Sometimes it is useful to arrange the data from a matrix such as the one above in a histogram, sometimes called a "bar graph." The histogram for the thirty-six segments is not perfectly symmetric, which itself suggests that the data is not "normally" or randomly arranged on the landscape.

The Kolgomorov-Smirnov test actually compares the cumulative distributions of randomly distributed data to the mound data. In this case what statisticians call the null hypothesis, or the hypothesis that the data is merely random, would be that there would be no difference between a plot of random data and a plot of the mound data. The "Test Statistic" is the largest absolute difference between the two distributions. In order to find the Test Statistic we calculate the cumulative frequency for lengths, the cumulative percentage for lengths, and then subtract the two, step by step, as we develop the cumulative distributions.

For the mound data we find that the absolute difference between predicated (where it is assumed that they will be uniformly distributed) and actual percentages is about 22.6%

We then check statistical tables in the back of any handy statistics book for a table of values for a Kolgomorov-Smirnov single sample test. We find that, for 36 observations, the difference one would expect between predicted and observed is 22.1 at the 5% confidence level and 26.5 at the 1% confidence level.

Thus we can say that the mound data is not uniformly distributed at a better than 5% confidence level, but not at the 1% confidence level.

There is a very similar Kolgomorov-Smirnov test for normalcy. In this case the Kolgomorov-Smirnov test verifies whether a sample could have come from a normally (randomly) distributed population. If the cumulative percentages of a normally distributed variable are plotted on normal probability graph paper, then a straight line results. The closer the mound data is to a straight line, then the more likely that it is the result of random processes.

In this case the data as plotted on probability paper is not a straight line. This suggests that we should calculate the largest absolute difference again, or the Test Statistic.

In this case the largest difference between predicted and observed data is calculated to be 16.7. We check our table for Kolgomorov-Smirnov values for thirty-six observations for normally distributed data and find that at a 10% confidence level the predicted figure is 13.4. At a 5% confidence level the prediction is 14.6. At a 1% confidence level the prediction is 17.0, which is only slightly larger than our calculated figure of 16.7 Therefore we are almost at the 1% confidence level (we are nearly 99% sure) in finding that the mound data is not normally distributed, as well as not uniformly distributed.

As an aside, may I point out that, by agreement in the scientific community, the confidence level one tries to achieve is that of 2%. We have exceeded the magic 2% confidence level in this case.

It seemed to be a good idea to check a second feature of the line segments drawn from mound to mound. The mounds in effect become points of intersection between the various line segments drawn from mound to mound. Angles are formed by the intersections of these line segments.

The same Kolgomorov-Smirnov test for uniformness and normalcy apply to the distribution of the angles at the mounds. This time I will not walk the reader through the numbers, but the calculation of the difference between the predicted and observed distribution of angles at the mounds again shows that the angles are not distributed randomly, nor are they uniformly distributed between 0 degrees and 120 degrees. These conclusions can be drawn at about the 1% confidence level.

Of course what these calculations do not do is explain the origin of the mounds nor do they indicate how we are to understand their observed grid. From the point of view of a practicing archaeologist, these calculations indicate that we should take a closer look. For example, if we were investigating features of this type in satellite photographs, our practical conclusion is that we need to go and take a look at ground level. If we cannot do that, then at least we need new photographs at much better resolution. It would even be good to have soil interface radar imagery, infrared imagery, and other images. Above all we need "ground truth," or direct observation of the mounds and their context, but that is likely years away.

High Probablility
of Artificiality
at Cydonia

Dr. Mark J. Carlotto

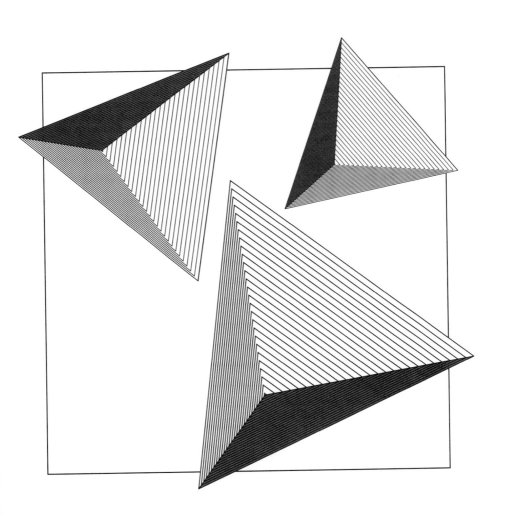

Since Viking first imaged the Face at Cydonia and nearby objects in 1976, several probes have been sent to Mars. The Pathfinder landing in the summer of 1997 marked the first successful mission to the Red Planet in over 20 years. Currently Global Surveyor is in orbit around Mars. This spacecraft contains among other experiments a high resolution camera capable of shedding new light on these enigmatic surface features. Because they control this instrument, the planetary science community not only participates in the debate over the Face's possible artificiality but also, in effect, judges it. Like a judge presiding over a murder trial, their demand for hard evidence has lead to the development of *The Case for the Face*.

There are two ways to build the case. One way is to show that a single piece of evidence is so strong that it in itself is sufficient to 'convict.' In *The Case for the Face*, however, "conviction" does not mean proving that one or more objects on Mars are artificial; rather it means establishing a reasonable probability that some of those objects may be artificial—a probability sufficient to warrant active, detailed investigation of the site. In their reports, Horace W. Crater, Stanley V. McDaniel, and James F. Strange follow this line of investigation.

Another way is to accept at the outset that the quality of the available data is not sufficient to provide a single piece of extraordinary evidence. In other words to recognize that there is no smoking gun, no eyewitness to the crime. Instead, we use the convergence of many lines of evidence, like fingerprints, blood samples, and other clues that might be found at the scene of a crime pointing inevitably toward only one plausible conclusion.

This article follows this second approach, summarizing the body of circumstantial evidence that has been developed over the past 20 years. It argues that the extraordinary claim that certain objects on the surface of Mars might be artificial is supported by an extraordinary amount of evidence. This evidence is derived primarily from two medium resolution (50 meter/pixel) images of the region and to a lesser extent from several lower resolution (> 100 meter/pixel) images. The figure on the following page is a mosaic derived from several Viking Orbiter frames from orbit 35 showing the objects under consideration on the surface of Mars. The image covers an area roughly 70 × 40 km in size. The Face, near the center of the picture, is located at approximately at 41degrees N latitude and 9.5 degrees W longitude. The figure on the following page shows 'The City,' a collection of formations originally identified by Richard Hoagland, located about 20 km southwest of the Face. Three objects comparable in size to the Face and a number of smaller mound-like objects shown on the following page (from 35A72) are considered here.

So What is the Evidence?

Clearly the formation known as the Face possesses all of the required features of a humanoid face: head, eyes, ridge-like nose, and mouth. Several years after Vincent DiPietro and Gregory Molenaar rediscovered the Face in the NASA archives, as part of a subsequent investigation artist James Channon found that measurements between the eyes, nose, mouth, chin, and crown of the head fall within classical human proportions. Noting that very small changes between facial proportions would completely change the visual impact, he expressed his belief that the Face was a precisely designed and deliberately executed structure. He also argued that the platform on which the Face is placed exhibits a high degree of architectural symmetry.

In addition to its gross humanoid features, the Face contains a number of subtle details or embellishments—details that should not be there if it is simply a naturally-occurring geological formation. (DiPietro and Molenaar noted a dark, rounded cavity within the eye socket that looks like the pupil within an eyeball). Several others have observed a series of broad parallel stripes across the Face. Using a method of image clarification called cubic spline interpolation, thin lines that intersect above the eyes and fine structure in the mouth that look like teeth have been revealed. These features are present in both of the key images (NASA Viking frames 35A72 and 70A13) and so are definitely not camera or processing artifacts. Logically these details should not be there. They should have been obliterated by erosional processes rather than preserved over time.

It has also been shown that the Face is not a "trick of light and shadow" as claimed by NASA in a remark originally attributed to NASA Viking project scientist Gerry Soffen. Using an

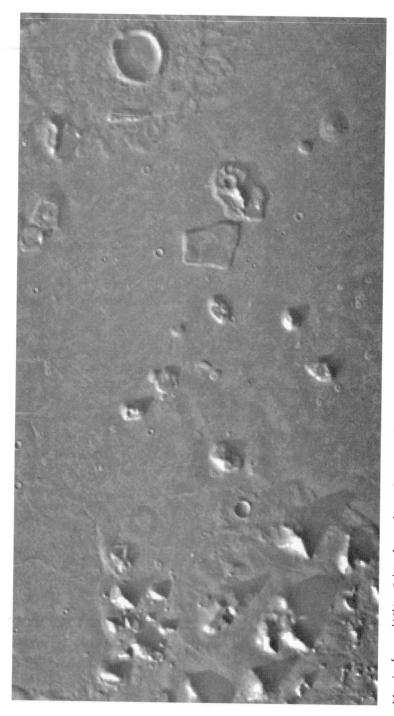

Mosaic of several Viking Orbiter frames from orbit 35 over the Cydonia region showing the 'Face on Mars.'

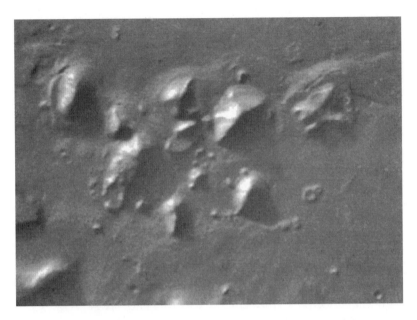

Portion of previous mosaic southwest of the Face showing a collection of objects known as 'The City.'

image processing technique known as shape-from-shading to derive the 3-D structure of the Face from its image, and computer graphics rendering techniques to generate synthetic views of the Face from its derived 3-D structure, it can be shown that the visual impression of a face persists over a wide range of sun angles and viewing geometries. This is not the case for naturally-occurring rock formations that look like faces when viewed in profile. The late Carl Sagan has even admitted to this, stating "I certainly agree that Gerry Soffen's 'trick of lighting' off-hand remark is in error; that is, the impression of the face persists over a variation of all three photometric angles."

Finally, using a technique known as fractal analysis to detect artificial objects in satellite imagery, the Face has been shown to be the least natural object over an area on Mars about 15,000 square kilometers in size.

DiPietro and Molenaar were the first to discover a large pyramidal formation south of the Face. Erol Torun has argued that this formation, termed the D&M pyramid afer its discoverers, cannot be explained by any known geological process on Mars.

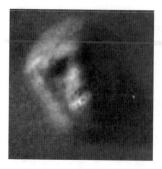 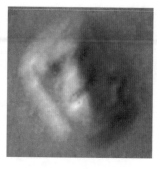

Two images of the Face from 35A72 (left) and 70A13 (right).

Southwest of the Face, Richard Hoagland discovered a collection of geometrically-shaped objects which he called the 'City.' One of these objects, the 'Fortress,' consists of straight sides or walls that surround an inner space. Detailed analysis reveals fine scale features in the form of regularly spaced markings that appear along two of its walls—again, features that should not be there if this is a natural landform. Southeast of the City and Face are several mound-like objects. One of these, the "Tholus," contains two sets of grooves that wind half-way up the object, one of which appears to lead into a opening in its side. Northeast of the Face, Hoagland noticed an elongated mesa topped by a sharp ridge-like feature running down its length located next to a large impact crater. Two geologists, James Erjavec and Ron Nicks, have yet to find a satisfactory explanation for this feature. They also have provided compelling evidence that differential erosion in itself could not have been responsible for the creation of these landforms as claimed by certain planetary geologists.

Comparative analysis reveals yet more interesting "coincidences." The Face and a rounded formation in the City are approximately the same in size, overall shape, and orientation, and both seem to be emplaced on a similar kind of platform. This resemblance suggests the possibility that the Face could have been carved from a pre-existing landform. The Fortress and an adjacent pyramidal object in the City are similar in size, overall shape, and orientation. This suggests that the Fortress may have been an enclosed pyramidal structure that collapsed inward and conversely that the pyramid next to the Fortress may be hollow. The Fortress, Face, rounded formation and pyramid in the City, though different in shape, are similar in size and orientation. Within and

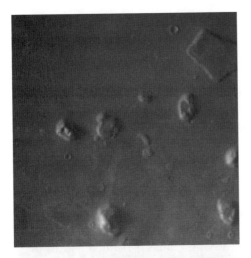

Fractal analysis results for Face and surrounding area. 35A72 and corresponding fractal model-fit image. Bright areas in model-fit image indicate where structure of the image intensity surface (which is related to the shape of the underlying terrain) does not fit a fractal model and thus is least natural by the fractal criterion.

around the City, McDaniel and Crater have found that a group of small mound-like objects, originally discovered by Hoagland, appears to be arrayed in a grid-like pattern. The orientation of this grid appears to match that of the Face and larger objects in City.

All of the above evidence is circumstantial. Each can be interpreted in more than one way. But if you put it all together, it points very strongly to the conclusion that these objects are more likely to be artificial constructions than natural formations. This probability can be quantified using a technique known as Bayesian reasoning. We assume that each piece of evidence is independent. If the weight of a single piece of evidence can be determined and can be assumed to be representative of the weight of the other evidence, then the odds (probability that the objects are artificial divided by the probability that they are natural) can be calculated. This has been done. Using rather modest assumptions it can be shown that even when we assume a prior odds of one in a million against artificiality (representative of an extraordinary claim), the evidence when combined overrides this extremely conservative assumption and yields odds of between 100 and 100,000 to one in favor of artificiality.

In evaluating the significance of this result, it will be helpful to consider a somewhat parallel case. The possible discovery of fossilized microbes in Martian meteorites was an exciting bit of news during the summer of 1996. Although it has generated a great deal of controversy, the idea has gained considerable momentum in the science community. But what is the evidence to support this claim? In the August 16, 1996 issue of the journal *Science,* a group of researchers headed by David S. McKay published an article entitled: "Search for Life on Mars: Possible Relic Biogenic Activity in Martian Meteorite ALH84001." The authors list the following pieces of evidence to support their claim (italics added):

(i)   An igneous Mars rock (of unknown geologic context) that was penetrated by a fluid along fractures and pore spaces, which then became the sites of secondary mineral formation and possible biogenic activity;

(ii) formation age for the carbonate globules younger than the age of the igneous rock;

(iii) SEM and TEM [electron microscope] images of carbonate globules and features resembling terrestrial microorganisms, terrestrial biogenic carbonate structures, or microfossils;

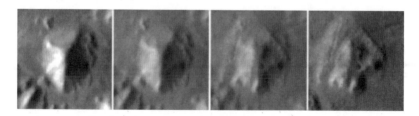

Sequence derived from coregistered images from 70A11 which fades from pyramid (left) to Fortress (right). The images have not been rotated or scaled in size.

(iv) magnetite and iron sulfide particles that could have resulted from oxidation and reduction reactions known to be important in terrestrial microbial systems; and

(v) the presence of PAHs [polycyclic aromatic hydrocarbons] associated with surfaces rich in carbonate globules.

They did not find live microbes. Their evidence is circumstantial. They go on to say that: "None of these observations is in itself conclusive for the existence of past life. Although there are alternative explanations for each of these phenomena taken individually, when they are considered collectively, particularly in view of their spatial association, we conclude that they are evidence for primitive life on early Mars."

Why, then, is the claim for artificial objects on Mars any different than that for microbial life? Clearly the evidence in both cases is circumstantial. It can be argued that given the amount of evidence summarized in this article that *The Case for the Face* is much stronger than that for microbes in a meteorite thought to be from Mars. The answer probably has something to do with the current belief of most planetary scientists that the likelihood of finding artificial structures on Mars is much lower than that of microbes. In other words, because they can't be there, they aren't. Nevertheless the hypothesis that the Face and other nearby objects on Mars are artificial can be tested. In Carl Sagan's last book, *The Demon Haunted World*, speaking of the hypothesis that some objects at Cydonia may be artificial, he states: "Unlike the UFO phenomena, we have here the opportunity for a definitive experiment. This kind of hypothesis is falsifiable, a property that brings it well into the scientific arena."

With the Mars Global Surveyor camera we can perform that experiment.

Evidence for Artificiality Provided by Fractal Analysis

BY DR. MARK J. CARLOTTO

Fractal analysis examines the brightness values of pixels within a square window that slides over the image. All square regions of a given size are examined in this way. Within the processing window an analysis of the area of the image intensity surface at different resolutions is performed. The area as a function of resolution is plotted on a logarithmic scale. The slope of a linear fit to this plot gives the fractal dimension. The deviation from the straight line fit is the model fit error. The model fit error is used as a measure of artificiality.

In order to determine the weight of the evidence provided by the fractal analysis a series of experiments were performed using de-classified national intelligence imagery containing a mix of manmade objects embedded in complex natural backgrounds. In these images the manmade objects are about the size (in pixels) of those on Mars and were imaged under similar lighting conditions. Three images were analyzed. The first was over a U.S. military base, Ft. Drum in New York (Figure 1). The image contained a variety of military hardware arrayed in an open area surrounded by trees. The fractal model fit image is shown in Figure 2. To determine the accuracy of the fractal technique a ground truth image was created by hand (Figure 3). Areas containing manmade objects are shown in white, other areas containing mostly natural background are black. Figure 4 plots the distribution of model fit error values for the two regions. The weight of the evidence is determined by the point where the two curves intersect. The weight is the area of the solid curve divided by the area of the dotted curve from the point where the two curves intersect to the right. The value calculated for this image was 3.28.

Two other images, one containing an SA-2 anti-aircraft site surrounded by brush and tropical vegetation (imaged in August 1962 near Havana, Cuba), the other containing a group of SCUD storage bunkers in the desert (imaged in February 1991 near Quebaysah, Iraq) were analyzed in the same way. The weights computed from these two images were 5.04 for Cuba, and 2.99 for Iraq.

Based on the results of these experiments we concluded that weights between 3 and 5 are reasonable for the fractal analysis technique and that the similarity in the performance curves suggests that the fractal technique can be extended and applied to Mars.

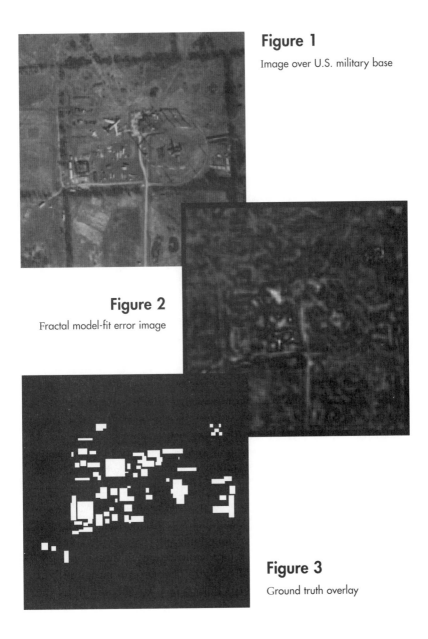

Figure 1

Image over U.S. military base

Figure 2

Fractal model-fit error image

Figure 3

Ground truth overlay

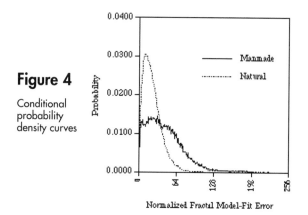

Figure 4

Conditional
probability
density curves

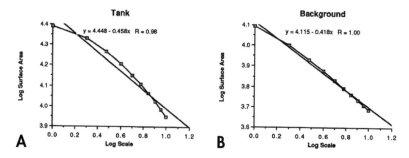

Fractal signatures for a tank and its surrounding natural background are shown in Figures A and B. The fractal signature plots a local property of the image such as its surface area within a region as a function of resolution. The deviation from a straight line fit is used as a measure of artificiality. The structure of a manmade object such as a tank causes the fractal signature to deviate from a straight line (Figure A). Natural terrain however follows a straight line characteristic (Figure B).

Figures C and D show the fractal signatures for the Face and Martian background. Like natural backgrounds on Earth the background on Mars has the same straight line characteristic (compare Figures B and D). And like the tank the fractal signature of the Face deviates from a straight line (compare Figures A and C). Applying the same criteria used for detecting manmade objects in terrestrial imagery to Viking suggests the Face on Mars may be an artificial structure.

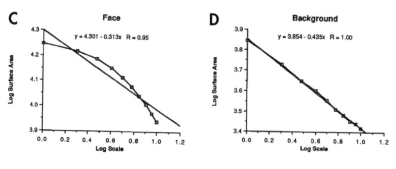

Appendices
& References

MARS: The Statistics

Compiled by Dr. Thomas Van Flandern
Former Director,
Celestial Mechanics Branch,
U.S. Naval Observatory

Fourth planet, located between Earth and Jupiter, adjoining the main asteroid belt
Equatorial radius = 3397 km = 0.53 of Earth's radius
Polar radius = 3372 km
Mass = 6.4×10^{23} kg = 0.11 of Earth's mass
Density = 3.9 g/cc
Surface gravity = 0.38 of Earth's
Surface temperature (normal range) = 183 to 268 K (-137 to +16 F)
Surface pressure = 0.007 to 0.010 bars
Atmosphere: carbon dioxide 95%, nitrogen 3%
                scale height 11 km
Escape velocity = 5.0 km/s
Rotation period = 24h 37m 23s
Inclination of equator to orbit = 24.0 deg.
Moons: Phobos at 9400 km, period = 7h 39m
          Deimos at 23,500 km, period = 30h 18m
Orbit: mean distance from Sun = 1.52 au = 228,000,000 km
         period = 687 days = 1.88 Earth years
         velocity = 24 km/s
         eccentricity = 0.093
         inclination = 1.85 deg.
         minimum distance from Earth = 56,000,000 km
         maximum distance from Earth = 377,000,000 km

The Cydonia Anomalies:
Frequently Asked Questions

COMPILED BY LAN FLEMING

Q: What exactly is this "Face on Mars" and who discovered it?

A: The "Face" is a land form that bears a striking resemblance to a human face. It is 2.5 kilometers long, 1 kilometer wide, and 400 meters high. It is located in an area of Mars' northern hemisphere called Cydonia Mensae (Cydonia Plain). It was discovered in 1976 by Viking project scientists in the 72nd photograph taken on the 35th orbit of Viking Orbiter A (Frame 35A72).

Q. Isn't it true that the human brain is "hard-wired" to see faces in random patterns?

A. If this were true, all of us would be forced to "see faces" constantly in random objects as we go about our daily business. Instead we have the ability generally to distinguish vague, imaginary faces from real ones.

Q. Aren't these so-called "investigators" actually nothing but believers and zealots who are out to exploit the "Face" for their own profit?

A. Members of the Society for Planetary SETI Research (SPSR) are all academically or professionally qualified individuals, many of whom have written and published peer-reviewed papers on this and other scholarly subjects. Their focus of interest is in scientific research.

Q. Isn't it just plain crazy to imagine that there could be artifacts of an intelligent civilization on the planet Mars?

A. Many reputable scientists, including Dr. Carl Sagan and the scientists who authored the prestigious Brookings Institution

Report on space policy for NASA in 1960, have proposed that such artifacts might be found on planets in the solar system.

Q: If an intelligent race built an enormous "Face" out in the middle of a Martian wasteland, wouldn't there be traces of some other intelligent activity?

A: There are many unusual features within a 20-mile radius of the "Face" that are under investigation.

Q: Do the investigators really believe that Martians built a "fortress?"

A: No. The commonly used names "Fortress," etc., were originally chosen merely for convenience by science writer Richard C. Hoagland.

Q: Isn't "image enhancement" just a way to fake photographs?

A: See the chapter "Image Enhancement: What It Is and How It Works" in The Case For The Face: Scientists Examine the Evidence for Alien Artifacts on Mars (Adventures Unlimited, 1998).

Q: Statistics are used to test predictions about events whose outcomes are unknown before the fact, while the mounds analyzed statistically by Dr. Crater have been there for a long time. How can statistics be relevant here?

A: The angular relationships discovered by Dr. Horace W. Crater were discovered as a result of predictions made on the basis of an initial analysis of four mounds. This is called an "a priori" (before the fact) statistical result and is not "a posteriori" (claiming significance after the fact).

Q: Haven't the investigators chosen some mounds for certain geometric relations while ignoring others?

A: All the 16 mounds in the area have been taken into account.

Q: On Earth one can see naturally occurring geometric regularities like hexagonal cracks in dried river beds, why not natural geometrical regularities on Mars?

A: Naturally appearing hexagonal patterns are on a different scale and are not nearly as precise as the patterns of mounds seen in Cydonia. If the mound pattern is natural, it is unlike any natural regularities with which we are familiar.

Q: Why is it surprising that fractal analysis has shown that the Face and a few of the other so-called anomalies in Cydonia are different from the surrounding land forms when there is bound to be much variation in the texture of any given natural landscape?

A: The fractal technique does not measure mere differences in texture, but the degree of non-fractal response of an object. The more non-fractal the response, the more likely it is that the object is artificial.

Q: Couldn't erosion explain all the seemingly odd land forms found in Cydonia?

A: When an "explanation" is used to explain everything regardless of details, it is no longer an explanation.

Q: If there are artificial structures in Cydonia, then who built them?

A: Assuming the objects are artificial, speculations as to who built them would have to await ground investigation by archaeologists.

Q: What is NASA's official position regarding Cydonia and the acquisition of new images?

A: NASA's official position is that "most scientists" think the Face is an optical illusion. However, we are unaware of any serious scientific study by NASA or others that has either established the natural origin of the Cydonia anomalies or refuted the analyses performed by those who conclude some of the objects may be artificial. Recently, SPSR representatives met with NASA's Director of Solar System Studies, Dr. Carl Pilcher, on Nov. 24, 1997, and he promised full and regular imaging of Cydonia to the best of the Mars Global Surveyor's ability. Dan Goldin, NASA Administrator, also announced new data release policies on Jan. 8, 1998 that should stop the initial sequestering of data by NASA contractors and provide the public with very rapid access to NASA-acquired data.

Q: What kind of evidence would it take to convince the Cydonia investigators that they were wrong and that there was nothing there unexplainable in terms of natural forces?

A: The hypothesis of possible artificiality could be falsified by new data that produces results contrary to the present data. Failing this, ground investigation by a manned mission could confirm or invalidate the hypothesis of artificiality using standard archaeological methods.

Q: If the artificiality hypothesis is disproved, wouldn't that mean this has all been a waste of time?

A: The methodologies developed by these investigations have wide general applicability to possible future cases requiring the analysis of anomalous objects on the surfaces of planets.

Mars Anomalies Research Chronology
Highlights from 1976 to the Present

COMPILED BY DR. MARK J. CARLOTTO

O pinions about the possibility of life on Mars have changed over the years—from Percival Lowell's canals, to the dead planet imaged by the early Mariner probes, to the enormous volcanoes, great canyon systems, and channels carved by water seen by Mariner 9 and Viking and now to the apparent sedimentary layers shown in the Valles Marinaris mountain peak by Mars Global Surveyor. Among Viking's discoveries was a formation resembling a gigantic humanoid head staring into space from the surface of Mars. Although NASA has evidently not taken the time to study the Face on Mars in any depth, it has been the focus of serious investigation outside of the "mainstream" planetary science community for almost twenty years. Professionals from diverse fields of study have examined the data and concluded that certain objects including the Face may be artificial in origin and deserve further study. This article summarizes the history of the discovery and investigation of these strange objects on Mars.

1976
The first picture of the Face on Mars is taken by the Viking orbiter on July 25. This image, Viking frame 35A72, shows the object in late afternoon sun, casting long shadows which cause the controversial features to stand out in vivid relief.

On December 15, while watching a NASA film, Walter Hain in Germany is impressed by an image of the Face.

1977
Vincent DiPietro, searching NASA files, locates a second image of Face (Viking frame 70A13).

1979
DiPietro and Gregory Molenaar develop the Starburst Pixel Interleave Technique (SPIT), a highly successful method of image enhancement and clarification, and begin studying the two Viking images.

Wir, vom Mars (We from Mars) is published by Walter Hain. A compilation of fact and myth about Mars, the book includes the suggestion that the Face may be artificial.

1980

DiPietro, Molenaar and physicist Dr. John E. Brandenburg publish *Unusual Martian Surface Features.* The book contains a detailed account of their image enhancement techniques and the results when applied to the Face. On June 16, at the 156th Meeting of the American Astronomical Society in College Park, Maryland, DiPietro and Molenaar present their work.

1981

In July, at the first Case for Mars conference in Boulder, Colorado, science writer Richard C. Hoagland meets DiPietro and Molenaar.

1982

DiPietro and Molenaar's work appears in a four-page article in the April issue of *Omni* magazine.

1983

On viewing more recent photographic enhancements, Hoagland becomes interested in the Face. He eventually identifies nearby objects of interest, naming the group the "City." The objects include the "Fortress," "Cliff" and seemingly pyramidal objects as well as smaller "mounds." Hoagland observes that the "City," Face and "Cliff" appear to be aligned with the summer solstice on Mars of several hundred thousand years ago.

In the summer, Hoagland joins with anthropologist Randolfo Pozos to organize a computer conference referred to as the Independent Mars Investigation. Hoagland makes the first conference entry in December.

1984

"Martian Chronicles" computer conference takes place during the first quarter of 1984. Participants include John E. Brandenburg, Lambert Dolphin, Bill Beatty, and James Channon along with DiPietro, Molenaar, Hoagland, and Pozos.

Thomas Rautenberg at the University of California at Berkeley discusses the formation of a parallel investigation (Mars Investigation Group) with Hoagland.

The results of the Independent Mars Investigation are presented by John Brandenburg at the "Case for Mars II" conference in Boulder, Colorado in July.

The August issue of *Soviet Life* magazine reports a discovery by Russian author, Vladimir Avinsky of what appear to be pyramids on Mars.

Discover magazine publishes a report on the Case for Mars II conference in September, but with no mention of the Independent Mars Investigation paper. In the same issue, astronomer Carl Sagan mentions "enigmatic landforms" on Mars and proposes joint U.S./Soviet mission to Mars.

In the fall, a meeting takes place in Washington, D.C. between Rautenberg, Sagan, international space policy consultant David Webb, and Louis Friedman, Executive Director of The Planetary Society. Friedman, shown images of the Face, is reported to have covered his eyes and refused to look. In an aside, Sagan confides to Webb, "These are very interesting, but if anyone asks me I will deny that the meeting took place."

1985

At the National Academy of Sciences meeting in Washington D.C. in January, Sagan discusses the Mars anomalies with Hoagland. Sagan makes an offer to review material on the subject that Hoagland will send him, and finishes by saying perhaps they will be "exchanging papers in the literature."

Instead of "papers in the literature," a series of newspaper articles critical of the Independent Mars Investigation are published during the spring. The University of California withdraws its sponsorship of Mars Investigation Group formed by Rautenberg. On June 2, a popularized article by Carl Sagan entitled "The Man in the Moon," is published in *Parade Magazine*. The article includes a version of Viking frame 70A13 which has been colorized in a manner that obscures the crucial shadows. Sagan identifies this image as showing that the "Face" is actually just an ordinary hill. He is harshly critical of the investigators, putting them in the same category as "flying saucer zealots," but mentioning none of them by name.

At the Washington, D.C. "Steps to Mars" conference in mid-July, interviews with Sagan and others indicate a growing resistance in the planetary science community toward investigation of the Mars anomalies.

1986

On July 23, 1986, Sagan and Vincent DiPietro meet at the National Academy of Sciences in Washington, D.C. DiPietro shows Sagan his enhancements of the face which reveal the "eyeball" detail.

Physicist and former member of the NASA astronaut corps, Dr. Brian O'Leary, organizes the Mars Anomalies Research Society. Its members include DiPietro, Brandenburg, Webb, Dr. Mark J. Carlotto, and others.

"The Curious Case of the Humanoid Face on Mars" by Hoagland is published in *Analog* magazine's November issue.

The Face on Mars, an account of the Independent Mars Investigation computer conference, is published by Chicago Review Press. Edited and with extensive commentary by anthropologist Randolfo Pozos, the book contains photographic documentation including SPIT-processed images as well as new image enhancements by Dr. Mark J. Carlotto. Artist/anthropologist James Channon analyzes the Face and finds to be in accord with classical humanoid proportions.

Planetary Mysteries by Richard Grossinger, including an account of the Mars anomalies, is published.

1987

A paper by Carlotto, "Digital Imagery Analysis of Unusual Martian Surface Features," is rejected by the planetary science journal *Icarus* with the excuse that it is "not of sufficient scientific interest."

Icarus also rejects O'Leary's paper, "Comments on Imagery of the Face on Mars and Nearby Objects" on similar grounds. This journal previously had published eleven papers by O'Leary.

The Monuments of Mars by Richard Hoagland is published by North Atlantic Press.

Baron Johannes von Buttlar publishes *Lieben auf dem Mars* (Life on Mars) in Germany. The book becomes a huge bestseller in Germany and is translated into many different languages.

1988

After peer review, the journal *Applied Optics* accepts Carlotto's paper. The paper is published in the May 15 issue.

Russian probes Phobos I and II are launched to Mars in July. Contact with Phobos I is lost while en route to Mars.

After a press conference at National Press Club in Washington D.C., *New Scientist* (July 7) and *Newsweek* (July 25) publish articles about the Face.

Erol Torun, a cartographer at the Defense Mapping Agency in Washington D.C., undertakes a geomorphological and geometric analysis of the object called the "D&M pyramid" (after DiPietro and Molenaar). He proposees a hypothetical model of the original shape of the formation, which appears to be geometrically sophisticated and to express numerous universal mathematical constants. He concludes that no known geological process can adequately account for the formation.

Following on Torun's hypotheses, Hoagland claims that the same universal constants may be found in geometric relationships between the D&M pyramid and other nearby objects. He calls this group of objects the "Cydonia complex" and argues that the latitude of the D&M pyramid may be expressed in terms of those constants.

Hoagland, Carlotto, and Torun present research results in December at NASA's Goddard Space Flight Center in Maryland.

A new paper by Carlotto and Michael Stein, titled "A Method for Searching for Artificial Objects on Planetary Surfaces," describing fractal analysis of the Face, is submitted to the journal *Nature* on December 18. The editor refuses to review the paper.

1989

In March, the Russian probe Phobos II is sent into an uncontrolled spin as it approached the tiny Martian moon Phobos. The failure of the probe is attributed to erroneous radio transmissions.

In April, Congressman Robert A. Roe, Chairman of the House of Representatives Committee on Science, Space, and Technology, meets with Hoagland, Carlotto, and Torun.

1990

The paper by Carlotto and Stein which had been rejected by *Nature*, "A Method for Searching for Artificial Objects on Planetary Surfaces," is peer-reviewed, accepted and published in the May issue of the *Journal of the British Interplanetary Society*. Dr. Brian O'Leary's paper that was rejected by *Icarus*, "Analysis of Images of the Face on Mars and Possible Intelligent Origin," appears in a revised version in the same issue.

In a revised version of his Cosmos television series, Carl Sagan adds film footage produced by Carlotto showing three-dimensional views of the Face on Mars.

1991

"The Cydonian Hypothesis" by Brandenburg, DiPietro and Molenaar is published in the spring issue of the *Journal of Scientific Exploration*. The authors propose that the Face is artificial and was built by a former race of indigenous Martians having a humanoid form.

Hoagland asserts that the geometry of the D&M pyramid and the "Cydonia Complex" reflects tetrahedral geometry, particularly the so-called "tetrahedral latitude" constant of 19.5 degrees, which is the latitude marked out by the base of a tetrahedron embedded in a sphere.

The Martian Enigmas by Mark Carlotto is published. The book presents Carlotto's extensive work on the Viking images, using different processing techniques than those employed by DiPietro and Molenaar.

1992

In February, an audience at Goddard Space Center in Maryland hears DiPietro present his research results.

Ananda Sirisena, a technical instructor at the UNISYS Europe Training Center, publishes "Intelligent Faces on Mars?" in the July/August issue of the British professional magazine *Image Processing*. In this article Sirisena outlines his discovery of several enigmatic 4-sided pyramidal formations on Mars, not located in the Cydonia area. He also identifies a possible second Face and a mysterious and provocative feature termed "The Sirisena Quadrangle."

The Mars Observer spacecraft, carrying a sophisticated new camera designed by Malin Space Science Systems, is launched toward Mars on September 25.

A new edition of *The Monuments of Mars* is published by North Atlantic Books in Berkeley, California.

Press coverage of the Mars Observer launch, plus information found in the new edition of Monuments, prompts Professor Stanley V. McDaniel at Sonoma State University to begin an independent evaluation of the research on the Mars anomalies.

1993

In April the journal *Digital Signal Processing* publishes an invited paper by Carlotto, "Digital Image Analysis of Possible Extraterrestrial Artifacts on Mars."

Don Ecker, the director of research for *UFO Magazine*, locates a report on the peaceful uses of outer space, developed for NASA by the Brookings Institution in 1960. The report includes the suggestion that scientists may consider suppressing the discovery of extraterrestrial life or artifacts in order to avoid hypothetical public unrest.

The Mars Observer spacecraft arrives at the Red Planet, but its transmissions cease on August 21, just prior to orbital insertion. Communication with the craft is never reestablished. Along with the mysterious loss of Phobos II, this prompts Hoagland to suggest that NASA may actually remain in clandestine communication with the craft and is covering up the truth about artificial structures on Mars.

In September, Mars anomaly researchers meet in Cody Wyoming at conference organized by Tom and Cynthia Fell.

In November, a Mars Forum is sponsored by the *International Tesla Society* in Colorado Springs, CO.

McDaniel's analysis of the independent Mars investigations and NASA's policy toward the anomalies is published by North Atlantic Books under the title *The McDaniel Report*.

1994

At McDaniel's suggestion, the Society for Planetary SETI Research (SPSR) is organized to study the Mars anomalies. Members are drawn from a variety of academic and professional fields.

SPSR members James Erjavec and Ronald Nicks begin work on a geological map of the Cydonia region. Physicist Horace W. Crater, also a member of SPSR, turns his attention to the small mound formations at Cydonia that had been previously noticed by Hoagland.

1995

Crater's analysis of the geometric relationships between the mounds indicate that they are not distributed according to chance expectation. McDaniel distributes two papers privately within the SPSR, "Geometric Solution to the Pentad" and "Geometric Construction of the Square Root 2 Rectangle," in which he proposes that a regular grid pattern based on the square root of 2 accurately fits the geometric distribution of the mounds.

In June, McDaniel and Crater present their results at the 14th meeting of the Society for Scientific Exploration in Huntington Beach, California. McDaniel and Crater begin work on a paper synthesizing their separate research results.

1996

In May, Carlotto and archaeologist James F. Strange of the University of South Florida, speak before the 15th meeting of the Society for Scientific Exploration in Charlottesville, Virginia. Carlotto's paper, "Do Certain Martian Surface Features Suggest an Extraterrestrial Hypothesis?" presents a probabilistic analysis of evidence for artificiality. Carlotto also presents new evidence resulting from a comparative analysis of several features. Strange's talk, "Can Archaeological Method Apply to Planetary SETI?" applies a different test of random distribution to the mounds studied by Crater and McDaniel and also discusses Torun's geometrical model of the D&M pyramid. The probability that some of the objects are artificial is supported in both cases.

A paper titled "Atmospheric Mass Loss on Mars and the Consequences for the Cydonian Hypothesis and Early Martian Life-Forms" by Helmut Lammer is published in the autumn issue of the *Journal of Scientific Exploration*. Lammer does not rule out the possibility that the anomalous objects may be artificial, but disputes Brandenburg's hypothesis that the Face and other structures on Mars were built by native Martians.

The Demon-Haunted World is published by Carl Sagan as one of his last public statements before his death. Although remaining highly skeptical he calls for more active investigation of the anomalies by NASA and concludes that the hypothesis of artificiality can be tested, thus opening the subject to scientific inquiry by the "mainstream."

In the fall, NASA launches Pathfinder, carrying a Mars rover, and Mars Global Surveyor, replacing the lost Mars Observer and carrying an identical camera.

The Mars 96 Orbiter, which was to work in cooperation with the Mars Global Surveyor, is launched by the Russians. The spacecraft fails to reach Earth orbit.

In a tour arranged by the UK Mars Network, McDaniel lectures on the Mars anomalies at Oxford University and universities and schools in Aylesbury, Canterbury, Glasgow, and London.

1997

Astronomer Thomas Van Flandern publishes a preprint of "New Evidence of Artificiality at Cydonia on Mars." Calculating the position of the Face prior to a Martian polar shift, the paper concludes that the Face would have been located on the old Martian equator and was then oriented north-south. Van Flandern notes that this is consistent with his exploded planet hypothesis, according to which Mars was the moon of a larger planet that exploded. Because a location on the equator would have been highly visible as seen from such a planet, Van Flandern concludes that a cultural rationale for the Face is thereby established.

Carlotto's paper, "Evidence in Support of the Hypothesis that Certain Objects on Mars are Artificial in Origin," is published by the *Journal of Scientific Exploration*. Carlotto analyzes all of the evidence to date using a Bayesian method for calculating probabilities. He concludes that the probability weighs in favor of possible artificiality and that the combined evidence satisfies Sagan's criterion for "extraordinary evidence."

Crater and McDaniel complete their analysis of the mound configuration at Cydonia. SPSR publishes a preprint, "Mound Configurations on the Martian Cydonia Plain." Their conclusion is that the mound formation cannot be accounted for by ordinary geomorphological causes and is highly anomalous.

A revised and expanded edition of Carlotto's *The Martian Enigmas* is published by North Atlantic Books. A video of McDaniel's lecture at Aylesbury in England is released by Amora International. Ltd. *QUEST for Knowledge Magazine,* a British science publication, publishes a special Mars anomaly edition containing articles exclusively by SPSR members. O'Leary embarks on a lecture tour of England. In September, McDaniel and Carlotto lecture at a Mars anomaly convention in Harpenden, England sponsored by TopEvents Ltd, publishers of *QUEST.*

In August, John Brandenburg's paper, "Mars as the parent body of the CI carbonaceous chondrites and implications for Mars biological and climatological history" is presented at a conference on "Instruments, Methods, and Missions for the investigation of Extraterrestrial Microorganisms" sponsored by the International Society for Optical Engineering in San Diego, California. Brandenburg concludes that meteorite evidence supports the likelihood of a long-term past environment on Mars favorable for the development and evolution of Martian life.

On November 11, Mars Global Surveyor images show sedimentary layers in Valles Marinaris peak, thousands of feet thick, supporting the likelihood of long-term standing water on Mars.

On November 24, at the invitation of Dr. Carl Pilcher, Acting Science Director for Solar System Exploration at NASA, six members of SPSR present summaries of their research. Attending are Dr. Pilcher, Dr. Joseph Boyce of NASA, and SPSR members DiPietro, Crater, Webb, Carlotto, Brandenburg, and McDaniel. At the conclusion of the meeting, Pilcher states that it is "official NASA policy" to photograph the anomaly area with the high resolution camera aboard the Mars Global Surveyor.

1998

Daniel Goldin makes NASA policy change announcement guaranteeing rapid access to all images obtained during future missions and stopping NASA subcontractors from withholding data and images from the public for extended periods.

References

Publications by Society for Planetary Research (SPSR) Members

Brandenburg, J.E., "Constraints on the Martian Cratering Rate Based on the SNC Meteorites and Implications for Mars Climactic History." *Earth, Moon and Planets*, Vol. 67, pp. 35-45, 1995.

Brandenburg, J.E., "Mars as the Parent Body of the Carbonaceous Chondrites and Implications for Mars Biological and Climactic History." *Proceedings of the SPIE*, Vol. 3111, pp. 69-80, July, 1997.

Brandenburg, J.E., "Possible Parent Body for the Carbonaceous Chondrites: Mars." American Geophysical Union Conference, Baltimore, MD, pp. 52A-4, June 1995.

Brandenburg, J.E., and DiPietro, V. "Did the Lyot Impact End the Liquid Water Era on Mars?" American Geophysical Union Conference, Baltimore, MD, P52A-3, June 1995.

Brandenburg, J.E., DiPietro, V., and Molenaar, G., "The Cydonian Hypothesis." *Journal of Scientific Exploration*, Vol. 5, No. 1, 1991.

Carlotto, Mark J., "Digital Imagery Analysis of Unusual Martian Surface Features." *Applied Optics*. Vol. 27, No. 10, 1988.

Carlotto, Mark J., "Evidence in Support of the Hypothesis that Certain Objects on Mars are Artificial in Origin," *Journal of Scientific Exploration*. Vol. 11, No. 2, 1997.

Carlotto, Mark J., *The Martian Enigmas: A Closer Look*. North Atlantic Books, Berkeley, CA, 1991, Revised Edition, 1997.

Carlotto, Mark J. and Stein, M. C., "A Method for Searching for Artificial Objects on Planetary Surfaces." *Journal of the British Interplanetary Society*, Vol. 43, No. 5, May, 1990.

Crater, Horace W., "A Probabilistic Analysis of Geomorphological Anomalies in the Cydonian Region of the Martian Surface." Paper delivered in Cody, Wyoming at the Moon/Mars conference, September 16, 1994.

Crater, Horace W., "A Statistical Study of Angular Placements of Features on Mars." Paper delivered at Society for Scientific Exploration meetings, June 15, 1995.

Crater, Horace W. and McDaniel, Stanley V., "Mound Configurations on the Martian Cydonia Plain: A Geometrical and Probabilistic Analysis." Submitted for publication, preprint published by SPSR, c/o Dr. Horace W. Crater, Rm. 204, The University of Tennessee Space Institute, Tullahoma, TN 37388.

DiPietro, V., Molenaar, G., & Brandenburg, J., Unusual Mars Surface Features. Mars Research, P.O. Box 284, Glenn Dale, MD 20769. First Edition, 1982; Fourth Edition, 1988.

Erjavec, J. and Nicks, R., "A Geologic/Geomorphic Investigative Approach to Some of the Enigmatic Landforms in Cydonia." in *The Martian Enigmas*. North Atlantic Books, Berkeley, CA, Revised Edition, 1997.

McDaniel, Stanley V., *The McDaniel Report: On the Failure of Executive, Congressional, and Scientific Responsibility in Setting Mission Priorities for NASA's Mars Exploration Program*. North Atlantic Books, Berkeley, CA, 1994.

O'Leary, B., "Analysis of Images of the Face on Mars and Possible Intelligent Origin." *Journal of the British Interplanetary Society*, Vol. 43, No. 5, May 1990.

O'Leary, B., *Exploring Inner and Outer Space*. North Atlantic Books, Berkeley, CA, 1989.

O'Leary, B., *Mars 1999*. Stackpole Books, Harrisburg, PA, 1987.

O'Leary, B., *Miracle in the Void*. Kamapua'a Press, Kihei, HI, 1994.

O'Leary, B., *The Second Coming of Science*. North Atlantic Books, Berkeley, CA, 1993.

Pozos, Randolfo R., *The Face on Mars: Evidence for a Lost Civilization?* Chicago Review Press, 814 N. Franklin, Chicago, IL 60610, 1986. Also available from North Atlantic Books, 2800 Woolsey Street, Berkeley, CA, 94705.

Sirisena, Ananda, "Intelligent Faces on Mars?" *Image Processing*, London, July/Aug., 1992.

Strange, James F. "Some Statistical Observations on the Distance between some of the Mounds at Cydonia." Paper presented before the Society for Scientific Exploration at Charlottesville, VA, May, 1996.

Strange, James F., *Archaeology, The Rabbis and Early Christianity*. Abingdon Press, Nashville, TN, 1981.

Strange., James F., "The Excavation of the Ancient Synagogue at Gush Hulau, Israel." The Meiron Excavation Project, Vol. V, 1990.

Torun, Erol, "The Geomorphology and Geometry of the D & M Pyramid." 1988. Appendices A and B added June and August, 1989. An updated version, 1996, is available on the World Wide Web at the following address: http://www.well.com/user/etorun/pyramid.html.

Van Flandern, T., Dark Matter, Missing Planets and New Comets, North Atlantic Books, Berkeley, CA, pp. 155-236, 1993.

von Buttlar, Baron Johannes, *Leben auf dem Mars* (Life on Mars—in German), Herbig Verlag, Munich, Germany, 1987; Revised Edition, 1997.

von Buttlar, Baron Johannes, *Terraforming* (in German), Heyne Verlag, Munich, Germany, 1996.

Websites of SPSR Members

Carlotto, Dr. Mark J.   http://www.psrw.com/~markc/marshome.html
Erjavec, James   http://www.psrw.com/~markc/Other/mars/erjavec.html
Fleming, Lan   http://www.VGL.org
McDaniel, Prof. Stanley V.   http://www.mcdanielreport.com
O'Leary , Dr. Brian   http://www.maui.net/~kamapuaa
Torun, Erol   http://www.well.com/user/etorun/pyramid.html
Van Flandern , Dr. Thomas   http://www.metaresearch.org

References & Related Publications

Adams, Douglas, *Hitchhiker's Guide to the Galaxy*. Ballantine Books, NY, NY, 1995.

American Society of Photogrammetry, *Manual of Photo Interpretation*. p. 109, 1960.

Avinsky, V., "Pyramids on Mars?," *Soviet Life*. August, 1984.

Baker, V.R., Strom, R.G., Gulick, V.C., Kargel, J.S., Komatsu, G., and Kale, V.S., "Ancient Oceans, Ice Sheets and the Hydrological Cycle on Mars." *Nature*, Vol. 352, August 15, 1991.

Burgess, Eric, *Return to the Red Planet*. Columbia University Press, NY, NY, 1990.

Caidin, M., Barbree, J., and Wright, S., *Destination Mars: In Art, Myth, and Science*. Penguin Studio, NY, NY, 1997.

Carr, Michael H., *The Surface of Mars*. Yale University Press, New Haven, CN, 1981.

Carroll, Michael, "Braking for Mars," *Popular Science*. pp. 62-63, February, 1998.

Cattermole, P., *Mars: The Story of the Red Planet*. Chapman and Hall, NY, NY, 1992.

Central Conference of American Rabbis, *Gates of Prayer: The New Union Prayer Book*. NY, NY, 1975.

Chandrasekhar S., *Hydrodynamic and Hydromagnetic Stability*. Oxford Univ. Press, 1961, (Chapter 2 discusses the Bernard convection problem.), Dover, 1981.

Channon, James, in Hoagland, Richard, *The Monuments of Mars: A City on the Edge of Forever*. North Atlantic Books, Berkeley, CA, pp. 166-69, 1987.

Clarke, Arthur C. and Kubrick, Stanley, *2001: A Space Odyssey*. New American Library, 1993.

Clarke, Arthur C., *The Snows of Olympus: A Garden on Mars*. W.W. Norton, NY, NY, 1995.

DiGregorio, Barry and Levin, Gil, *Mars: The Living Planet*. Frog, Ltd., Berkeley, CA, 1997.

Fiebag, Johannes, "Analysis Of Tectonic Directional Pattern (Richtungsmuster) On Mars: No Indication Of Artificial Structures In The Southern Cydonia Region." in *Astronautik Heft* 1, pp. 9–13, 1990.

Feldenkrais, Moshé, *The Elusive Obvious*. Meta Publications, Santa Cruz, CA, 1981.

Forget, F. and Pierrehumbert, Raymond, "Warming Early Mars with Carbon Dioxide Clouds that Scatter Infrared Radiation." *Science*, 278: (5341) 1273 (in Reprints), Nov. 14, 1997.

Foster, G. V., "Non-human Artifacts in the Solar System." *Spaceflight*, Vol. 14, pp. 447-453, Dec., 1972.

Ghyka, Matila, *The Geometry of Art and Life*. Dover paperback reprint, (Esp. Chapter VIII "Greek and Gothic Canons of Proportion."), 1946.

Greeley, R., and Iverson, J.D., *Wind as a Geological Process on Earth, Mars, Venus, and Titan*. Cambridge University Press, Cambridge, England, 1985.

Grossinger, Richard, *Planetary Mysteries*. North Atlantic Books, Berkeley, CA, 1987.

Guest, E. and Butterworth, P. S., "Geological Observations in the Cydonia Region of Mars from Viking." *Journal of Geophysical Research*, Vol. 82, No. 28, Sept., 30, 1977.

Hain, W., *Wir, vom Mars* (We, from Mars), Ellenberg Verlag, Cologne, Germany, 1979.

Harp, Elmer, Jr., "Threshold Indicators of Culture in Air Photo Archaeology: A Case Study in the Arctic." Foley, J. D., and Van Dam, A., *Fundamentals of Interactive Computer Graphics*. Addison-Wesley, Reading, MA, 1983.

Hartmann, Wm. K., "Red Planet Rendezvous." *Astronomy*, pp. 50-53, March, 1998.

Hoagland, Richard C., *The Monuments of Mars: A City on the Edge of Forever*. North Atlantic Books, 2800 Woolsey Street, Berkeley, CA 94705. First Edition, 1987; Second Edition, 1992; Third Edition, 1996.

Horn, B. K. P., "Understanding Image Intensities." *Artificial Intelligence*, Vol. 8, pp. 201-231, 1977.

Horn, B. K. P., "Hill Shading and the Reflectance Map." Image Understanding Workshop, Palo Alto, CA, 1979.

Hoover, Richard B., Editor, "Instruments, Methods and Missions for the Investigation of Extraterrestrial Microorganisms," *Proceedings of the International Society for Optical Engineering*, Vol. 3111, July, 1997.

Hoover, Richard B., "Meteorites, Microfossils and Exobiology," *Proceedings of the International Society for Optical Engineering*, Vol. 3111, pp. 115-136, July, 1997.

Kerridge, John F., and Matthews, Mildred Shapeley, *Meteorites and the Early Solar System*. Univeristy of Arizona Press, Tucson, AZ, 1988.

Lammer, H., "Atmospheric Mass Loss on Mars and the Consequences for the Cydonian Hypothesis and Early Martian Life Forms," *Journal of Scientific Exploration*, Vol. 10, No. 3, 1996.

Legon, John A. R., "A Ground Plan at Giza." *Discussions In Egyptology 10*, 1988, pp. 33-39.

Legon, John A. R., "The Giza Ground Plan and Sphinx." *Discussions In Egyptology 14*, 1989, pp. 53-60.

Legon, John A. R., "The Geometry of the Bent Pyramid." *GM*, 116, 1990, pp. 65-72.

Levin, G. and Straat, P, "A Reappraisal of Life on Mars." *Proceedings of the NASA Mars Conference*, July, 1986. Published by the American Astronomical Society, Vol. 71, Science and Technology Series.

Levin, G., "The Life on Mars Dilemma and the Sample Return Mission." Workshop on Mars Sample Return Science held at the Lunar and Planetary Institute, LPI Report No. 88-07.

Levin, G., "The Viking Labeled Release Experiment and Life on Mars." in "Instruments, Methods and Missions for the Investigation of Extraterrestrial Microorganisms," *Proceedings of the International Society for Optical Engineering*, Vol. 3111, p. 146-161, July, 1997.

Malin, M.C., "The Face on Mars." (unpublished). Online version can be found at http://barsoom.msss.com/education/facepage/face.html, 1996.

Mason, B., *Principles of Geochemistry*, John Wiley & Sons, New York City, NY, 1982.

McGill, G.E., "The Martian Crustal Dichotomy," Lunar and Planetary Institute Technical Report 98-04, 1989.

McKay, D.S., Gibson, E.K., Thomas-Keprta, K.L., Vali, H., Romanek, C.S., Clemett, S.J., Chillier, X.D.F., Meachling, C.R. and Zare, R.N., "Search for Past Life on Mars: Possible Relic Biogenic Activity in Martian Meteorite ALH84001," *Science*, Vol. 273, 16, August, 1996.

Morris, Robert C., "Sedimentary and Tectonic History of the Ouachipa Mountains," in Dickenson, Wm. R., editor, *Tectonics and Sedimentation*. SEPN, Tulsa, OK, pp. 120-142, 1974.

Murray, B. , Malin, M. and Greeley, R., *Earthlike Planets: Surfaces of Mercury, Venus, Earth, Moon, Mars*. W. H. Freeman, San Francisco, CA, 1981.

Nagy, Bartholomew, *Carbonaceous Meteorites*, Elsevier Scientific Publishing Co., NY, NY, 1975

Norton, O. R., *Rocks from Space*. Mountain Press Publishing Co., Missoula, Montana, 1994.

Pentland, A., "The Transform Method for Shape-From-Shading," MIT Media Lab Vision Sciences Tech. Report 106, July 15, 1988.

Parker, T.J., Gorsline, D.S., Saunders, R.S., Pieri, D.C. and Schneeberger, D.M., "Coastal Geomorphology of the Martian Northern Plains." *J. Geophys. Res.*, 82, No. E6, pp. 11,061-11,078, 1993.

Peli, T. and Lim, J., "Adaptive Filtering for Image Enhancement." *Optical Eng.*, Vol. 12, No. 1, 1982.

Pittendrigh, Colin et. al., ed., Biology and the Exploration of Mars: Report of a Study Held under the Auspices of the Space Science Board, National Academy of Sciences National Research Council, 1964-1965." Chapter entitled "Remote Detection of Terrestrial Life," 1965.

Rieder, R, Economou, T., Wanke, H., Turkevich, A., Crisp, J., Bruckner, J., Dreibus, G., and McSween Jr., H. Y, 1997, "The Chemical Composition of Martian Soil and Rocks Returned by the Mobile Alpha Proton X-ray Spectrometer: Preliminary Results from the X-ray Mode," *Science*, v. 278, p. 1771-1774.

Robinson, Kim Stanley, *Red Mars*. Bantam, NY, NY, 1993.

Robinson, Kim Stanley, *Green Mars*. Bantam, NY, NY, 1994.

Robinson, Kim Stanley, *Blue Mars*. Bantam, NY, NY, 1996.

Sagan, C. and Wallace, D., "A Search for Life on Earth at 100 Meter Resolution," *Icarus*. Vol. 15, pp. 515-554, 1971.

Sagan, Carl, "The Man in the Moon." *Parade Magazine*. June 2, 1985.

Sagan, Carl, *The Demon-Haunted World: Science as a Candle in the Dark*. Random House, NY, NY, 1996.

Sagan, Carl., letter to Mark Carlotto dated September 10, 1986.

Schreiber, W., "Image Processing for Quality Improvement." *Proceedings IEEE*, Vol. 66, No. 12, Dec. 1978.

Schultz, P.H. and Lutz, A.B., "Polar Wandering on Mars", *Icarus*, 73, pp. 91-141, 1988.

Shklovskii, I. S. and Sagan, Carl, *Intelligent Life in the Universe*. Dell, NY, NY, 1967.

Stein, M. C., "Fractal Image Models and Object Detection." *Society of Photo-optical Instrumentation Engineers*, Vol. 845, pp. 293-300, 1987.

Stuart, J. T., "On the Cellular Patterns in Thermal Convection." *Journal of Fluid Mechanics*, Vol. 18, pp. 481-498, 1964.

Sturrock, P.A., "Applied Statistical Inference," *Journal of Scientific Exploration*, Vol. 8, No. 4, 1994.

Suppe, John, *Principles of Structural Geology*. Prentice Hall, Edgerton, New Jersey, 1985.

Tom, V., "Adaptive filter techniques for digital image enhancement." *Proceedings SPIE*, Vol. 528, 1985.

Tom, V., Merenyi, R., Carlotto, M. and Heller, W., "Advanced Enhancement Techniques for Digitized Images." 15th Symposium on Nondestructive Evaluation, San Antonio, TX, April, 1985.

van Dyke, Milton (Assembler), *An Album of Fluid Motion*. Parabolic Press, Stanford, CA, 1982.

Vinogradov, A. P. and Ronov, A. B., 1956, "Composition of the Sedimentary Rocks of the Russian Platform in Relation to the History of its Tectonic Movements," *Geochemistry*, no. 6, pp. 533–559.

Vogt, Evon Z., Ed., *Aerial Photography in Anthropological Field Research*. Harvard University Press, Cambridge, MA, 1974.

Wang, D., Vagnucci, A. and Li, C., "Digital Image Enhancement: A Survey." *Computer Vision, Graphics, and Image Processing*, Vol. 24, pp. 363-381, 1983.

Wilson, D. R., *Air Photo Interpretation for Archaeologists*. St. Martin's Press, New York, NY, p. 186, 1982.

Zubrin, Robert and Wagner, Richard. *The Case for Mars: The Plan to Settle the Red Planet*. Free Press, NY, NY 1996.

Related Web Sites

http://cmex-www.arc.nasa.gov (Center for Mars Exploration—includes links to most of the major Pathfinder and Global Surveyor sites.)

http://www.gsfc.nasa.gov/education/education_home.html (Educational and space image resources from National Space Science Data Center)

http://www.psrw.com/~markc/marshome.html (Face on Mars Homepage from Mark Carlotto, also has copies of his refereed journal articles.)

http://photojournal.jpl.nasa.gov (JPL's Planetary Photojournal—many beautiful images and extensive data from all of the planets.)

http://barsoom.msss.com (Malin Space Science Systems Mars images—Global Surveyor images and analysis from the MGS Camera operator.)

http://www.mcdanielreport.com (Stanley McDaniel discusses the science and politics of Cydonia.)

How You Can Help

If you or your group would like to support the efforts to resolve the Cydonia investigatioon, please contact the number below to get a faxed or emailed list of possible constructive actions you can take.

To Contact Authors

For interviews with authors for magazines, newspapers, television or radio, or for book, movie, CD-ROM, foreign or reprint rights, please contact project agent Stephen Corrick at Mind Into Matter (773) 381-1122, fax (773) 381-1899 or e-mail Hoomai@aol.com.

About The Authors

- Dr. John E. Brandenburg is a plasma physicist and rocket propulsion system developer who works for a NASA sub-contractor.

- Dr. Mark J. Carlotto is an image scientist with twenty years experience in digital satellite remote sensing. His work has appeared in *OMNI*, *Newsweek* and in Carl Sagan's "Cosmos" series.

- Dr. Horace Crater is a quantum physicist, an expert in relativistic quantum mechanics and a professor at the University of Tennessee Space Institute.

- Vince DiPietro is an engineer and image processing specialist, long-time contractor at NASA's Goddard Space Flight Center and the man who most directly brought the Mars Face to public attention.

- Dan Drasin is an original member of the Mars Investigation, and is an imaging expert who works for New Dimensions Radio.

- James Erjavec, MS, is a geologist and specialist in mapping and computer graphics who is working on US government compliance projects for the State of Ohio.

- Lan Fleming, MS, is an engineer and computer systems analyst, for the Intelligent Systems Laboratory at NASA's Johnson Space in Houston.

- Harry Moore, MS, is an engineering geologist and head of the geotechnical office for the Tennessee Department of Transportation.

- Chris O'Kane is a long-time Mars researcher and photographic specialist whose work with English school children has received broad national recognition.

- Dr. Brian O'Leary is a space scientist, former professor at Cornell and several other university space science programs and, in 1967-68, a member of the NASA Astronaut Corps.

- Dr. Randolfo Pozos is an anthropologist and co-organizer of the original Independent Mars Investigation.

- Ananda Sirisena has been an image processing engineer and trainer for Unisys and is a long-time Mars researcher.

- Cesar Sirvent is a graduate student in Physics at the University of Zaragosa, Spain, and former director of the science magazine, *Lumen*.

- Dr. James V. Strange is a Biblical archaeologist and Professor, and a former Dean and Former Chair of the Department of Religious Studies at the University of South Florida.

- Dr. Mitchell R. Swartz is a ScD and MD with an emphasis in biomedical engineering and radiation imaging techniques.

- Erol Torun is a cartographer and physical scientist with a specialty in geomorphology for the Defense Mapping Agency.

- Dr. Tom Van Flandern is a Former Director of the Celestial Mechanics Branch of the US Naval Observatory and currently is Head of the MetaResearch Foundation.

- Baron Johannes von Buttlar is a Fellow of the Royal Astronomical Society and is Europe's most widely published science writer.

- Dr. David Webb is a member of the National Commission on Space and has pioneered several college-level space science programs.

- Dr. Michael Zimmerman is a professor and former chair of the Department of Philosophy at Tulane University.

About the Editors

- Professor Stanley V. McDaniel is the former chairman of the Philosophy Department at Sonoma State University in California, where he taught courses in logic, theory of knowledge, philosophy of science and eastern philosophy for over twenty-five years. He is the author of *The McDaniel Report* on the Martian anomalies.

- Monica Rix Paxson is the author of several published books and the editor/developer of many more. Her editorship of *The Case for the Face* fits perfectly with her lifetime goal of introducing books and ideas that will ultimately have wide cultural impact.

Acknowledgements

The editors, and authors, gratefully acknowledge the contributions, in many discussions over the past four years, of those members of SPSR who are not directly represented by articles in this volume—Dr. Marie Kagan, Gerry Zeitlin, Gregory Molenaar, Dr. Alexey Arkhipov, Dr. Conley Powell, Dr. Charles Walker, Dr. Kenneth Wheaton, Dr. Lambert Dolphin, Dr. Johannes Fiebag. We also express our heartfelt appreciation to Mr. Stephen Corrick, without whose tireless work as agent this material might never have seen publication. We wish to extend our thanks to all those others who, in the two-decade history of the Mars anomaly problem, even though sometimes outside the limits of scientific protocol, have kept the public aware of and interested in the mysteries of Mars through their many speculations and bold leaps of imagination. Also we do not fail to remember Tom Rautenberg and Roger Keeling, early supporters of the Mars research projects. In the UK we acknowledge the efforts of the UK Mars Network, which led among other things to various lectures by our members in England and Scotland: Malcolm Smith, David Eccott, and Robert Johnston. We are deeply appreciative of NASA Administrator Daniel Goldin and of David McKay and his associates, whose brave announcement of microfossils in ALH84001 brought Mars science back to "life." Finally, we thank Drs. Carl Pilcher and Joseph Boyce of NASA, and Mr. Glenn Cunningham of the Jet Propulsion Laboratory, for their outstanding scientific integrity in responding to our research with the promise that NASA will, without question, make every possible effort to uncover the truth that lies hidden in the northern plains of Mars.

Index

NEW BOOKS FROM AUP

THE CASE FOR THE FACE
Scientists Examine the Evidence for Alien Artifacts on Mars
edited by Stanley McDaniel and Monica Rix Paxson
Mars Imagery by Mark Carlotto
The ultimate compendium of analyses of the Face on Mars and the other monuments in the Cydonia region. *The Case For the Face* unifies the research and opinions of a remarkably accomplished group of scientists, including a former NASA astronaut, a quantum physicist who is the chair of a space science program, leading meteor researchers, nine Ph.D.'s, the best-selling science author in Germany and more. The book includes: NASA research proving we're not the first intelligent race in this solar system; 120 amazing high resolution images never seen before by the general public; three separate doctoral statistical studies demonstrating the likelihood of artificial objects at the Cydonian site to be over 99%; and other definitive proof of life on Mars. Solid science presented in a readable, richly illustrated format. This book will also be featured in a Learning Channel special featuring Leonard Nimoy.
320 PAGES. 6X9 PAPERBACK. ILLUSTRATED. INDEX & BIBLIOGRAPHY. $17.95. CODE: CFF

ATLANTIS IN AMERICA
Navigators of the Ancient World
by Ivar Zapp and George Erikson
This book is an intensive examination of the archeological sites of the Americas, an examination that reveals civilization has existed here for tens of thousands of years. Zapp is an expert on the enigmatic giant stone spheres of Costa Rica, and maintains that they were sighting stones found throughout the Pacific as well as in Egypt and the Middle East. They were used to teach star-paths and sea to the world-wide navigators of the ancient world. While the Mediterranean and European regions "forgot" world-wide navigation and fought wars the Mesoamericans of diverse races were building vast interconnected cities without walls. This Golden Age of ancient America was merely a myth of suppressed history—until now. Profusely illustrated, chapters are on Navigators of the Ancient World; Pyramids & Megaliths: Older Than You Think; Ancient Ports and Colonies; Cataclysms of the Past; Atlantis: From Myth To Reality; The Serpent and the Cross: The Loss of the City States; Calendars and Star Temples; and more.
360 PAGES. 6X9 PAPERBACK. ILLUSTRATED. BIBLIOGRAPHY & INDEX. $17.95. CODE: AIA

ANCIENT MICRONESIA
& the Lost City of Nan Madol
by David Hatcher Childress
Micronesia, a vast archipelago of islands west of Hawaii and south of Japan, contains some of the most amazing megalithic ruins in the world. Part of our *Lost Cities of the Pacific* series, this volume explores the incredible conformations on various Micronesian islands, especially the fantastic and little-known ruins of Nan Madol on Pohnpei Island. The huge canal city of Nan Madol contains over 250 million tons of basalt columns over an 11 square-mile area of artificial islands. Much of the huge city is submerged, and underwater structures can be found to an estimated 80 feet. Islanders' legends claim that the basalt rocks, weighing up to 50 tons, were magically levitated into place by the powerful forefathers. Other ruins in Micronesia that are profiled include the Latte Stones of the Marianas, the menhirs of Palau, the megalithic canal city on Kosrae Island, megaliths on Guam, and more.
256 PAGES. 6X9 PAPERBACK. HEAVILY ILLUSTRATED. INCLUDES A COLOR PHOTO SECTION. BIBLIOGRAPHY & INDEX. $16.95. CODE: AMIC

THE ENERGY GRID
Harmonic 695, The Pulse of the Universe
by Captain Bruce Cathie.
This is the breakthrough book that explores the incredible potential of the Energy Grid and the Earth's Unified Field all around us. Bruce Cathie's first book *Harmonic 33*, was published in 1968 when he was a commercial pilot in New Zealand. Since then Captain Bruce Cathie has been the premier investigator into the amazing potential of the infinite energy that surrounds our planet every microsecond. Cathie investigates the Harmonics of Light and how the Energy Grid is created. In this amazing book are chapters on UFO propulsion, Nikola Tesla, Unified Equations, the Mysterious Aerials, Pythagoras & the Grid, Nuclear detonation and the Grid, maps of the ancients, an Australian Stonehenge examined, more.
255 PAGES. 6X9 TRADEPAPER. ILLUSTRATED. $15.95. CODE: TEG

THE BRIDGE TO INFINITY
Harmonic 371244
by Captain Bruce Cathie
Cathie has popularized the concept that the earth is criss-crossed by an electromagnetic grid system that can be used for anti-gravity, free energy, levitation and more. The book includes a new analysis of the harmonic nature of reality, acoustic levitation, pyramid power, harmonic receiver towers and UFO propulsion. It concludes that today's scientists have at their command a fantastic store of knowledge with which to advance the welfare of the human race.
204 PAGES. 6X9 TRADEPAPER. ILLUSTRATED. $14.95. CODE: BTF

BRUCE L. CATHIE
THE BRIDGE TO INFINITY

HARMONIC 371244

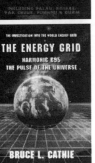

24 HOUR CREDIT CARD ORDERS—CALL: 815-253-6390 FAX: 815-253-6300
EMAIL: AUPHQ@FRONTIERNET.NET HTTP://WWW.AZSTARNET.COM/~AUP

BOOKS ON MARS & SPACE

THE MARTIAN ENIGMAS
A Closer Look
by Mark J. Carlotto
The second edition of Carlotto's large format book with state-of-the-art digital image processing of the controversial Vik
photos of the famous Face, pyramids, and other unusual objects on Mars. A literal coffee-table photo book of pyramids, the f
roads and unusual structures on Mars. Packed with illustrations and photographs. This new edition contains additional resea
supporting evidence that we are not alone.
207 PAGES. 8x10 TRADEPAPER. ILLUSTRATED. $18.95 CODE: MAR

THE MCDANIEL REPORT
by Stanley V. McDaniel
This large format, tradepaper book is an analysis of the Cydonia Martian images and a condemnation of NASA and its failu
to seriously look into the possible evidence for artificial structures on Mars. Originally prepared as a briefing on the "Marti
Hypothesis" for government officials, this scientific document, well illustrated with maps, charts and photos, belongs in eve
"extraterrestrial archaeology" library.
172 PAGES. 8XL1 TRADEPAPER. ILLUSTRATED. APPENDIX. $20.00. CODE: TMR

EXTRATERRESTRIAL ARCHAEOLOGY
David Hatcher Childress

With 100s of photos and illustrations, Extraterrestrial Archaeology takes the reader to the strange and fascinating worlds of Mars, t
Moon, Mercury, Venus, Saturn and other planets for a look at the alien structures that appear there. Using official NASA and Sov
photos, as well as other photos taken via telescope, this book seeks to prove that many of the planets (and moons) of our solar syste
are in some way inhabited by intelligent life. The book includes many blow-ups of NASA photos and detailed diagrams of stru
tures—particularly on the Moon.
- NASA PHOTOS OF PYRAMIDS AND DOMED CITIES ON THE MOON.
- PYRAMIDS AND GIANT STATUES ON MARS.
- HOLLOW MOONS OF MARS AND OTHER PLANETS.
- ROBOT MINING VEHICLES THAT MOVE ABOUT THE MOON PROCESSING VALUABLE METALS.
- NASA & RUSSIAN PHOTOS OF SPACE-BASES ON MARS AND ITS MOONS.
- A BRITISH SCIENTIST WHO DISCOVERED A TUNNEL ON THE MOON, AND OTHER "BOTTOMLESS CRATERS."
- EARLY CLAIMS OF TRIPS TO THE MOON AND MARS.
- STRUCTURAL ANOMALIES ON VENUS, SATURN, JUPITER, MERCURY,URANUS & NEPTUNE.
- NASA, THE MOON AND ANTI-GRAVITY. PLUS MORE. HIGHLY ILLUSTRATED WITH PHOTOS, DIAGRAMS AND MAPS!
304 PAGES. 8x11 PAPERBACK. BIBLIOGRAPHY, INDEX, APPENDIX. $18.95. CODE: ETA

DARK MATTER, MISSING PLANETS & NEW COMETS
Paradoxes Resolved--Origins Illuminated
by Tom Van Flandern
In recent years, astronomy's main theory of cosmology, the Big Bang, has been challenged by many. Astronomer Van Flande
joins these arguments with a new "Meta Model." The book shows new evidence for the asteroid belt as a "planetary break-up;" ar
argues that comets may develop in a different manner from that previously thought. This book gives the latest information abo
the possible existence of a tenth planet. A scholarly debate on the current issues in astronomy. Amongst those presented are: th
moons of Mars, Neptune's retrograde moon, the nature of Jupiter's Great Red Spot.
428 PAGES. 6x9 TRADEPAPER. ILLUSTRATED. BIBLIOGRAPHY. $18.95. CODE: DARK

PARADIGM WARS
Consciousness Shifts on the Road to the Millenium
by Mark B. Woodhouse

This thick book is a comprehensive overview of New Paradigm thought and how it clashes with the old belief system of th
West. The author explores a wide range of topics including modern physics and Eastern mysticism, reincarnation, Kirli
photographs, paranormal research, millennial prophecies, psychic healing, and more. Included is a chapter on UFOs, alien
government cover-ups and abductions. Probably the most important chapter is a new perspective on the geometry of the struc
tures on Mars. With 25 pages of sacred geometry and the Martian artifacts for researchers into Extraterrestrial Archaeolog
632 PAGES. 6x9 PAPERBACK. ILLUSTRATED. $22.50. CODE: PDW

THE SECOND COMING OF SCIENCE
by Brian O'Leary, Ph.D.
Former astronaut O'Leary, takes the reader through the new science with first hand accounts with Sai Baba, the Face on Mar
Marcel Vogel on crystals, crop circles, object materializations, more.
204 PAGES. 6x9 PAPERBACK. ILLUSTRATED. $12.95. CODE: SCS

THE SECOND COMING OF SCIENCE VIDEO
with Brian O'Leary, Ph.D.
Former astronaut O'Leary, author of *Exploring Inner & Outer Space*, takes the readers of his books on a visual tour through th
new science with a look at Sai Baba, the Face On Mars, Marcel Vogel on crystals, crop circles, object materializations, more.
90 MINUTES. VHS VIDEO CASSETTE. $29.95. CODE: SCSV

24 HOUR CREDIT CARD ORDERS—CALL: 815-253-6390 FAX: 815-253-6300
EMAIL: AUPHQ@FRONTIERNET.NET HTTP://WWW.AZSTARNET.COM/~AUP

One Adventure Place
P.O. Box 74
Kempton, Illinois 60946
United States of America
Tel.: 815-253-6390 • Fax: 815-253-6300
Email: aup@azstarnet.com
http://www.azstarnet.com/~aup

ORDERING INSTRUCTIONS

➤ Remit by USD$ Check or Money Order
➤ Credit Cards: Visa, MasterCard, Discovery, & American Express Accepted
➤ Prices May Change Without Notice

SHIPPING CHARGES

United States

➤ Postal Book Rate { $2.50 First Item / 50¢ Each Additional Item
➤ Priority Mail { $3.50 First Item / $2.00 Each Additional Item
➤ UPS { $3.50 First Item / $1.00 Each Additional Item

NOTE: UPS Delivery Available to Mainland USA Only

Canada

➤ Postal Book Rate { $3.00 First Item / $1.00 Each Additional Item
➤ Postal Air Mail { $5.00 First Item / $2.00 Each Additional Item
➤ Personal Checks or Bank Drafts MUST BE USD$ and Drawn on a US Bank
➤ Canadian Postal Money Orders OK
➤ Payment MUST BE USD$

All Other Countries

➤ Surface Delivery { $6.00 First Item / $2.00 Each Additional Item
➤ Postal Air Mail { $12.00 First Item / $8.00 Each Additional Item
➤ Payment MUST BE USD$
➤ Checks MUST BE USD$ and Drawn on a US Bank
➤ Add $5.00 for Air Mail Subscription to Future Adventures Unlimited Catalogs

SPECIAL NOTES

➤ RETAILERS: Standard Discounts Available
➤ BACKORDERS: We Backorder all Out-of-Stock Items Unless Otherwise Requested
➤ PRO FORMA INVOICES: Available on Request
➤ VIDEOS: NTSC Mode Only
PAL & SECAM Mode Videos Are Not Available

European Office:
Adventures Unlimited, PO Box 372, Dronten, 8250 AJ, The Netherlands
South Pacific Office
Adventures Unlimited NZ
221 Symonds Sreet Box 8199
Auckland, New Zealnd

Please check: ☑

☐ This is my first order   ☐ I have ordered before   ☐ This is a new address

Name
Address
City
State/Province ___ Postal Code
Country
Phone day ___ Evening
Fax

Item Code	Item Description	Price	Qty	Total

Please check: ☑

☐ Postal-Surface
☐ Postal-Air Mail (Priority in USA)
☐ UPS (Mainland USA only)
☐ Visa/MasterCard/Discover/Amex

Subtotal ➤	
Less Discount-10% for 3 or more items ➤	
Balance ➤	
Illinois Residents 6.25% Sales Tax ➤	
Previous Credit ➤	
Shipping ➤	
Total (check/MO in USD$ only) ➤	

Card Number
Expiration Date

10% Discount When You Order 3 or More Items!

Comments & Suggestions	Share Our Catalog with a Friend